Maximising Quality and Outcomes Framework Quality Points

The QOF clinical domain

Anita Sharma
General Practitioner
Oldham

Forewords by

Shauna Dixon
Chief Executive
NHS Oldham

and

Tanya Claridge
Associate Director, Quality and Clinical Governance
NHS Oldham

Radcliffe Publishing
London • New York

Radcliffe Publishing Ltd
33–41 Dallington Street
London
EC1V 0BB
United Kingdom

www.radcliffepublishing.com

Electronic catalogue and worldwide online ordering facility.

British Library Cataloguing in Publication Data

A catalogue record for this book is available from the British Library.

ISBN-13: 978 184619 491 7

The paper used for the text pages of this book is FSC® certified. FSC (The Forest Stewardship Council®) is an international network to promote responsible management of the world's forests.

Typeset by Phoenix Photosetting, Chatham, Kent
Printed and bound by TJI Digital, Padstow, Cornwall

Contents

Foreword by Shauna Dixon

I was delighted to be invited to write the foreword to this book by Dr Anita Sharma, who is a highly respected general practitioner in Oldham and who provides high-quality, impartial and professional support to NHS Oldham.

The Quality and Outcomes Framework (QOF), as a national improvement programme designed to improve health and overall standards of care provided in general practice, represents a large investment in the quality of primary care provision. The response of general practices to the implementation of the QOF provides demonstrable evidence of not only their ability to meet new challenges and their willingness to compare their performance with their peers, but also their overall commitment to improving the quality of care they provide to their practice population, thereby reducing inequity and variation in healthcare provision.

I believe that *Maximising Quality and Outcomes Framework Quality Points* provides an accessible educational resource to all general practitioners, their trainees and their support staff in maximising the benefit of the QOF, both for their practice and – ultimately – for the patients they serve.

Shauna Dixon
TD DL, MSc, RN, RM, RHV, FloD
Chief Executive, NHS Oldham
April 2011

Foreword by Tanya Claridge

The Quality and Outcomes Framework (QOF) provides a unique opportunity to influence national improvement in population health and outcomes. It also provides an agreed framework by which practices can compare, with others, their performance relating to consistent standards across multiple chronic disease areas, and receive incentive payments for their achievements. It also, and just as importantly, provides clearly described, best-practice standards by which the care of individual patients should be managed.

Maximising Quality and Outcomes Framework Quality Points provides chronic disease group-specific guidance and techniques designed to support and improve QOF performance. These techniques support practice level achievement, for instance, in terms of disease register validation and coding accuracy; more importantly, they also support the quality of the care received by individual patients, including the identification of 'added value' interventions and activity, above and beyond the requirements of the QOF.

Maximising Quality and Outcomes Framework Quality Points provides a key one-stop resource for all general practitioners and their staff to support the delivery of the QOF within their practice.

Tanya Claridge
PhD, BNurs (Hons), RGN, RHV
Associate Director, Quality and Clinical Governance
NHS Oldham
April 2011

Preface

The Quality and Outcomes Framework (QOF) is a system to reward general practices financially for providing quality care to their patients. It is a fundamental part of the general medical services (GMS) contract, introduced in April 2004.

The QOF measures achievements with points against a range of indicators and payment is awarded according to the level of achievement. Evidence suggests that linking financial incentives to quality achievements has improved the overall quality of primary care and reduced inequalities in primary care delivery in the UK.

Improving the quality of primary care is an important objective and its significance was reinforced in the review of the National Health Service – the one aim and one objective of this book. The QOF is estimated to have saved up to 10 000 lives a year since its introduction and following the 'do something extra for your patients' written in every chapter will continue to save more lives. I have added extra read codes in most templates to maximise points and improve quality care.

It should be noted that the author assumes that the reader's practice is fully computerised and is able to create templates.

This book gives you practical guidance and tips as to how to score maximum on all the clinical indicators. Setting up a disease register, ensuring that you have an accepted definition of the condition, arranging a practice meeting to discuss registers, motivating all team members to use and think templates, cross-checking with hospital letters and discharge summaries, conducting a repeat prescription search, actively screening at-risk patients and ensuring an efficient call and recall system are the basic rules which apply to each and every clinical indicator.

The main and rewarded activity lies in treating patients to target and near target levels. The book gives you tips as to how to achieve these. The reader gets an insight as to where the targets come from, should they be different for elderly, how achievable the targets are in primary care and what guidelines are in place.

To benefit your patients, you readers have to add two ingredients. First, you have to add a mastery of the clinical skills of patient interviewing, history taking, physical examination without which you can not begin the process of maximising QOF. Secondly you must add the practice of continuous, life-long, self-directed learning without which you will rapidly become dangerously out of date. There are references at the end of each chapter for those who wish to learn more.

If you are able to identify where and why are you falling short of your standards and able to implement a process for improving performance, the book would have served its purpose well.

I regard this book as the start of an evolutionary process and the first of many editions. I encourage readers to write to me with constructive comments and suggestions.

At the time of writing this book I was waiting for the announcement from the NHS Employers and the BMA's General Practitioners Committee for the changes to the GMS contract for the year 2011/12. The next edition will update you with changes in the QOF clinical indicators. In the meantime, the new QOF clinical indicators will be made available at www.radcliffepublishing.com/qofindicators

Anita Sharma
Oldham
April 2011

About the author

Anita Sharma MBBS, MD, DRCOG, MFFP has been a general practitioner in Oldham for more than 22 years and loves every second of working as a GP.

She is an undergraduate trainer attached to the University of Manchester and a trainer in family planning. She is the GP editor for the *British Journal of Medical Practitioners*, *Junior Dr*, the magazine for trainee doctors, and the LMC newsletter. She writes regularly in various GP magazines on clinical and practice developmental issues.

Anita has served as a local medical committee locality member for the last seven years and is a GP appraiser for Oldham Primary Care Trust. She is also the chairperson of BMA Rochdale Division and organises various educational and social activities.

With the help and support of her patient participation group, she organises various fundraising activities and raises money for Cancer Research. She has donated the royalties of her recently published book, *COPD in Primary Care* (Radcliffe Publishing; 2010), to the 'Breathe Easy Group'.

Acknowledgements

Every piece of writing takes time – time that could have been spent with my husband and children.

My heartfelt gratitude goes to my husband Ravi, a consultant physician, for his continued support and for doing my household duties while I battled with my computer.

Above all, I should like to thank my son Neel, who is currently doing core medical training at Lewisham and Guy's Hospital, London, and my daughter Ravnita, an anaesthetist in Manchester, for putting up with my laptop addiction; they never once suggested that I should seek professional help.

I would particularly like to thank Matthias Hohmann, a GP principal in Oldham with interests centred on palliative care. He is Macmillan GP for NHS Oldham and Macmillan GP advisor for Greater Manchester and Cheshire.

Primary care trusts have a duty to ensure that they pay practices their correct entitlement and to do so they require additional information. I am very grateful indeed to John Stephen Kelly, GP principal in Oldham, GP LIFT Champion and QOF clinical assessor, for explaining the purpose of the visit and the assessment process.

With value for money and quality improvement as the main political drivers, the QOF is seen as a tool to incentivise improved quality of care. My special thanks to Philip Trewinnard, GP principal in Oldham, for explaining points, pounds and prevalence.

I am very grateful to Pat Beecroft, Quality and Outcomes Primary Care Lead Clinical Governance, NHS Oldham, for providing the support material.

Finally, as will become apparent to all who read this book, I have long been driven by high-quality personal care, continuity of care and a commitment to individual patients that make being a GP a profession rather than just a job. I sincerely hope that you, the readers, agree that this has been time well spent.

Anita Sharma

CHAPTER 1

QOF clinical indicators: 2009/10

The Quality and Outcomes Framework (QOF) was introduced as part of the 2004 GP contract. It currently offers practices up to 1050 points if the delivery of care is of a high standard on a range of services. Payments per point vary with relative practice prevalence and the patient list size. In 2004/05, payment was £77.50 per point, yielding £80 000 per annum potential gross income. In 2005/06, this was increased to £124.60 per point, yielding a potential gross income of £130 000 per annum for average sized practices.

New indicators were added in 2006, 2008 and 2009/10, with further changes planned for 2011/12. The points are linked to the clinical and organisational structure and patients' experience of the practice.

Each QOF point is currently worth £127.29. The practice agrees in advance with the primary care organisation the total number of QOF points it is aiming for in the coming year. Seventy per cent of the payment is made to the practice on a monthly basis, with the balance being paid once the practice has proved that the target points have been achieved.

The QOF of the general medical services (GMS) contract for 2009/10 came into effect on 1 April 2009. The clinical domain covers the areas shown in Table 1.1.

Table 1.1 Quality and Outcomes Framework: clinical domain categories, 2009/10

Clinical domain	Points
Asthma	45
Atrial fibrillation	27
Cancer	11
Cardiovascular disease – primary prevention	13
Coronary heart disease – secondary prevention	87
Chronic kidney disease	38
Chronic obstructive pulmonary disease (COPD)	30
*Contraception	10
Dementia	20

(continued)

Depression	53
Diabetes mellitus	100
Epilepsy	15
Heart failure	29
Hypertension	81
Hypothyroidism	7
Learning disabilities	4
Mental health	39
Obesity	8
Palliative care	6
Smoking	60
Stroke and TIA	24

*The contraception indicators are listed as part of the 'additional services' section of the framework.

Points are attached to each indicator and the number of points achieved determines the sum earned.

All clinical indicators are organised by disease categories. The QOF expects the primary care physician to provide a high quality of care in the categories listed in Table 1.1.

These categories were selected on the basis of good evidence of the health benefits from improved primary care, and where the disease area is a priority because of the substantial burden, in terms of morbidity and healthcare expenditure in particular, and if there is an accepted national clinical guideline.

The indicators chosen are largely process based, and much of the effort in earning points boils down to good data collection. The framework endorses the advice of the guidelines on the specific disease to make an objective diagnosis.

The **key aims of QOF** clinical indicators are to:
➤ prevent the disease developing in the first place
➤ slow down the progression of the disease
➤ make an early diagnosis and provide ongoing management as per accepted national guidelines by the primary care team
➤ reduce the complications associated with the disease
➤ reduce hospital admissions and deaths by providing better primary care.

The incentive to improve diagnosis is contained in the process of prevalence. Once diagnosed the patients should receive timely and appropriate investigations, with effective treatment and follow-up by the primary care team to reduce the risk of progression and complications.

In 2009/10, 72 points were removed from the following indicators, as shown in Table 1.2.

Table 1.2 Quality and Outcomes Framework: indicator points removed, 2009/10

Indicator	Previous value	Current value	Points removed
BP4	20	18	2
CHD6	19	17	2
AF3	15	12	3
SMOKING3	33	30	3
SMOKING4	35	30	5
CON1	1	0	1
CON2	1	0	1
Patient Experience2	25	0	25
Patient Experience6	30	0	30

Achievements in the clinical domain of the QOF fell from 97.8% in 2008/09 to 95.9% in 2009/10 with scores markedly lower in the newest indicators introduced in the last round of negotiations including diabetes and depression screening. Average practice achievement in the 8305 practices in England was 93.7% of all QOF points available, equivalent to a £2125 loss for the average practice. The DM23 indicator (percentage of patients with diabetes in whom the last HBA1c is 7% or less in the previous 15 months) scored the lowest of all clinical indicators, with practices scoring 83.5% of the points available. The National Institute for Health and Clinical Excellence (NICE) has recommended increasing this target to 7.5% from next year. Another indicator where practices scored less was DEP3. Practices scored only 64.4% of the points available for DEP3, which offers 20 points for the percentage of patients who are reassessed 5–12 weeks after the first assessment of depression and anxiety severity using a validated assessment tool.

It is proposed that NICE should be involved in reviewing existing indicators and piloting new indicators. This has been welcomed by GPs because the achievement of the target of some of the indicators is currently impossible.

QOF changes and new indicators

The following new indicators will be reviewed prior to the start of 2011/12.

Anxiety and depression: one new indicator worth 20 points
DEP3

In those patients with a new diagnosis of depression and assessment of severity recorded between the preceding 1 April and 31 March, the percentage of patients who have had a further assessment of severity 5–12 weeks (inclusive) after the initial recording of the assessment of severity. Both assessments should be completed using an assessment tool validated for use in primary care.

Points 20   **Thresholds 40–90%**

Primary prevention of cardiovascular disease: two new indicators worth 13 points

PP1

In those patients with a new diagnosis of hypertension (excluding those with pre-existing coronary heart disease (CHD), diabetes, stroke and/or transient ischaemic attack (TIA)) recorded between the preceding 1 April and 31 March, the percentage of patients who have had a face-to-face cardiovascular risk assessment at the outset of diagnosis using an agreed risk assessment tool. At the outset of diagnosis means as within three months of the initial diagnosis.

Points 8   **Thresholds 40–70%**

PP2

The percentage of people diagnosed with hypertension diagnosed after 1 April 2009 who are given lifestyle advice in the preceding 15 months for increasing physical activity, smoking cessation, safe alcohol consumption and healthy diet.

Points 5   **Thresholds 40–70%**

Diabetes: 7 new points plus 28 current points

DM23

Replaces DM20. The percentage of patients with diabetes in whom the last HBA1c is 7 or less (or equivalent test/reference range depending on local laboratory) in the previous 15 months.

Points 17   **Thresholds 40–50%**

DM24

New. The percentage of patients with diabetes in whom the last HBA1c is 8 or less (or equivalent test/reference range depending on local laboratory) in the previous 15 months.

Points 8   **Thresholds 40–70%**

DM25

This replaces DM 7. The percentage of patients with diabetes in whom the last HBA1c is 9 or less (or equivalent test/reference range depending on local laboratory) in the previous 15 months.

Points 10   **Thresholds 40–90%**

COPD: 2 new points, one revised indicator

COPD 13

Replaces COPD11. The percentage of patients with COPD who have had a review, undertaken by a healthcare professional, including an assessment of breathlessness using the MRC dyspnoea score, in the preceding 15 months. Two additional points.

Points 9   **Thresholds 50–90%**

Heart failure: 9 new points, one new indicator
HF4

The percentage of patients with a current diagnosis of heart failure due to LVD who are currently treated with an ACE inhibitor or angiotensin receptor blocker, who are additionally treated with a beta blocker licensed for heart failure, or recorded as intolerant to or having a contraindication to beta blockers.

Points 9   **Thresholds 40–60%**

CKD: 11 new points
CKD5

The percentage of patients on the CKD register with hypertension and proteinuria who are treated with an angiotensin converting enzyme inhibitor or angiotensin receptor blocker unless a contraindication or side-effects are recorded.

Points 9   **Thresholds 40–80%**

CKD6

A new indicator added: the percentage of patients on the CKD register whose notes have a record of an albumin:creatinine ratio (or protein:creatinine ratio) value in the previous 15 months.

Points 6   **Thresholds 40–80%**

Sexual health-contraception: 8 new points plus 2 points from current CON indicators, CON1 and CON2 to be removed
SH1

The practice can produce a register of women who have been prescribed any method of contraception at least once in the last year.

Points 4

SH3

The percentage of women prescribed an oral or patch contraceptive method in the last year who have received information from the practice about long-acting reversible methods of contraception in the previous 15 months.

Points 3   **Thresholds 40–90%**

SH4

The percentage of women prescribed emergency hormonal contraception at least once in the year by the practice who have received information from the practice about long-acting reversible methods of contraception at the time of, or within one month of, the prescription.

Points 3   **Thresholds 40–90%**

Future changes
➤ There is a considerable overlap of some of the indicators, for example, the blood pressure indicators in the hypertension, coronary heart disease, stroke and diabetes domains.

Two QOF indicators for measuring blood pressure, BP4 and CKD2 worth a total of 14 points, may be removed from 2012/13 to make room for new indicators. It is felt that these two indicators have high achievement and low exception reporting rates.

➤ A big question mark is hanging over the removal of SK7, which records cholesterol levels in patients with TIA or stroke.

➤ The new public health White Paper, *Healthy Lives, Healthy People,*[1] pledges to devote at least 15% of QOF payments to primary prevention by 2013. This will include assigning at least £1 in every £7 of QOF funding to public health and primary prevention indicators from 2013.

➤ The National Institute for Health and Clinical Excellence (NICE), an independent organisation that provides national advice to the NHS and local government on the promotion of good health and the prevention and treatment of ill health, is planning to make recommendations for amending and replacing clinical indicators in the QOF. NICE has a comprehensive programme and recommends the NHS to meet the quality, innovation, productivity and prevention (QIPP).

➤ QOF may be cut to fund commissioning.

➤ The Department of Health plans to shift the focus of the QOF from processes to patient outcomes. Indicators must produce a clinical outcome. The QOF advisory committee has warned that an outcome-based QOF will be very difficult to design.

Reference

1 Department of Health. *Healthy Lives, Healthy People: Our strategy for public health in England.* Cm. 7895. London: TSO; 2010.

Useful information

➤ *Quality and Outcomes Framework guidance for GMS contract 2009/10. Delivering investment in general practice.* www.nhsemployers.org

➤ National Institute for Health and Clinical Excellence. *About NICE.* www.nice.org.uk/aboutnice (accessed 13 July 2010).

➤ National Institute for Health and Clinical Excellence. *Health regulators.* www.nhs.uk/NHSEngland/thenhs/healthregulators/Pages/nice.aspx (accessed 13 July 2010).

CHAPTER 2

How to achieve maximum QOF points

When it was introduced, the aim of the QOF was to resource practices to deliver high-quality care to patients by helping them employ the staff they need. The QOF has had a hugely positive impact on patient care.

Critics argue that the framework is turning GPs into automatically programmed machines pursuing money at the expense of good patient care. Most GPs say that high-quality care is not synonymous with practice profits either by maximising points or achieving framework thresholds. They are focussed to provide high-quality care. Quality of care has improved for some clinical areas since the framework was introduced.[1] There are indications that the framework is associated with better recorded care, enhanced processes, improved intermediate outcomes and reduction in inequalities and that it provides value for money in some but not all its clinical domains.[1] It has helped consolidate evidence-based care.

So, if the QOF is all about high-quality care, improved intermediate outcomes and reduction in inequalities, which most GPs are endeavouring to provide, why do they fail to achieve the maximum points? Missing a single patient in a large practice makes little difference. But in a small practice one patient may represent 33% of the denominator, so if you miss that patient you can never achieve a 70% score.

This chapter provides some tips to help you succeed in achieving maximum points.

Tips

Prevalence

The value of each point is determined by the prevalence. If your prevalence is low in a specific disease area based on national average, the value of the points for that disease drops and you get paid less. The prevalence could be low because of poor communication with your patients, no or a poor system to review practice records or an inaccurate data entry.

➤ Improve patient communication and reach all those who might be at a risk of certain diseases, and make sure they are given information that would help diagnose the illness.

➤ Use a set of key messages for patients designed to prompt them into questioning whether they might have an undiagnosed illness. Use practice leaflets, display boards and your website to aid communication with your patients. Simple questions like 'Do you cough or wheeze?', 'Are you a smoker or an ex smoker?', 'Do you cough up lots of sputum?' may prompt your patients to consider whether they might have chronic obstructive pulmonary disease. Simple questions such as 'When was the last time you had your blood pressure measured or fasting blood sugar checked?' may pick up some undiagnosed essential hypertension patients or diabetics.

➤ Ensure that the person(s) entering data into the computer is/are familiar with the read codes.

➤ Encourage team working by involving staff, developing/delegating specific roles and addressing training needs, through in-house, local or national courses, to make sure that the disease register is kept accurate and up to date.

➤ Define individual staff roles and keep everyone informed about the clearly defined roles.

➤ Remember, many diagnoses are made outside your practice – a hospital outpatient clinic, at the time of discharge from hospital, A&E attendance or out-of-hours service, for example. There should be a system in place to check and highlight the diagnosis. This should ideally be done by either a clinician, a nurse or a healthcare assistant to minimise the potential for error, as this could cost your practice dearly.

➤ Carry out regular audits to show that changes introduced have been effective, for example, the result of albumin:creatinine ratio is entered in the CKD template, the ECHO result in the heart failure template.

➤ Carry out regular audits of the medications patients are taking to make sure they are coded correctly. For example, run a search on patients with inhalers and make sure they have a read code of asthma or chronic obstructive pulmonary disease.

➤ Provide incentives for staff by rewarding them with a bonus.

➤ Actively screening patients will also increase your prevalence. For example, CKD is common in patients with cardiovascular disease. Checking creatinine and eGFR could pick up CKD patients.

Prevalence and payment

When the GMS contract was introduced in 2004, GP leaders agreed that QOF pay should be adjusted to account for prevalence. This recognised the additional work-load from targeting a large number of patients with a particular disease. Square root adjustment to rein in high-prevalence practices and a 5% uplift to protect practices from losing out on QOF pay was applied.

Some GPs felt that this was unfair. They argued that practices with three times the prevalence had three times the work and deserved three times the reward. So, in October 2008, the General Practitioners' Committee (GPC) scrapped the adjustments and switched to weighting pay according to raw prevalence.

Rapidly growing list size can distort the prevalence calculations. Poor timing of data collection resulted in some practices recording artificially high disease prevalence. Practice list size and disease registers are not counted at the same time for QOF purposes. Prevalence is calculated by dividing the number of patients on a disease register on 31 March by the practice's registered population on 1 January. As a result, expanding practices can record an abnormally high prevalence. If the list size grows between these dates, prevalence for disease areas will be extraordinarily high and this could result in some practices loosing thousands of pounds.

Removal of the square rooting in 2009/10 that damped QOF pay weighting further increased payment variation. In 2010/11, the 5% uplift will also be lost.

From 2010/11, pay will be weighted for the first time according to the raw prevalence, and the mechanism for supporting low prevalence practices will be removed. This change will make QOF pay reflect the workload and payment will be directed to the practices that need it the most.

Ensure an efficient call and recall system

There is little point calling patients for checks if there is no system to alert you if they do not attend. The new contract has specific time limits for every indicator.

There should be an efficient system for recall.

Depression 3, introduced in 2009/10, is worth 20 points for assessing severity of depression 5–12 weeks after diagnosis. If you have no efficient call and recall system you can easily loose points for this new indicator.

New patients

All new patients, including those in nursing and residential homes, registering with the practice must be added to the disease specific register. The best tactic here is to give any patient joining the practice a new patient health questionnaire asking about any existing illness and the medications they are on.

Hospital letters/discharges

Clinicians should ensure that any mention of heart disease, hypertension and COPD are correlated with the register.

Repeat prescription search

Searching patients on repeat medications like antihypertensive, insulin or oral medication for diabetics or asthma inhalers and checking if they are on the register is essential. This must be done every six months.

Practice meeting

Arrange a regular practice meeting to discuss registers. Every member of the practice team must have a read code training. Introduce 'Think template' to your staff.

This is a team effort.

Working as a team will increase your chances of success. Remember, patients and their carers are also members of the team.

Delegate

Your district nurse or community matron can easily update the stroke/heart failure template of a housebound patient. **Just make sure you are delegating to the right person.**

Patient education

Educate the patients; explain the real risks of not complying with medication and attending regular follow-ups. You should also emphasise the targets and the real numbers – for example, HBA1c level, blood pressure, cholesterol target. Explanation ensures compliance, fewer missed appointments and maximum points.

Teaching practice

It is proven that training practices score higher on QOF. Glasgow researchers discovered higher QOF figures in practices taking part in undergraduate teaching, postgraduate teaching, Scotland's Programme for Improving Clinical Effectiveness, Scottish Primary Care Collaborative and the RCGP Quality Practice Award scheme.[2] Researchers found that practices in more affluent areas were more likely to undertake postgraduate training compared with practices in deprived areas. However, deprivation did not affect practices' performance on QOF.[2] Involvement in GP training and undertaking audits improves the QOF figures of small- and medium-sized practices.[2]

So, if you are a small- or medium-sized practice, give it a go and get involved in teaching.

Average age of GP

It has been observed that that delivered quality of care is lower in practices where the average age of GP is high (*I can only assume poor use of computerisation by an older GP*). Think of employing a young GP to boost your income!

Coding errors

It is easy to make mistakes in coding. A small error in coding can lead to lost money. If you want to see the financial benefits, it is important to get the coding right.

Coding should ideally be done by a clinician. This may be possible in a large practice, with one GP supervising the coding, but not in a single-GP or medium-sized practice. QOF is becoming more complex, with more changes to be introduced over the coming years, so it is important to invest in a data input clerk who understands read codes, templates and QOF.

Invest

Buy some useful gadgets like an ECG machine. Why are you still sharing spirometer? Start screening smokers and ex-smokers 'in-house' – you will pick up some COPD patients.

National guidelines

Keep yourself up to date with national guidelines and provide cost-effective treatment.

Exception reporting

The QOF allows practices to exception report specific patients from data collection to calculate the score. Exception reporting is justifiable if a patient's blood pressure cannot be lowered to a target level without fainting or falling episodes. It is clinically justifiable not to treat high cholesterol with statin in a cancer patient. Then there is patient's choice. If a patient chooses not to take antihypertensive or cholesterol lowering drugs, do an exception coding. Why should a GP be penalised if he or she cares for those patients who choose not to take the prescribed medication?

The exception codes fall in to persisting and expiring codes. Try not to choose a persisting code because that will increase your workload. It is better to use the adverse reaction to B blocker code (U60B7) rather than a B blocker not tolerated code (8173).

Some GPs have played on the exception reporting approach, which clearly is unethical. Some mangers think practices evade criticism of their clinical care by exception reporting.

The Department of Health is considering scrapping exception reporting. Exception reporting rates have risen for the first time in three years.

The figures released by the NHS Information Centre show that the average exception rate rose to 5.41% in 2009/10, up from an all-time low of 4.87% in the previous year.[3]

Eight of the 16 clinical indicator domains had reported increased exception reporting in 2009/10 compared with the previous years. The NHS Information Centre said the rise was due to new outcome-based indicators – depression, diabetes, heart failure and chronic obstructive pulmonary disease had new or revised indicators added in 2009/10. Out of these, the heart failure domain had the biggest change from 2008/09. Exception reporting rose to 17.2%, compared with 9.2%. The new heart failure indicator 4 had an exception reporting rate of 37.8%.

Just because some GPs have misused exception reporting, it does not mean that the rest of the hardworking, caring and conscientious GPs should be penalised.

References

1 Gillam S, Siriwardena N. Should the Quality and Outcomes Framework be abolished? *BMJ.* 2010; **340**: 1338–9.
2 Mackay DF, Watt GCM. General practice size determines participation in optional activities: cross sectional analysis of a national primary care system. *Primary Healthcare Research and Development.* 2010; **11**: 271–9.
3 NHS. The Information Centre. *The Quality and Outcome Framework Exception Reporting 2009/10.* 26 October 2010.

CHAPTER 3

QOF: Good or bad?

The QOF, introduced as part of the GMS contract, came into being in 2004. When it was introduced, the QOF aimed to reward practices for providing high-quality care to their patients. It is a voluntary incentive scheme and now accounts for around 15% (£1 billion) of all expenditure on primary care in England.[1]

Under the QOF, achievements are measured against a range of evidence-based indicators – clinical, organisational, education and training, information for patients, practice management, medicine management, patient experience, additional services and contraception – with points allocated for each indicator. Practices are paid according to their level of the achievement. Prevalence data forms an integral part of the QOF in determining the payment.

Six years on, most of us would say that since its introduction there has been a consistent level of good-quality service provision in general practice. GPs have delivered good evidence-based care to their patients.

The Royal College of General Practitioners has set out the values that define the GP – high-quality personal care, continuity of care and a commitment to individual patients – that makes being a GP a good profession rather than just a job.[1] Since the introduction of the QOF, GPs have redefined their roles in terms of good-quality care.

What is good about QOF?

Most of us would say the QOF is a successful development. It has delivered a quality service based on evidence. Evidence suggests that QOF indicators have had a positive benefit in motivating patients to stop smoking.[2] The QOF is estimated to have saved up to 10 000 lives a year since its introduction.[3]

Indicators with largest potential benefit are:

➤ primary prevention for hypertension, saving 12 lives per 100 000 population
➤ influenza immunisation, saving six lives per 100 000
➤ B blockers in CHD, saving six lives per 100 000.

The first evidence that the QOF has narrowed health inequalities by cutting admissions and deaths from heart disease, especially in deprived areas, has come from a new study.[4] This study demonstrates that the QOF has been successful in reducing health disparities and has resulted in improved CHD outcomes especially in deprived areas.[4]

The purpose of the QOF is about quality improvement. Some argue that removing incentives may lead to a decline in performance level.

The QOF has narrowed health inequalities by cutting admissions and deaths from heart disease, especially in deprived areas.[5] Researchers at the London Health Observatory calculated practice-level deprivation scores for 1531 practices (98%) of all GP practices in the capital over a period of three years and studied the association between achievements in 12 clinical CHD indicators and the outcomes. The impact was the strongest in the most deprived areas. The researchers found more than twice the reduction in admission and deaths from CHD.[6] The QOF has been one of the most successful elements of the GP contract, and has helped raised standards as well as focus high-quality care where it is most needed.

What is bad about QOF?

Some say that the QOF should be about incentivising good care to our patients at all times, not focussing on computer screens and tick-boxing compliance, or nagging patients for not attending for follow-ups.

The report from the King's Fund GP enquiry, *Tackling Health Inequalities in General Practice*,[7] criticised the QOF and long-term condition care. 'Continuity of care was higher for aspects of care linked to incentives and those not linked to incentives fell since the introduction of QOF', the report said. Continuity of care declined significantly with patients' evaluation, falling by 4.1 percentage points in 2005 and 4.3 in 2007.

The National Audit report mentioned that the new contract had cost £1.76 billion more than expected while the QOF had only brought moderate improvement in outcome.[8] The incentives in the QOF have improved care but may not have offered value for money.[8]

Some argue that exception reporting has at times been abused to achieve points. Data falsification and deliberate fraud to reach QOF targets contributes to a high level of attainment of quality targets.

The QOF penalises small practices. High-performing small practices are being held back because thresholds are set too low to reward their achievements. Practices with fewer than 3000 patients had greater variation in performance than larger practices. Small practices made up 45.1% of the bottom 5% of QOF achievers, but also accounted for 46.7% of the top 5%.[9]

Indicators of poor value

An analysis of nine indicators showed that the indicators in diabetes, coronary heart disease, hypertension and stroke were cost-effective in only one-third of practices.[10] The QOF DM15 indicator, which rewards for the percentage of diabetic patients with proteinuria or albuminuria who are treated with either an ACE inhibitor or an ARB, was cost-effective in only 36% of practices. The stroke 10 indicator for recording stroke patients receiving anticoagulants also scored low and was cost-effective in only 40% of practices.

Researchers at the University of York calculated the cost-effectiveness of indicators based on the £20 000 per quality adjusted life year (QALY) threshold used by NICE and found that, on average, the nine indicators studies were cost-effective in only 45% of practices.[10]

Cost-effective QOF indicators

The percentage of practices where indicators are the least cost-effective at the £20 000 per QALY threshold are shown in Table 3.1.

Table 3.1 Practices where indicators are the least cost-effective at the £20 000 per QALY threshold

Indicator	Percentage of practices
CHD9	45.59
CHD10	47.59
CHD11	42.20
BP5	52.8
DM15	36.32
DM21	**54.07**
STROKE 12	39.8

The least cost-effective indicator subject to the value for money thresholds was DM21 (diabetic retinopathy).

NICE in QOF

A consultation was launched by the Department of Health in England in October 2008 on proposals that NICE should be responsible for the QOF revisions in the future. NICE is an established organisation with specific expertise and a track record of producing evidence-based policies. The aim is to establish a more independent process, to improve transparency and to ensure the best use of the annual investment.

A Primary Care QOF Indicator Advisory Committee was set up by NICE in April 2009. To ensure cost-effectiveness, produce guidance on implementation, review all existing indicators and support the development of new indicators by piloting the new indicators, a contract with an external academic body was agreed. The academic body is a group made up of the National Primary Care Research and Development Centre at Manchester University, the Royal College of General Practitioners and the York Health Economics Consortium. It could take approximately two years from proposal to incorporation.

The government appears to support the use of QALY within the QOF. QALY is a measure of disease burden, including both the quality and quantity of life lived. It is used in assessing the value for money of a medical intervention.

The consensus is that the QOF should address inequalities in care. Emerging evidence seems to suggest that QOF targets can reduce health inequalities, albeit over a period of time.[11] The government's view is that the QOF is successfully closing the gap in practice performance and that cost-effectiveness is one of a range of criteria for prioritising indicators.

Some GPs argue that NICE has got things wrong in the past and might stray from the initial aim and objective of the QOF, which was to reward practices for providing high-quality care. Plans to remove and add new indicators will make it harder to achieve. So far, the QOF has worked because GPs believe that indicators matter to the patients. It is therefore important that any future changes in indicators must have the full support of GPs.

This revision of the system for the QOF appears to have been driven by the Darzi Report in England.[12] No one seems to know where Scotland, Wales and Northern Ireland fit in this change with regard to the QOF and NICE.

The most important criticism is that if the present system is working, why make it more bureaucratic? Any changes made to the QOF must be for the better.

References

1 Royal College of General Practitioners. *Developing the Quality and Outcomes Framework: proposals for a new independent process: consultation response and analysis.* London: Department of Health; 2009.
2 National Institute for Health and Clinical Excellence. *Brief Interventions and Referral for Smoking Cessation in Primary Care and Other Settings: NICE guideline PH1.* London: NHICE; 2006. www.nice.org.uk/guidance/PH1
3 Primary care and financial incentives cut heart disease deaths and admissions. *Journal of epidemiology and community health.* 7 September 2010. group.bmj.com/… group.bmj. com/…/JECH%20-%207%20Sept%202010%20- %20Primary%20care%20financial %20incentives%20cut%20heart%20disea…
4 Kiran T, Hutchings A, Dhalla IA, *et al.* The association between quality of primary care, deprivation and cardiovascular outcomes: a cross sectional study using data from the UK Quality and Outcomes Framework. *J Epidemiol Community Health.* 2010; **64**: 927–34.
5 Royal College of General Practitioners. *Leading the Way. High Quality Care For All Through General Practice.* 2010. Available at: www.rcgp.org.uk/pdf/1146-1510_ Political_Manifesto_Web_key_documents.pdf (accessed 23 March 2010).
6 Dhalla I, Hutchings A, Dhalla IA. Impact of a one point increase in QOF CHD achievement. *J Epidemiol. Community Health.* 2010; **64**:921–34.
7 QOF may perpetuate health inequalities. www.gponline.com/News/…/QOF-may-perpetuate-health-inequalities
8 www.pulsetoday.co.uk/story.asp?storycode=4117959
9 QOF penalises small practices/GP newspaper news/Healthcare. 2 September 2010. www.gponline.com/search/Articles/phrase/QOF…/2010/50/
10 Walker S, Mason AR, Claxton K, *et al.* Value for money and the Quality and Outcomes Framework in primary care in the UK NHS. *Br J Gen. Pract.* 2010; **60**(574): 213–20.
11 Doran T, Fullwood C, Kontopantelis E, *et al.* Effect of financial incentives on inequalities in the delivery of primary care in England: analysis of clinical activity indicators for the quality and outcomes framework. *The Lancet.* 2008; **372**(9640): 728–36.
12 Darzi A. *High Quality Care for All: NHS next stage review final report. Cm. 7432.* London: Department of Health; 2008.

CHAPTER 4

Points and pounds

Philip Trewinnard

Whilst there have been improvements in patient care as a result of the QOF, the financial benefits for practices have been considerable. Since the beginning of the QOF the points achieved by practices have been converted to pounds per point to produce the final payment to practices.

The initial payments per point were £77.50 in the first year, increasing to £124.60 in subsequent year and in the year 2010/11 each point value is £127.29.

This figure is, however, based on an average practice list size of 5891 patients; and from this figure a contractor population index is calculated. This figure is the practice's registered population divided by 5891 for practices in England and Wales and the index is used to allocate payments to practices relative to their list size.

There is a comparable figure in Scotland, where the average list size used for the contractor population is 5095, and in Northern Ireland, where the average list size used is 4937.

The practice list size which is used for this calculation is supplied to the Quality Management and Analysis System (QMAS) from the National Health Applications and Infrastructure Services (NHAIS), the national practice payments system, and is the registered list size on 1 January in each year.

Below are two examples of the contractor population index calculation and pounds per point for two practices. Both calculations are based on the England and Wales average list size: Practice A has a list size of 3200 and Practice B 11 000.

Practice A

(practice list size) / (national average list size) = contractor population index

3200/5891 = 0.5432

(contractor population index) x £127.29 = (£ per point)

0.5432 x £127.29 = £69.14

(continued)

Practice B

(practice list size) / (national average list size) = contractor population index

11 000/5891 = 1.867

(contractor population index) x £127.29 = (£ per point)

1.867 x £127.29 = £237.68

An alternative way of looking at this is on the basis of pounds per registered patient. Using the figure for 2010/11 this is calculated as follows.

£127.29/5891 = £0.021 per patient x registered list size:

Practice A

£0.021 x 3200 = £69.14

Practice B

£0.021 x 11 000 = £237.68

This figure of points to pounds applies to all the non-clinical areas of the QOF, i.e. the organisational domains, the patient experience domain and the additional services domain. It does not apply in the same way to the clinical domains, where there is an additional financial variable related to prevalence, which has not always been straightforward in its application.

Points, pounds and prevalence

Having done all the clinical work, at the end of the QOF year there is a final adjustment for all of the clinical domains which depends on the practice's prevalence for that disease, apart from palliative care

The prevalence is calculated from the register size (number of patients with a read coded diagnosis qualifying under the business rules) as a percentage of the practice population. The data is extracted by QMAS.[1]

For example

Asthma register size: 160 patients

Registered patients: 3200

Practice raw prevalence: 160/3200 = 0.05

In most cases the practice population is the total practice registered list size; however, five clinical indicator domains relate to specific age groups – diabetes, epilepsy, chronic kidney disease, obesity and learning disabilities – and in these the practice population is not used. The diabetic register relates to patients aged 17 and above; the epilepsy chronic kidney disease and learning disabilities registers apply to patients aged 18 and above; and the obesity register applies to patients age 16 and above. For these conditions the NHS Information Centre produces prevalence information based on appropriate age-banded list size information.

From 2009, the prevalence data is now calculated at the same time as the submission of achievement on 31 March (the end-of-year submission).

National Prevalence Data

The National Prevalence Data is calculated from the final QMAS submissions and is used to calculate a prevalence factor used to arrive at the final payments for each clinical domain. The prevalence figures based on the QOF registers may differ from figures from different sources such as epidemiology and statistically produced figures because of coding issues or differences in disease definitions.

The National Prevalence levels for the year 2009/10 are shown in Table 4.1.

Table 4.1 National raw prevalence levels1

Clinical area	Sum of register counts	Prevalence (%)
Coronary Heart Disease	1 885 089	3.4
Cardiovascular Disease – Primary Prevention	340 056	0.6
Heart Failure	393 290	0.7
Heart Failure due to LVD	214 654	0.4
Stroke or Transient Ischaemic Attacks (TIA)	921 819	1.7
Hypertension	7 321 472	13.4
Diabetes Mellitus (Diabetes) (ages 17+)	2 338 813	5.4
Chronic Obstructive Pulmonary Disease	861 341	1.6
Epilepsy (ages 18+)	332 001	0.8
Hypothyroidism	1 603 670	2.9
Cancer	775 623	1.4
Palliative Care	74 907	0.1
Mental Health	424 223	0.8
Asthma	3 254 562	5.9
Dementia	249 463	0.5
Depression (ages 18+)	4 648 287	10.9
Chronic Kidney Disease (ages 18+)	1 817 871	4.3
Atrial Fibrillation	761 965	1.4
Obesity (ages 16+)	4 634 408	10.5
Learning Disabilities (ages 18+)	179 064	0.4
Smoking Indicators	12 488 033	–

Based on the practice list size and the disease register size a figure for the practice prevalence can be calculated. This figure is divided by the figure for national prevalence to produce the figure for the prevalence factor. In the early years of the QOF the square root of this figure was used to calculate the final payment – in effect, taking the square root of practice prevalence compared with the national prevalence brought high figures down towards a prevalence factor of 1 and a low prevalence up towards a prevalence factor of 1.

> **For example**
>
> If the ratio of pratice:national prevalence is 2, the square root prevalence factor is 1.41. Thus the prevalence factor has been reduced.
>
> If the ratio of the practice:national prevalence is 0.5 the square root prevalence is 0.7071. Thus the prevalence factor has been increased.

For the year 2009/10 a different formula was used, with a 5% cut-off applied at the bottom of the national range of prevalence, and from 2010/11 the prevalence factor will rely entirely on raw practice and raw national prevalence.

This figure is then used to calculate the payment for each clinical disease indicator group.

> **For example**
>
> Diabetes indicator payment = clinical points for diabetes achieved x practice prevalence factor for diabetes x practice pounds per point

The significance of the prevalence factor

Since the change in the way prevalence factors are calculated the size of the disease registers has increased in its significance in financial terms, provided that the level of achievement is maintained. However, as practices increase their register sizes and further work is put into disease validation not only will practice prevalence increase but also national prevalence, as this figure is derived from the practice prevalence.

This is of increased significance to practices which have small practice registers, as they will need to identify more cases to maintain their prevalence factors. This will particularly be an issue for practices with a healthy young population such as university practices. Primary care trusts have been able to use a mathematical formula to advise practices about the financial implications of the change in prevalence factor. Inevitably there is potential for practices with high disease registers to increase practice income – although it must be remembered that increased register size will increase workload and only improve income if the levels of achievement are maintained.

Reference

1 NHS Information Centre. www.ic.nhs.uk/webfiles/QOF/2009-10/Prevalence%20 tables/QOF0910_National_Prevalence.xls

Useful reading

➤ QOF Guidance 2009 1-48 GMS Guidance: www.nhsemployers.org/Aboutus/.../ QOF_Guidance_2009_final.pdf
➤ The new GMS contract: www.bma.org.uk/images/focusoninfo0204_tcm27_189061. pdf

CHAPTER 5

Asthma

Definition

Asthma is a chronic inflammatory airway disease. Asthma by definition is a variable condition and encompasses the following.

➤ Inflammation of the airways involving eosinophils, T lymphocytes and activated mast cells.

➤ Hyper responsiveness of the airways to a wide variety of exogenous and endogenous stimuli. This may include smoke, exercise, dust, aerosol spray, cold air or fog.

➤ Variable airway obstruction which may vary spontaneously from none to severe and improves after suitable therapy.

Prevalence

Asthma is one of the most common chronic diseases in the UK,[1] with 5.2 million people suffering from asthma.[2] The number of adults with asthma in the UK has increased by 400 000 since the last audit of UK asthma in 2001.[2] It is not known why the number has increased, but it may be that children with asthma are growing up to become adults with asthma. Asthma affects at least 15% of children in their childhood.[3] About 60% of adults with asthma in UK are women.[2] Each year, a GP with 2000 patients will see approximately 85 patients with asthma and each of these will consult three times on average.[2] Up until the late 1970s it was generally believed that asthma in old age was rare. However, it is now recognised that it can begin at any age, and the prevalence in those over aged 70 or over is estimated to be 6.5%.[4]

Occupational asthma may account for 9–15% of adult onset asthma.[5]

Why included in QOF

Asthma is included in the QOF for the following reasons.

➤ Asthma responds very well to appropriate medication and can be managed in a primary care setting.

➤ In 2002, there were over 69 000 hospital admissions due to asthma. These admissions could have been reduced or avoided by providing better care in the primary care sector.

➤ Poor adherence to inhaled corticosteroids is common and is related to an increase in A&E visits. Compliance with inhalers and using the inhaler correctly can improve the disease control and lower the hospital attendance and emergency admissions.[6]

➤ Education of patients and relatives is important and GPs are best placed to deliver and reinforce that message.

➤ Routine structured review, as opposed to opportunistic review, is associated with a favourable clinical outcome and this is only deliverable with a structured call and recall system. Seasonal variations in asthma are widely recognised. Individual seasonal histories are important for the management of asthma.[7]

➤ Obesity is associated with asthma, although the cause–effect relationship, if one exists, is still obscure. The BTS/SIGN guidelines recommend weight reduction to improve asthma control – easily deliverable in the primary care sector.

➤ The UK ranks high in the global league table of asthma prevalence,[8] but recent trends have indicated a plateau or even a fall in cases of childhood asthma – could this be due to early diagnosis by GPs since its introduction in the QOF?[9]

The facts

➤ Approximately 1600 people die from asthma each year in the UK.[10]

➤ Each year, 18 million working days are lost due to asthma.[10]

➤ The annual cost of asthma to the NHS exceeds £850 million.[10]

➤ Fifty per cent of those who thought their asthma was well controlled had woken up with a cough and wheeze meaning poorly controlled asthma in the previous 30 days.[11]

➤ Uncontrolled asthma places a significant burden on children and their families.

➤ The impact of an asthma attack influences choice of holiday destinations and also leisure activities.[12]

➤ Monthly peak flow testing during the winter, the cold and flu season, can improve symptom control in patients with asthma compared with normal care.[13]

QOF: asthma indicators

Indicators and points: total points 45

Records

ASTHMA 1

The practice can produce a register of patients with asthma, excluding patients with asthma who have been prescribed no asthma-related drugs in the previous 12 months.

Points 4

The diagnosis of asthma is a clinical one. It is important to get the diagnosis right before adding the patient to the register. Symptoms of wheezing, tight chest and cough worse at night and early morning in response to exercise, allergen, cold air and breathlessness suggest asthma. Other features that increase the suspicion of asthma are family history of atopic disorder or asthma, history of atopic disorder and widespread expiratory wheeze on auscultation.[14]

The register should be checked annually and those patients who have not asked for asthma-related drugs in the last 12 months should be removed from the register.

The BTS/SIGN asthma guidelines give pointers to asthma diagnosis in children such as dry cough, wheeze and breathlessness.[14]

Initial management
ASTHMA 8

The percentage of patients aged eight years and over diagnosed as having asthma from 1 April 2006 with measures of variability or reversibility.

Points 15   **Payment stages 40–80%**

In a new patient with a history suggestive of asthma, a peak flow measurement should be performed. Record the best of the three readings. Using an inhaler and spacer device, give four to six puffs of salbutamol inhaler and check the peak flow again. An increase in peak flow rate of 20% is highly supportive of asthma.

If reversibility is not demonstrable, prescribe a peak flow meter and ask the patient to chart the peak flow twice daily – on rising and at around 6–7 p.m. – and record the best of the three blows.

➤ A diurnal variability of greater than 20% over three days in a week for two weeks is typical of asthma.

➤ An increase in peak flow rate of 20% (or 15% with a 200 mL improvement in FEV1) after a high dose of short-acting bronchodilator through a spacer is suggestive of asthma.

➤ A fall in FEV1 or PFR of 20% after six minutes' running in children is suggestive of asthma.

➤ Carry out a positive histamine challenge test (performed in hospital). This is reserved for cases where the diagnosis is in doubt.

➤ A proportion of asthma patients will have COPD – they will show a large reversibility 400 mL or more on FEV1 but do not return to over 80% predicted FEV1. These patients should be on both registers.

Ongoing management
ASTHMA 3

The percentage of patients with asthma between the ages of 14 and 19 in whom there is a record of smoking status in the previous 15 months.

Points 6   **Payment stages 40–80%**

Smoking cessation is an important part of asthma management and it is justifiable for the contract targets to include recording of smoking status.

There is value in asking about smoking at each annual review, as at any given time about 70% of smokers wish to quit.

ASTHMA 6

The percentage of patients with asthma who have had an asthma review in the previous 15 months.

Points 20   **Payment stages 40–70%**

The aim of the annual review is to optimise the patient's treatment and minimise the symptoms. The review should include the following.
➤ Ask RCP3 questions.
➤ Check compliance. Compliance with treatment can be difficult to ascertain and should always be considered in patients with poor asthma control.
➤ Check inhaler technique. This is particularly important with children. Parents and children should be involved in the choice of inhaler device prescribed. Ask your nurse to check the inhaler technique on two or three occasions in the first month of prescription to make sure the correct technique is used.
➤ Check peak flow.
➤ Optimise treatment, if symptomatic, as per guidelines.
➤ Ask smoking history and advise cessation. Even brief smoking cessation advice from a GP is effective in getting people to stop.
➤ Make sure the patient knows their expected peak flow rate, has a peak flow meter and a self-management plan.
➤ Advise/provide flu immunisation.
➤ Parents of children who are allergic to house dust mites should be advised about replacing carpets with wooden or laminate floors, washing bed linens at high temperatures, encasement of duvets, pillows and mattress with protective covers and removing the soft toys from the bed and freezing in a plastic bag at −18°C for 6–8 hours and defrosting naturally to kill the mites.[15]
➤ For children sensitive to cats and dogs, parents should be advised to remove the pet from the house; however, it will take six months for the pet allergen levels to fall and benefits noticed.
➤ Make sure patient leaves the surgery with an appointment for their next asthma review.

Maximising quality points
➤ Ensure there is a system for recording new diagnosis, hospital discharges and newly registered patients. H33 is the read code for asthma. If you are a trainer or interested in research or audits in different types of asthma, use the following read codes:
— late onset asthma: H331-1
— exercise induced asthma: 173A
— occupational asthma: 173c
— allergic asthma: H330-1
— aspirin induced asthma: 1780.

(*My fourth-year medical student ran an audit on late onset asthma. Because it was read coded, searching of patients was easy.*)

➤ Do not use the read code 14B4 – H/O asthma.
➤ By all means use the read code 1J70 – suspected asthma – while waiting for the home peak flow diary readings.
➤ Identify patients on repeat inhalers – to increase your prevalence. Reception staff should be told to flag up patients requesting repeat prescriptions.
➤ Authorise the inhalers for six months only. This flags up asthma review.
➤ New onset allergic rhinitis in adulthood may be due to occupational exposure and may precede occupational asthma. A history of worsening symptoms during working hours or relief when away from work is suggestive of occupational asthma. Increase your prevalence by screening these patients with peak flow charts at and away from work.
➤ Offer an appointment which suits the patient to avoid 'did not attend' (DNA) incidence. There is a reluctance of people to attend asthma review if they are asymptomatic.
➤ Invite schoolchildren during school holidays or after school hours.
➤ Make sure your nurse is properly trained.
➤ Patients who have had a recent hospital admission, A&E attendance or are asking for frequent supplies of short acting inhalers must be asked to attend for review. Enter an alert message on the patients' medical records and prescribing screen. The BTS recommends that patients should be seen by their GP or specialist asthma nurse within two working days following a hospital discharge.[14]
➤ Review by telephone is not acceptable as the inhaler technique cannot be checked.
➤ Ensuring influenza immunisation and pneumococcal immunisation if indicated will earn extra points. The influenza vaccine is recommended in children with asthma as influenza infection can lead to asthma exacerbation.

The RCP three questions

➤ Have you had difficulty sleeping because of your asthma symptoms, including coughing? (Yes/No)
➤ Have you had your usual symptoms during the day (cough, chest tightness or breathlessness? (Yes/No)
➤ Has your asthma interfered with your activities (housework, work, school, sport, social, etc.)? (Yes/No)

Template GMS: Asthma (V16)

Prompt	Code	Date	Coded subsets
Exception report: asthma quality indicator	(9hA)		Except. asthma QI: Pt unsuit. (9hA1)
			Except. asthma QI: Pt inf. dis. (9hA2)
Ethnic category – 2001 census	(9i)		*See ethnicity template, Chapter 17*
Asthma monitoring check done	(9OJA)		Asthma monitoring by nurse (66YQ)
			Asthma monitoring by doctor (66YR)
			Refuses asthma monitoring (9OJ2)
Asthma resolved	(212G)		
Asthma annual review	(66YJ)		
Smoking status			*See smoking template, Chapter 25*
O/E HEIGHT	(229)		
O/E WEIGHT	(22A)		
BMI	(22K)		
WAIST CIRCUMFERENCE	(22N0)		
WAIST CIRCUMFERENCE DECLINED	(81Af)		
WAIST HIP RATIO	(22N7)		
PATIENT ADVISED REG. DIET	(8CA4)		
PATIENT ADVISED REG. EXERCISE	(8CA5)		
ALCOHOL CONSUMPTION			*See Alcohol, Chapter 27*
PATIENT ADVISED ABOUT ALCOHOL	(8CAM)		
SYSTOLIC BP	(2469)		
DIASTOLIC BP	(246A)		
O/E PULSE RATE	(242)		
Spirometry rev. +ve	(33G1)		
Refer spirometry	(8HRC)		
PEFR	(339A)		
PEFR (EN 13826)	(339p)		
Predicted peak flow	(339H)		
Days < 80% PEFR	(66Yc)		
Asthma limiting activities	(663P)		Asthma limiting activities (663P)
			Asthma not limiting activities (663Q)
Asthma disturbing sleep	(663N)		Asthma disturbing sleep (663N)
			Asthma not disturbing sleep (663O)
Asthma daytime symptoms	(663q)		Asthma never causes daytime symptoms (663s)
			Asthma daytime symptoms 1–2 per month (663t)
			Asthma daytime symptoms 1–2 per week (663u)
			Asthma daytime symptoms most days (663v)
Home PFR meter	(663S)		
Home nebuliser	(6638)		
Nebulisation since last appointment	(663c)		
Oral steroids last used	(6633)		

(continued)

Prompt	Code	Date	Coded subsets
Using spacer	(6631)		
Bronchodilator used > 1/day	(663L)		Bronchodil. > 1/day (663L) Bronchodil. 1/day max. (663M)
Inhaled steroids use	(663g)		Not using inhaled steroids (663g0) Using inhaled steroids – normal dose (663g1) Using inhaled steroids high dose (663g2) Increases inhaled steroid approp. (663g3)
Inhaler technique – good	(663H)		Inhaler tech. good (663H) Inhaler tech. poor (663I) Inhaler tech. moderate (66Y4)
HEALTH EDUCATION ASTHMA	(679J)		
Asthma A&E attended since last visit	(663m)		
Emergency asthma admission since 1st appointment	(663d)		
Asthma management plan given	(663U)		
Influenza vaccination	(65E)		*Influenza coded subsets same as in CHD template, Chapter 9*
PNEUMOCOCCAL VACCINATION	(6572)		*Pneumococcal coded subsets same as in CHD template, Chapter 9*
Asthma medication review	(8B3j)		
Asthma F/U	(66YK)		
Asthma annual review	(66YJ)		
DNA ASTHMA CLINIC	(9N4Q)		
ASTHMA MONITOR 1st LETTER	(90J4)		
ASTHMA MONITOR 2nd LETTER	(90J5)		
ASTHMA MONITOR 3rd LETTER	(90J6)		

(Add the capitalised prompts to your template to maximise points and quality care)

Do something extra

➤ Provide pneumococcal vaccine if the patient has both COPD and asthma or is over the age of 65.

    This will earn extra points.

➤ Smoking cessation is an integral part of the management of any respiratory condition. If the patient smokes, they should be encouraged not to and advice should be recorded. They should be referred to a smoking cessation clinic run by the primary care trust or an in-house clinic.

➤ Overweight and obese patients should be offered dietary and health education and exercise advice.

➤ Checking blood pressure may score extra points if the patient is on the hypertension/CKD register. Do not be afraid to come out of the asthma template and use the other indicated specific disease template. (The patient may have more than one chronic disease.)

➤ It is often the high-risk patients who do not attend review. These patients should be flagged up electronically so that the asthma review can be done opportunistically.

➤ Every patient should have a personalised action plan, with details of regular medication, how to recognise and what to do when the asthma gets out of control and when and how to seek medical help when needed.[16,17]

➤ Combination inhalers have been shown to be more cost-effective compared with using separate inhalers. They improve compliance too.

➤ Combination inhalers can be used as both preventive and reliever treatment. For example, the Symbicort SMART regime can be used as a twice a day preventer, to be increased and used as a reliever when the patient's asthma gets out of control.

➤ Issue an extra reliever inhaler so that the patient always has a spare one.

➤ Patients on high doses of inhaled steroids – over 1000 μg in adults or 400 μg beclomethasone or equivalent in children – have the potential for reduced bone mineral density and this should be monitored[18] and the patient referred for dual energy X-ray absorptiometry (DEXA) if indicated.

➤ Check height routinely in children on high doses of inhaled steroids.

➤ Asthma exacerbation in pregnancy increases the risk of foetal mortality and some patients' asthma gets worse during pregnancy. Make sure exacerbation is aggressively managed in a pregnant woman to reduce the risk of foetal hypoxia.

High-risk patients

➤ Using excessive amounts of beta 2 agonists.

➤ Frequent A&E attendances.

➤ Recent hospital admission.

➤ Severe asthma.

➤ Psychiatric history, drug abusers, excessive alcohol consumption.

References

1 British Thoracic Society. *The Burden of Lung Disease*. London: British Thoracic Society; 2001.

2 Asthma UK. *Where Do We Stand? Asthma in the UK Today*. London: Asthma UK; 2006. Available at: www.asthma.org.uk

3 General Practice Airways Group. *Opinion. Management of Asthma in Children*. GPIAG Opinion No. 4. 2006.

4 Dyer C. Asthma: diagnosis and management in the older person. *Prescriber*. 2006; 38–41. Available at: www.escriber.com

5 SIGN and BTS. 2009. Available at: www.sign.ac.uk

6 Williams LK, Peterson EL, Pladevall M, *et al*. Relationship between adherence to inhaled corticosteroids and poor out-comes among adults with asthma. *J Allergy Clin. Immunol*. 2004; **114**: 1288–93.

7 Fleming DM, Cross KW, Sunderland R, *et al*. Comparison of the seasonal patterns of asthma identified in general practitioner episode, hospital admission and deaths. *Thorax*. 2000; **55**: 662–5.

8 International Study of Asthma and Allergies in Childhood (ISAAC) Steering Committee. Worldwide variation in prevalence of symptoms of asthma, allergic rhinoconjunctivitis and atopic eczema. *Lancet.* 1998; **351**: 1225–32.

9 Anderson H, Gupta R, Strachan D, *et al.* 50 years of asthma: UK trends from 1995 to 2004. *Thorax.* 2007; **62**: 85–90.

10 Department for Work and Pensions. *What is Asthma.* Available at: www.dwp.gov.uk/publications/specialists-studies/.../a-z/asthma/

11 Price D, Ryan D, Pearce L, *et al.* The AIR study: asthma in real life. *Asthma J.* 1999; **4**: 74–8.

12 Sennhauser FH, Braun-Fahrlander C, Wildhaber, JH. The burden of asthma in children: a European perspective. *Paediatr. Respir. Rev.* 2005; **6**: 2–7.

13 Janson SL, McGrath KW, Covington JK, *et al.* Objective air way monitoring improves asthma control in the cold and flu season. A cluster randomised trial. *Chest.* 2010; **138**: 1148–55.

14 BTS guidelines on the management of asthma. *Thorax.* 2008; **63**(Suppl. 1V): iv1–121.

15 Warner J. Controlling indoor allergens. *Paediatr. Allergy Immunol.* 2000; **11**: 208–19.

16 Asthma UK. *Be in Control: personal asthma action plan.* Available at: www.asthma.org.uk/all_about_asthma/publications/be_in_control_perso.html (accessed 22 March 2011).

17 Primary Care Respiratory Society. *Opinion. Personal Asthma Action Plans.* PCRS-UK Opinion No. 12. 2007. Available at: www.pcrs-uk.org (accessed 22 March 2011).

18 National Osteoporosis Society guidelines. www.nos.org.uk/

Useful reading

➤ British Thoracic Society/Scottish Intercollegiate Guidelines Network asthma guidelines. Available at: www.brit-thoracic.org.uk/ClinicalInformation/Asthma/AsthmaGuidelines/tabid/83/Default.aspx

➤ Global Initiative for Asthma (GINA) guidelines. Available at: www.ginasthma.com/

➤ Asthma UK website: www.asthma.org.uk

➤ Primary Care Respiratory Society: www.pcrs-uk.org/index.php

CHAPTER 6

Atrial fibrillation

Atrial fibrillation (AF) is the most common cardiac arrhythmia encountered in clinical practice. It is classified under the following headings.

➤ **Paroxysmal:** if the episode terminates spontaneously within seven days, most often within 48 hours.

➤ **Persistent:** if the arrhythmia lasts longer than seven days and requires electrical or pharmacological cardioversion for termination.

➤ **Permanent:** if it does not terminate despite attempted cardioversion.

Prevalence

The overall incidence of AF is 11.5 per 1000 person-years in males and 8.9 per 1000 person-years in females. AF is increasingly common in old age. It affects about 5% of people over the age of 65 and almost 10% of those over the age of 80.[1]

The lifetime risk of developing AF is 23.8% and 22.2% in a 55-year-old man and woman respectively.[2]

The prevalence rate in primary care is 1.2%.

Why included in QOF

➤ AF is associated with increased mortality and morbidity. Diagnosis of AF between the ages of 55 and 64 years is associated with a shortening of life span by around six years for men and nine years for women.[3] Its inclusion in the QOF means early detection, aiming to reduce the morbidity and mortality.

➤ AF increases the risk of ischaemic stroke. Between 15% and 20% of all ischaemic strokes are due to AF. It is hoped that its inclusion will reduce the risk of ischaemic strokes.

➤ AF-related strokes have a worse prognosis for recovery and require longer hospital stays.[1]

➤ AF may be a presenting feature of a myocardial infarction or pulmonary embolism.

➤ Obesity is a strong risk factor of AF.[4] The rising levels of obesity in the Western world can partly explain the recent increase in AF. The primary care team is best placed to give health promotion advice.

➤ The evidence for the pharmacological treatment of patients with AF is strong and benefits are proven. A rapid assessment, an immediate action and treating patients with anti-thrombotic and anti-arrhythmic therapies, a realistic goal, can be delivered effectively by a GP.

➤ AF increases the risk of congestive heart failure three- to fourfold. Hopefully its inclusion in the QOF will enable prevention and early management of heart failure.

➤ About 1% of all NHS expenditure in the UK is due to AF, thus reflecting the huge public health burden.[5] The QOF financial incentive may lessen the NHS financial strain.

The facts

➤ AF is often seen in patients with coronary artery disease (CAD), hypertension and heart failure.

➤ One-third of patients with heart failure have AF.

➤ Female gender is a risk factor for paroxysmal atrial fibrillation and drug induced vascular arrhythmias.

➤ Illicit drugs and alcohol are especially common precipitating factors in younger patients.

➤ The Department of Health and NICE are keen to see GPs ramp up the prescribing of warfarin, which the department estimates could prevent up to 10 000 strokes a year.[6]

➤ The estimated total cost of maintaining one patient on warfarin for one year is £383, including monitoring.

➤ The cost per stroke due to AF is approximately £11 900 in the first year after the occurrence of stroke.

➤ All patients, whether symptomatic or presenting with an incidental finding, must be referred to the rapid access chest clinic as an emergency for confirmation of diagnosis.

➤ Stroke risk assessment using the CHADS2 score is vital. If the score is 2 or higher anti-coagulation therapy should be considered.

QOF: atrial fibrillation indicators

Indicators and points: total points 27

AF1

The practice can produce a register of patients with atrial fibrillation.

Points 5

As with other clinical domains, the compilation of register will enable appropriate advice and management and reduce the risk of AF-related strokes, which bear the worst prognosis.

A register is a prerequisite for an efficient call and recall system.

AF4

The percentage of patients with atrial fibrillation diagnosed after 1 April 2008 with electrocardiography or specialist-confirmed diagnosis.

Points 10   **Payment stages 40–90%**

➤ AF is usually detected by an irregular pulse.
➤ If AF is suspected an electrocardiogram (ECG) must be performed, either in-house or in a hospital ECG department. Once confirmed, read code the diagnosis.
➤ Holter ECG monitoring is useful in patients with suspected spontaneously cardioverted paroxysmal AF and daily symptoms, while longer periods of monitoring are required in those with less frequent episodes of AF. ECG monitoring is also useful for detecting asymptomatic AF in patients with previous AF paroxysms.[7]

AF3

The percentage of patients with atrial fibrillation who are currently treated with anti-coagulation drug therapy or an anti-platelet therapy.

Points 12   **Payment stages 40–90%**

The prevention of thromboembolism is an essential and crucial part of management in all patients. The risk factors can identify patients who are at high, intermediate or low risk of developing AF.

Warfarin is better than aspirin in reducing the risk of ischaemic stroke by approximately 40%.[8] Adequate therapy with an adjusted dose of warfarin (INR of 2–3) prevents two-thirds of cases of ischaemic stroke and reduces all cause mortality.[8]

Patients who are taking triple therapy, a combination of warfarin, clopidogrel and aspirin, have a threefold risk of bleeding complications compared with those just receiving warfarin. Combination therapy should be given only for a short period of time[9] – **keep a close eye on these patients**. The recommended anti-thrombotic therapies for thromboprophylaxis are shown in Table 6.1. Table 6.2 shows the CHA2DS2-VASc categories.

Table 6.1 Approach to thromboprophylaxis in patients with atrial fibrillations[10]

Risk category	CHA2DS2-VASc score	Recommended anti-thrombotic therapy
'Major' risk factor or > 2 'clinically relevant non-major' risk factors	> 2	Oral anti-coagulant with INR 2.0–3.0 (target 2.5)
'Clinically relevant non-major' risk factor	1	Either oral anti-coagulant **or** aspirin 75–325 mg daily Preferred: oral a anti-coagulant rather than aspirin
No risk factors	0	Either aspirin 75–325 mg **or** no anti-thrombotic therapy Preferred: no anti-thrombotic therapy rather than aspirin

Table 6.2 The CHA2DS2-VASc for stroke risk assessment

Letter	Clinical feature	Points awarded
C	Congestive heart failure/LV dysfunction	1
H	Hypertension (systolic > 160 mm Hg)	1
A	Age ≥ 75 years	2
D	Diabetes mellitus	1
S	Stroke/TIA	2
V	Vascular disease (PAD)	1
A	Age 65–74 years	1
Sc	Sex category (Female)	1
		Maximum 9 points

A patient scoring 2 or more points should be considered for anti-coagulation therapy.

Studies suggest that only 46% of patients with AF aged over 75 in primary care are taking warfarin.[11] NICE is to pilot indicators designed to drive up GP use of warfarin after the Department of Health estimated the move could prevent up to 10 000 strokes per year.

Maximising quality points

➤ Read code once the ECG confirms the diagnosis. Make sure there is a system in place for checking the A&E and hospital letters and ECG reports.

➤ Exception reporting, although important, should be used wisely and not excessively.

➤ AF can usually be detected if a patient presents with dyspnoea, dizziness, chest discomfort and an irregular pulse. Refer this patient for an ECG for confirmation of diagnosis. This will help you increase your prevalence.

➤ Family history is a significant factor in the development of AF. Actively screen patients who have a family history of AF. Consider doing an ECG – this might increase your prevalence.

➤ AF is less common in the South Asian (Indian subcontinent) and Afro-Caribbean population. You may be able to explain at the time of the practice QOF visit why your prevalence is low if your registered population has as large number of these patients.

➤ Address lifestyle issues such as excessive alcohol consumption and obesity. This will help you increase your obesity indicator and alcohol DES (if in your area).

➤ Chase all DNAs – send out appointments by post, ask the practice nurse to phone the patient or involve the community matron if the patient is housebound.

➤ Exception reporting can be done on those patients who refuse to attend for review and have been invited on three occasions during the preceding 12 months. Patients who are on maximum tolerated therapy, patients in whom the medication is not clinically appropriate or those who are terminally ill can be excluded too, **but** be prepared to explain at the time of the QOF visit.

> If a patient refuses ECG investigation for confirmation of diagnosis or refuses treatment, enter a code of informed dissent. This should be recorded clearly in the medical records.
> Authorise the medication for 6 months only. This flags up when review is due.
> Ensuring influenza and pneumococcal vaccines are given will earn extra points.
> Use the GRASP-AF (Guidance in Risk Assessment for Stroke Prevention in AF) tool. This is available www.improvement.nhs.uk/heart/

The tool will apply a CHADS2 risk stratification score to your patients with AF and identify patients who are at high risk and not on warfarin, helping you to achieve the full 10 points of indicator 3 easily.

Template GMS: Atrial fibrillation (V16)

Prompt	Code	Date	Coded subsets
Exception report: atrial fibrillation quality indicator	(9hF)		Except. atr. fib. QI: Pt uns. (9hF0) Except. atr. fib. QI: inf. diss. (9hF1)
Ethnic category – 2001 census	(9i)		See ethnicity template, Chapter 17
SMOKING STATUS			See smoking template, Chapter 25
ALCOHOL CONSUMPTION			See Alcohol, Chapter 27
O/E WEIGHT	(22A)		
O/E HEIGHT	(229)		
BODY MASS INDEX	(22K)		
PATIENT ADVISED REG. DIET	(8CA4)		
PATIENT ADVISED ABOUT ALCOHOL	(8CAM)		
PATIENT ADVISED REG. EXERCISE	(8CA5)		
WAIST CIRCUMFERENCE	(22N0)		
WAIST CIRCUMFERENCE DECLINED	(81Af)		
WAIST HIP RATIO	(22N7)		
SYSTOLIC BP	(2469)		
DIASTOLIC BP	(246A)		
O/E PULSE RATE	(242)		
THYROID FUNCTION TEST	(442J)		
SERUM T4 LEVEL	(4426)		
SERUM T3 LEVEL	(4424)		
SERUM TSH LEVEL NORMAL	(442A0)		
FBC	(424)		
LFT	(44D)		
SERUM CREATININE	(44J3)		
SERUM CHOLESTEROL	(44P)		
Atrial fibrillation resolved	(212R)		
ECG: atrial fibrillation	(3272)		
12 LEAD ECG	(321B)		ECG coded subsets same as in CHD template, Chapter 9
ECHO ABNORMAL	(58531)		US heart scan (5853) ECHO request (33BD) ECHO shows LVDDF (585g)

(continued)

Prompt	Code	Date	Coded subsets
STANDARD CHEST X-RAY	(539)		Chest X-ray normal (5352-1)
			Chest X-ray abnormal (5353)
			Chest X-ray requested (5351)
Anticoagulation contraindicated	(8I2R)		Anticoag. prescrib. by 3rd party (8B2K)
			Anticoag. contraind. (8I2R)
			Anticoag. declined (8I3d)
			Anticoag. not indic. (8I6N)
			Anticoag. not tolerat. (8I7A)
Advice about taking aspirin	(67I8)		H/O aspirin allergy (14LK)
			OTC aspirin (8B3T)
			Salicylate prophyl. (8B63)
			Aspirin prophyl. contraind. (8I24)
			Aspirin prophyl. refused (8I38)
			Aspirin not indic. (8I66)
			Aspirin not tolerat. (8I70)
			AR-salicylate (TJ53)
			[X]Salic. cause adv. eff. (U6051)
			[V]PH of aspirin allergy (ZV148)
Warfarin contraindicated	(8I25)		H/O warf. allergy (14LP)
			Warf. contraind. (8I25)
			Warf. declined (8I3E)
			Warf. not indic. (8I65)
			Warf. not tolerat. (8I71)
			AR-warf. (TJ421)
			[V]PH warf. allergy (ZV14A)
AR-anticoagulants	(TJ42)		AR-anticoag. (TJ42)
			AR-nicoumalone (TJ422)
			AR-phenindione (TJ423)
			AR-anticoag. NOS (TJ42z)
			[X]Anticoag. cause adv. eff. (U6042)
Clopidogrel prophylaxis	(8B6P)		Clop. contraind. (8I2K)
			H/O clop. allergy (14LQ)
			Clop. declined (8I3R)
			Clop. not indic. (8I6B)
			Clop. not tolerat. (8I72)
			[V]P/H clop. allergy (ZV14B)
			[X]Clop. cause adv. eff. their use (U6048)
H/O Dipyridamole allergy	(14LX)		Dipy. contraind. (8I2b)
			Dipy. declined (8I3n)
			Dipy. not indic. (8I6a)
			Dipy. not tolerat. (8I7J)
			AR-dipyridamole (TJC44)
			[X]Coronary vasodil. adv. eff. NEC (U60C3)
General medical referral	(8H41)		Cardiology ref. (8H44)
			Ref. for ECG (8HR1)
			Private ref. to cardiologist (8HVJ)
			Ref. to GPwSI card. (8H4R)

(continued)

Prompt	Code	Date	Coded subsets
MEDICATION REVIEW DONE	(8B3V)		
ATRIAL FIBRILLATION MONITORING 1st LETTER	(90s0)		
ATRIAL FIBRILLATION MONITORING 2nd LETTER	(90s1)		
ATRIAL FIBRILLATION MONITORING 3rd LETTER	(90s2)		
ATRIAL FIBRILLATION VERBAL INVITE	(90s3)		
ATRIAL FIBRILLATION TELEPHONE INVITE	(90s4)		
INFLUENZA VACCINATION	(65E)		*Influenza vaccination coded subsets same as in CHD template, Chapter 9*
PNEUMOCOCCAL VACCINATION	(6572)		*Pneumococcal vaccination coded subsets same as in CHD template, Chapter 9*

(Add the capitalised prompts to your template to maximise points and quality care)

Do something extra

➤ Although not a quality indicator, it is best practice to run an echocardiography (ECHO) for all new AF patients if stroke risk is in question, as per the NICE guidance. This would exclude valvular issues. Make sure the ventricular rate is under some control prior to sending the patient for ECHO.

➤ Invest in an ECG machine. Even if you are not an expert in ECG interpretation, you cannot miss the rapid, irregular fibrillatory waves typical in AF. ECG will also pick up asymptomatic patients.

➤ Once AF is confirmed, undertake further investigations such as full blood count (FBC), urea and electrolytes (U&E) and liver and thyroid function tests (TFT and LFT).

➤ Take a chest X-ray where thoracic pathology is suspected as a cause of AF.

➤ Patients with AF who remain symptomatic despite rate management should be referred for electrophysiological assessment and possible ablation.

➤ Patients with a 'high risk' of bleeding requiring extra caution can be predicted carrying out doing a new validated bleeding risk score scheme called HAS-BLED (hypertension, abnormal liver/renal function, stroke, bleeding history, labile INR, elderly, drugs/alcohol – one point given to each factor if present).[12]

References

1 Lakatta EG, Levy D. Arterial and cardiac aging: major shareholders in cardiovascular disease enterprises. *Circulation*. 2003; **107**: 139–46. Available at: www.circ.ahajournals/org/cgi/content/full/107/1/139

2 Lip GY, Tse HF. Management of atrial fibrillation. *Lancet*. 2007; **370**: 604–18. Available at: www.ncbi.nlm.nih.gov/pubmed/17707756

3 Benjamin EA, Wolf PA, D'Agostino RB, *et al.* Impact of atrial fibrillation on the risk of death: the Framingham heart study. *Circulation.* 1998; **98**: 946–52.

4 Braunwald E. Shattuck Lecture: cardiovascular medicine at the turn of the new millennium: triumphs, concerns and opportunities. *N. Engl. J Med.* 1997; **337**: 1360–9.

5 Iqbal MB, Taeja AK, Lip GYH, *et al.* Atrial fibrillaion: strategies in primary care: routine investigations in atrial fibrillation. *Arch. Intern. Med.* 1994; **154**: 1449–57. Available at: www.medscape.com/viewartical/510211_4

6 www.pulsetoday.co.uk/story.asp? (June 2010).

7 Hindricks G, Piorkowski C, Tanner H, *et al.* Symptom guided assessment of atrial fibrillation recurrence after radiofrequency pulmonary vein ablation: is it a reliable strategy? *Circulation.* 2005; **112**: 307–13. Available at: www.scielo.br/scielo.php?pid=S0066-782X20060000500015

8 Lip GYH, Watson T. Stroke prevention in atrial fibrillation – things can only get better. *Thromb. Res.* 2006; **118**: 321–33.

9 Hansen ML, Sorenson R, Mette T, *et al.* Risk of bleeding with single, dual or triple therapy with warfarin, aspirin and clopidogrel in patients with atrial fibrillation. *Arch. Intern. Med.* 2010; **170**: 1433–41.

10 Camm AJ, Kirchhof P, Lip GYH, *et al.* Guidelines for the management of atrial fibrillation: the Task Force for the Management of Atrial Fibrillation of the European Society of Cardiology (ESG) *Eur. Heart J.* 2010; **19**: 2369–429. Available at: www.ncbi.nlm.gov/pubmed/20802247

11 Jeffrey S, Barclay L. Warfarin superior to aspirin for stroke prevention in AF. BAFTA trial published. *Lancet.* 2007; **370**: 493–503.

12 Lip GYH, Frison L, Halperin JL, *et al.* Comparative validation of a novel risk score [HAS-BLED] for predicting bleeding risk in anticoagulated patients with atrial fibrillation. *J Am. Coll. Cardiol.* 2011; **57**: 173–80.

Useful reading

➤ Atrial Fibrillation Association: *Information and Support for Professionals and Patients.* Available at: www.atrial-fibrillation.org.uk (accessed 22 March 2011).

➤ British Heart Foundation. For leaflets, booklets, posters, factsheets for professionals and patients: www.bhf.org.uk

➤ National Institute for Health and Clinical Excellence and the National Collaborating Centre for Chronic Conditions. *The Management of Atrial Fibrillation: NICE guideline CG36.* London: NIHCE; 2006. Available at: www.nice.org.uk/nicemedia/pdf/cg036fullguideline.pdf and www.content.onlinejacc.org/cgi/content/abstract/57/2/173.

CHAPTER 7

Cancer

The number of patients with cancer and the number of patients surviving cancer is growing dramatically. Continuity of care is very important and most GPs wish to be involved in the ongoing care of their registered patients who have cancer.[1]

A 2000 UK report on cancer treatment concluded that 'as many as 70% of patients might safely stop hospital follow ups without detriment to the desired outcomes of early recognition of recurrence or new disease, psychological support, opportunities for audit and research and training'.[2]

Why included in QOF

➤ More than 80% of patients with common cancers first present to their GP with symptoms.[3]

➤ The GP's role in relation to cancer covers the full spectrum of care – prevention, screening, detection, treatment and palliative care – and that includes psychological and emotional support not only to the patient but also to their families and carers.

➤ GPs have a place in the follow-up of many patients with cancer. This is to detect recurrence and monitor the effects of treatment. In a study in Glasgow, most patients with early breast cancer consulted their GPs more than 10 times during the year after diagnosis – almost double the number of consultations with hospital specialists.[4] The long-held tradition of providing routine follow-up care in the hospital sector has been challenged lately following the results of two randomised controlled trials carried out in the UK and Canada.[5] Both trials confirmed that the follow-up of patients with breast cancer in the primary care is a safe alternative to a specialist follow-up.

➤ Patients trust their GP to provide the competent care and support as some may have other healthcare needs on top of their cancer.[6]

➤ The supportive and coordinating role of GPs led to cancer's inclusion in the QOF.

➤ Continuity of care is of paramount importance. The GP is able to facilitate communication between specialists and members of multi-disciplinary team making sure that the patient receives timely and high-quality care.

➤ GPs are well placed to promote healthy lifestyle changes such as stopping smoking, reducing sun exposure and obesity – risk factors for cancer.

The facts

➤ Twenty per cent of the average GP's patients will be smokers and 30% will be overweight with a Body Mass Index (BMI) > 25 kg/m^2.[7] Smoking and obesity are both risk factors for cancer.

➤ The lifetime population risk of developing breast cancer is one in nine.[8]

➤ Familial breast and ovarian cancer susceptibility syndrome due to altered BRCA1 and BRCA2 genes accounts for up to 80% lifetime risk of developing breast cancer and a 20–40% lifetime risk of developing ovarian cancer.[8]

➤ Early cancer detection has favourable outcome. Randomised controlled trials of breast cancer[9] and colorectal cancer screening have demonstrated that detecting cancers earlier has significant effects on mortality.[10] NICE has recently published referral guidelines for suspected cancers.[11]

➤ Few cancer patients have close contact with their GP during the course of palliative treatment, as the oncologists and the nurses in the outpatient clinic take care of their problems, and do not visit their GP during the hospital-based treatment.

➤ Most cancer patients view their GP as having an important supportive role as hospital specialists do not have time to offer psychological support.[12]

➤ In a study of 103 women treated for gynaecological cancer and attending a hospital clinic for follow-up, 28% were willing to consider follow-up by their GP.[13]

➤ The benefits of GP follow-up is adequate time to discuss the problem and the likelihood of being seen on the same day. Because GPs know their patients well, they tend to fit in and address the urgent problems on the same day.

QOF: cancer indicators

Indicators and points: total points 11

Records

CANCER1

The practice can produce a register of all cancer patients, defined as a 'register' of patients with a diagnosis of cancer excluding non-melanotic skin cancers from 1 April 2003.

Points 5

A register is important to ensure that the patient gets appropriate medical care, psychological support, regular routine visits and tests if needed. This can be done by involving a multi-professional team with different roles and responsibilities. Monitoring the effects of treatment and early detection of recurrence is only possible if there is a register.

The aim of maintaining a register is to produce a recognisable improvement in the quality of cancer care by the primary healthcare team. Practices should make sure that they have a system in place for correctly coding any new diagnosis of cancer.

Ongoing management

CANCER3

The percentage of patients with cancer, diagnosed within the last 18 months, who have a patient review recorded as occurring within six months of the practice receiving confirmation of the diagnosis.

Points 6   **Payment stages 40–90%**

This is the key role of primary care physician. The number of patients surviving cancer is growing dramatically. The GP must not lose contact with the patient even if the patient is undergoing radiotherapy or chemotherapy. The review must include an assessment of any support needs of the patient and carer and a review of coordination with secondary care.

All cancer patients should be discussed in a multi-disciplinary team meeting attended by all the professionals involved in the care of the patient to identify and address the patient's and carer's needs.

Maximising quality points

➤ All cancers are diagnosed in secondary care. Read code the hospital letter once the diagnosis is confirmed.
➤ The register is a useful tool and it must be kept up to date.
➤ Verify the register by comparing national prevalence rates for all cancers for all ages against national prevalence statistics. For example, the national prevalence of cancer for the year 2009/10 was 14.08 per 1000, which for a practice of 5000 patients would give around 70 cases. If your practice has a higher than average age band, you should have more cases on your list. If your prevalence is low, check your system of recording and coding.
➤ Do a computer search of patients on drugs such as Tamoxifen and the anti-androgens. Read code if not done already to increase your prevalence.
➤ Non-melanotic skin cancers such as squamous cell carcinoma and basal cell carcinoma do not count.
➤ Make sure you have a system in place such that the named read code receptionist brings the hospital letter with a diagnosis of cancer to your attention. All new patients registered with a cancer diagnosis must be checked when the last review was done. A cancer review must be done within six months of the diagnosis. Update your practice nurse, healthcare assistant and summarising staff about this important QOF point.
➤ Ask the district nurse attached your practice whether she is doing home visits on any registered cancer patient of yours.
➤ *In my small practice I read code all the cancer diagnoses. Losing a six-month window for even one patient can make me lose points.*

➤ Check your 8BAV code (cancer care review) every three months. This will identify patients who have not had a cancer review recorded within six months of the cancer diagnosis.

➤ Pick up early anxiety and depression symptoms and treat. By entering the read code of anxiety and depression you increase your depression prevalence.

➤ Provide influenza and pneumococcal vaccination .Check with the hospital first if the patient is having chemotherapy.

➤ Avoid using code 9h81 (cancer patient unsuitable) or 9h82 (cancer informed dissent) to remove the patient from the denominator – you could be in trouble at the time of the QOF visit.

Template GMS: Cancer (V16)

Prompt	Code	Date	Coded subsets
Exception reporting: cancer quality indicator	(9h8)		Except. cancer QI: Pt unsuitable (9h81) Except. cancer QI: inf. dis. (9h82)
Ethnic category – 2001 census	(9i)		See ethnicity template, Chapter 17
O/E WEIGHT	(22A)		
O/E HEIGHT	(229)		
BODY MASS INDEX	(22K)		
WAIST CIRCUMFERENCE	(22N0)		
SMOKING STATUS			See smoking template, Chapter 25
ALCOHOL CONSUMPTION			See Alcohol, Chapter 27
PATIENT ADVISED REG. DIET	(8CA4)		
PATIENT ADVISED REG. EXERCISE	(8CA5)		
PATIENT ADVISED ABOUT ALCOHOL	(8CAM)		
Cancer care review	(8BAV)		
Ds 1500 completed	(9EB5)		
PRESCRIPTION PAYMENT EXEMPTION	(9DD)		
Cancer diagnosis discussed	(8CL0)		
Medication review done	(8B3V)		
Cancer care review	(8BAV)		
REFERRAL TO MACMILLAN NURSE	(8HH6)		
UNDER CARE OF MACMILLAN NURSE	(9NNS)		(enter the name)
DISTRICT NURSE	(03FG)		(enter the name)
REFER TO DIETICIAN	(8H76)		(enter the name)
HAS A CARER	(918F)		
Carer's DETAILS	(9180)		Carer's details subsets same as in mental health template, Chapter 22
SUICIDE RISK	(1BD4)		
SUICIDE ATTEMPT	(TK)		
WORK STATUS	(13J)		Work status coded subsets same as in mental health template, Chapter 22
REFER TO SOCIAL WORKER	(8H75)		
SOCIAL WORKER	(03AQ)		
PREFERRED PLACE OF DEATH	(94Z0)		Preferred place of death coded subsets same as in palliative care template, Chapter 24

(continued)

Prompt	Code	Date	Coded subsets
INFLUENZA VACCINATION	(65E)		Influenza coded subsets same as in CHD template, Chapter 9
PNEUMOCOCCAL VACCINATION	(6572)		Pneumococcal vaccination coded subsets same as in CHD template, Chapter 9

(Add the capitalised prompts to your template to maximise points and quality care)

Do something extra

➤ Good quality care can only be achieved by setting aside time to meet with all professionals involved in the care. Enter in the medical records the names of involved, including the Macmillan nurse, district nurse, dietician and carer. By entering the read codes you are less likely to forget the names of the involved professionals and the carer.

➤ Most cancers arise sporadically, probably due to a combination of environmental factors like smoking, external radiation and inherited genetics. Reminding patients about lifestyle factors will go a long way to reducing their risks.

➤ Obesity is a key risk factor. Involve a health trainer or dietician.

➤ At the review, take the opportunity to elicit any family history of cancer and insert the codes into the records of any family members who are also registered in the practice. For example, those with first degree relatives with breast cancer or relatives with familial polyposis. Familial breast and ovarian cancer susceptibility syndrome due to altered BRCA1 and BRCA2 genes accounts for up to 80% lifetime risk of developing breast cancer and a 20–40% lifetime risk of ovarian cancer. The cancer genetics referral guidelines are available from regional genetic centres to advise on referring a patient to a genetic department. NICE has published guidelines on the management of familial breast cancer, which stratify familial risk into low, moderate or high risk.[14]

➤ It is important to know the carer. By adding the following codes and the name of the carer, you and your team are less likely to forget the name:
— has a carer: 918F
— carer: 918A (you can enter the carer's name).

➤ Social worker input regarding claiming the fees and allowances is valuable:
— refer to social worker: 8H75
— social worker: 03AQ (*enter the name*).

➤ It is worth adding the following codes as they may prove useful when doing a review:
— chemotherapy: 8BAD0
— radiotherapy: 5151
— metastatic cancer: BB13
— palliative care: ZV57C.

➤ Remember, the patient is entitled to free prescriptions if under 60 under the new rules of prescription payment exemption. Prescription payment exemption – 9DD.

➤ Make sure there is an arrangement in place for prescription collection and delivery to the patient.

➤ Keep yourself up to date with recent developments in various cancer managements.

➤ Everyone involved with the patient care must know patient's preferred place of death. If the patient wishes to die at home enter the read code 94Z1.

➤ Provide influenza vaccination to the carer.

References

1 Grunfeld E, Mant D, Vassey MP, *et al*. Specialist and general practice views on routine follow up of breast cancer patients in general practice. *Fam. Pract.* 1995; **12**: 60–5.

2 Royal College of General Practitioners and Faculty of Clinical Oncology, Royal College of Radiologists. *Cancer Care Follow Up: an evolving service*. London: RCGP and RCR; 2000.

3 Fergusson RJ, Gregor A, Dodds R, *et al*. Management of lung cancer in South east Scotland. *Thorax*. 1996; **51**: 569–74.

4 Macleod U, Ross S, Twelves C, *et al*. Primary and secondary care management of women with early breast cancer from affluent and deprived areas. *BMJ*. 2000; **320**: 1442–5.

5 Grunfeld E. Cancer survivorship: a challenge for primary care physicians. *Br J Gen. Pract*. 2005; **55**: 741–2.

6 Anvik T, Holtedahl KA, Mikalsen H. When patients have cancer, they stop seeing me – the role of general practitioner in early follow-up of patients with cancer – a qualitative study. *BMC Family Practice*. 2006; **7**: 19.

7 Cancer Australia. *The Primary Care Perspective on Cancer*. 2003. Available at: www.canceraustralia.gov.au/.../cancer-control.../national-cancer-control-initiative-reports/

8 Qureshi N. The current state of cancer family history collection tools in primary care: a systematic review. *Genetics in Medicine*. 2009; **11**: 495–506.

9 Nystrom L, Retqvist LE, Wall S, *et al*. Breast cancer screening with mammography: overview of Swedish randomised trials. *Lancet*. 1993; **341**: 973–8.

10 Towler B, Irwig L, Glasziou P, *et al*. A systematic review of the effects of screening for colorectal cancer using occult blood test, Hemoccult. *BMJ*. 1998; **317**: 559–65.

11 National Institute for Health and Clinical Excellence. *Referral Guidelines for Suspected Cancer: NICE guideline CG27*. London: NHICE; 2005.

12 Bulsara C, Ward AM, Joske D. Patient perceptions of the GP role in cancer management. *Aust. Fam. Phys.* 2005; **34**: 299–300.

13 Papagrigoriadis S, Heyman B. Patient's views on follow-up of colorectal cancer; implications for risk communication and decision making. *Postgrad. Med. J.* 2003: **79**: 403–7.

14 National Institute for Health and Clinical Excellence. *Familial Breast Cancer: the classification and care of women at risk of familial breast cancer in primary, secondary and tertiary care: NICE guideline CG27*. London: NHICE; 2006.

Useful reading

➤ NHS Improvement – cancer: www.improvement.nhs.uk/cancer/

CHAPTER 8

Cardiovascular disease: primary prevention

The revised QOF (April 2009) rewards practices for performing face-to-face formal cardiovascular (CV) risk assessment in all new patients diagnosed with hypertension. In England there is also a drive, using a systematic strategy, to identify people aged 40–74 years who are likely to be at high risk and offer advice on reducing risk and treatment for lipid modification and blood pressure lowering where appropriate. This is funded through locally enhanced services (LES) money.

Why included in QOF

There is a linear relationship with increasing blood pressure on premature morbidity and mortality in the UK.[1] A 2 mm Hg rise in systolic blood pressure results in a 7% increase in risk of death from ischaemic heart disease and a 10% increase in the risk of death from stroke.[2] It is believed that the financial incentive in the QOF may lessen the strain on the NHS.

There is strong evidence that GPs with a team of other healthcare professionals, including pharmacists, can significantly improve long-term outcomes.

Maximising quality points

➤ Flag up all patients with hypertension and do a CV risk assessment at the time of routine hypertension monitoring.
➤ Enter read code CV risk assessment 662K on the hypertension template.
➤ Run a computer search and identify all patients in the age group 40–74 years. Invite them for a full health check and fasting blood tests.
➤ Enter an alert message on the screen of 40–74 year-olds so that reception staff can fit these patients in (opportunistically or booked appointment).
➤ Remember, recent ex-smokers still carry some excess risk compared with never smokers. Run a computer search of all smokers and invite them for a risk assessment.

➤ Enter a read code on those patients who have declined – 9Oh9-1. They may need an explanation as to why you are focussing on the lifestyle modifications – they are the ones most likely to gain.

➤ Involve your community pharmacist. Patients can be advised to have the risk assessment done when having anti-hypertensive prescriptions made up or when pharmacists undertake medication use review (MUR). (*This has worked well in my practice as my pharmacist is based in my health centre.*)

➤ Make sure your healthcare assistant and practice nurse have completed the appropriate training for CV risk assessment.

➤ The cardiovascular disease (CVD) risk assessment tool, Framingham 1991 – a 10-year risk equation[3] – can be loaded on the practice computer – this makes it easier for the nurses and healthcare assistants to calculate the risk. The risk calculator is not appropriate for older people or people in high-risk ethnic groups.[4,5]

Cardiovascular risk charts

Using the 10-year risk as the basis of cardiovascular risk assessments and charts limits the usefulness of risk estimates. Some argue that the risk charts are 'biased by age'. People in their seventies are inevitably assessed as being at high risk but those under 40 are rarely judged at risk. It has been suggested that the cardiovascular risk charts should be based on lifetime risk estimates. It is hoped that lifestyle in risk assessment will help address the age-based bias.

QOF: cardiovascular disease, primary prevention

Indicators and points: total points 13

PP1

In those patients with a new diagnosis of hypertension (excluding those with pre-existing CHD, diabetes, stroke and/or TIA) recorded between the preceding 1 April to 31 March: the percentage of patients who have had a face-to-face cardiovascular risk assessment at the outset of diagnosis (within three months of the initial diagnosis) using an agreed risk assessment tool.

Points 8   **Payment stages 40–70%**

NICE recommends that the Framingham 1991, 10-year risk equation is used.[3] This is available at: www.bnsoc.org/cardiovascular_Risk_Charts_and_calculators.stm

CVD risk[3] = 10-year risk of fatal and non-fatal stroke, including TIA + 10 year risk of coronary heart disease. CHD risk includes the risks of death from CHD, including silent myocardial infarction, angina and coronary insufficiency (acute coronary syndrome).

Most computer systems provide a Framingham-based risk score. QRISK2 is another predictor of cardiovascular risk. NICE and the Department of Health in England have jointly agreed to use the Framingham 10-year risk equation. Scotland uses ASSIGN.

NICE recommends using lipid modifying drugs for treating all adults over 40 with a 20% or greater CVD risk.[1] Treatment with 40 mg Simvastatin is recommended as first line therapy.

PP2

The percentage of people with hypertension diagnosed after 1 April 2009 who have been given lifestyle advice during the last 15 months for increasing physical activity, smoking cessation, safe alcohol consumption and healthy diet.

Points 5   **Payment stages 40–70%**

Before initiating statin therapy for primary prevention, all other modifiable risk factors should be considered and management optimised. Nurse-led clinics are vital for achieving this indicator target.

People at high risk should be advised as follows.[5]

➤ To eat at least five portions of fruit and vegetables per day.
➤ To take 30 minutes of physical activity per day, of moderate intensity to the point of mild breathlessness, at least five days per week – brisk walking, cycling or using stairs.
  — Physical activity of 10 minutes or more accumulated throughout the day is as effective as longer sessions.
➤ To eat a diet in which total fat intake comprises no more than 30% of the total energy intake, with saturated fats 10% or less of total energy intake and dietary cholesterol intake less than 300 mg/day.
➤ To eat at least two portions of fish per week, including a portion of oily fish – limited to two portions per week in pregnant women.
➤ Not to smoke.[6]
➤ To manage weight[6] – in patients with a BMI of > 25 kg/m[2].
➤ To limit alcohol intake to 1–2 units or less/day for women and 2–3 units or less/day for men.[6]
➤ To sleep for seven hours a day.[7] Long and short sleep duration is a potential risk factor for CVD. Sleeping for more or less than seven hours a day may be an indication of an underlying risk of CVD.

Template GMS: CVD primary prevention (V16)

Prompt	Code	Date	Coded subsets
Exception report: CVD quality indicator	(9hJ)		CVD high risk review declined (8IAK) CVD risk assess. declined (9Oh9) Except. CVD QI (9hJ0) Except. CVD QI: inf. dis. (9hJ1)
Risk review	(6A40)		
Ethnic category – 2001 census	(9i)		See ethnicity template, Chapter 17
FAMILY HISTORY IHD	(ZV173)		
FAMILY H/O HYPERCHOL.	(1269)		
O/E Height	(229)		
O/E Weight	(22A)		
BMI	(22K)		(Target < 25 kg/m[2])

(continued)

Prompt	Code	Date	Coded subsets
*Waist circumference	(22N0)		(see below)
WAIST HIP RATIO	(22N7)		
PATIENT ADVISED REG. DIET	(8CA4)		
PATIENT ADVISED REG. EXERCISE	(8CA5)		
PATIENT ADVISED ABOUT ALCOHOL	(8CAM)		
Systolic Blood Pressure	(2469)		(Target BP to 140/90 or below)
Diastolic Blood Pressure	(246A)		
24 HOUR BP MONITOR	(662L)		
AVE DAY SYSTOLIC	(246Y)		
AVE DAY DIASTOLIC	(246X)		
AVE NIGHT SYSTOLIC	(246b)		
AVE NIGHT DIASTOLIC	(246a)		
O/E PULSE RATE	(242)		
REFER FOR ECG	(8HRI)		
12 LEAD ECG	(321B)		ECG coded subsets same as in CHD template, Chapter 9
STANDARD CHEST X-RAY	(535)		Standard chest X-ray coded subsets same as in CHD template, Chapter 9
URINE PROTEIN TEST+	(4674)		Urine protein coded subsets same as in CKD template, Chapter 10
URINE ALBUMIN:CREAT RATIO	(46TC)		
URINE MICROALBUMIN	(46W)		Urine microalbumin coded subsets same as in CKD template, Chapter 10
Smoking status			See smoking template, Chapter 25
Alcohol consumption			See Alcohol, Chapter 27
Advice about taking aspirin	(6718)		OTC aspirin (8B3T) Salicylate prophyl. (8B63) Aspirin not indic. (8I66) Aspirin prophyl. refused (8I38) Aspirin not tolerat. (8I70)
Statin prophylaxis	(8B6A)		Statins contraind. (8I27) Statins declined (8I3C) Statins not indic. (8I63) Statins not tolerat. (8I76) Adver. reaction to Simva (TJC24) Adver. reaction to Pravas (TJC25) Statin cause adver. eff. ther. (U60CA)
Serum cholesterol	(44P)		(No target recommended)
Serum LDL	(44P6)		(No target recommended)
Serum HDL	(44P5)		
Serum triglyceride	(44Q)		
Serum cholesterol:HDL ratio	(441F)		
12 LEAD ECG	(321B)		ECG coded subsets same as in CHD template, Chapter 9
REFER FOR ECG	(8HR1)		
Serum urea level	(44J9)		

(continued)

Prompt	Code	Date	Coded subsets
Serum creatinine	(44J3)		
Serum potassium	(44I4)		
Serum sodium	(44I5)		
GFR	(451E)		
LFT	(44D)		
CK	(44H4)		
Serum ALT	(44GB)		
Random blood sugar	(44g0)		
Fasting glucose	(44g1)		
THYROID FUNCTION	(442J)		
Life style counselling	(67H)		
JBS cardiovascular risk < 10% 10 years	(662k)		JBS cardiovascular risk < 10% 10 yrs (662k) JBS cardiovascular risk 10–20% in 10 yrs (662l) JBS cardiovascular risk > 20–30% in 10 yrs (662m) JBS cardiovascular risk > 30% in 10yrs (662n) CVD risk assess. declined (90h9)
CVD follow up	(66f1)		
CVD RISK INVITE	(9m2)		
CARDIOVASCULAR DISEASE RISK ASSESSMENT TELEPHONE INVITE	(9m20)		
CARDIOVASCULAR DISEASE RISK ASSESSMENT VERBAL INVITE	(9m21)		
CARDIOVASCULAR DISEASE RISK ASSESSMENT 1st INVITE	(9m22)		
CARDIOVASCULAR DISEASE RISK ASSESSMENT 2nd INVITE	(9m23)		
CARDIOVASCULAR DISEASE RISK ASSESSMENT 3rd INVITE	(9m24)		
INFLUENZA VACCINATION	(65E)		Influenza vaccination coded subsets same as in CHD template, Chapter 9
PNEUMOCOCCAL VACCINATION	(6572)		Pneumococcal vaccination coded subsets same as in CHD template, Chapter 9

*   Waist Circumference target:
        Europoids Male < 94 cm; Female< 80 cm
        South Asians and Chinese Male < 90cm; Females < 80cm

(Add the capitalised prompts to your template to maximise points and quality care)

Do something extra

➤ Run a computer search of patients who have microalbuminuria or a family history of hypercholesterolemia or ischaemic heart disease (IHD) and assess their CV risk.

➤ Statin therapy is recommended as part of the management strategy for the primary prevention of CVD for adults who have a 20% or greater 10-year risk of developing CVD.

➤ Primary prevention treatment is Simvastatin 40 mg. If there are potential drug interactions or Simvastatin 40 mg is contraindicated or not tolerated, a lower dose or alternative preparation may be chosen.

➤ Stick to the recommended strategy – there are no specific cholesterol treatment targets. No repeat lipid monitoring is recommended and no intensifying of lipid lowering therapy should be undertaken.

➤ There is no proven benefit of taking aspirin. Discuss the role of aspirin for primary prevention in patients taking over-the-counter medication. In primary prevention there is less favourable risk–benefit ratio.[8]

References

1 National Institute for Health and Clinical Excellence. *Hypertension: management of hypertension in adults in primary care: NICE guideline CG34*. London: NHICE; 2006.

2 Lewington S, Clarke R, Qizilbash R, *et al*. Age specific relevance of usual blood pressure to vascular mortality: a meta-analysis of individual data for one million adults in 61 prospective studies. *Lancet*. 2002; **360**: 1903–13.

3 Anderson KM, Odell PM, Wilson PW, *et al*. Cardiovascular disease risk profiles. *Am. Heart J*. 1990; **121**(1 Pt 2): 293–8.

4 National Institute for Health and Clinical Excellence. *Statins for the prevention of cardiovascular events: NICE technology appraisal TA94*. London: NHICE; 2006.

5 National Institute for Health and Clinical Excellence. *Lipid Modification: NICE guideline CG67*. London: NHICE; 2008.

6 Joint British Societies. JBS 2: Joint British Societies guidelines on prevention of cardiovascular disease in clinical practice. *Heart*. 2005; **91**(Suppl. V): v1–v52.

7 Hitt E. Increased CVD risk associated with shorter and longer sleep duration. *Sleep*. 2010; **33**: 1037–42.

8 Belgent C, Blackwell L, Collins R, *et al*. Aspirin in the primary and secondary prevention of vascular disease: collaborative meta-analysis of individuals of individual participant data from randomised trials. *Lancet*. 2009; **373**: 1849–60.

Useful information

For health professionals

➤ *Identifying and supporting people most at risk of dying prematurely*. NICE public health guidance 15 (2008): www.nice.org.uk/guidance/PH15

➤ *Alcohol-use disorders: preventing harmful drinking*. NICE public health guidance 24 (2010): www.nice.org.uk/guidance/PH24

➤ *Cardiovascular risk assessment and the modification of blood lipids for primary and secondary prevention of cardiovascular disease*: www.nice.org.uk/guidance/CG67

For patients

➤ Food Standards Agency. *Healthy Diet*. Available at: www.eatwell.gov.uk/healthydiet/ (accessed May 2009).

➤ Food Standards Agency. *Saturated Fat*. Available at: www.eatwell.gov.uk/healthydiet/ fss/fats/satfat/ (accessed May 2009).

➤ HEART UK. *Healthy Eating Fact Sheet F06*. Available at: www.heartuk.org.uk/images/ uploads/healthylivingpdfs/HUK_factsheet_F06_PlantSterols.pdf (accessed May 2009).

CHAPTER 9

Coronary heart disease: secondary prevention

Definition

Ischaemic heart disease (IHD) is characterised by ischaemia to the heart muscle due to coronary artery disease. It is more common in men and those with a family history of the disease.[1] IHD may be present with angina pectoris, unstable angina, acute coronary syndrome or myocardial infarction.[2]

Prevalence

One point four million people currently alive in the UK have had a myocardial infarction (MI).[3]

Every year in the UK there are 43 000 new cases of angina in women and 52 000 in men. The incidence rises with age.[4]

More than 2 million people suffer from angina in the UK and 4–6% of these die annually.[5]

Variation in coronary heart disease (CHD) mortality is largely caused by factors such as housing, education and employment. The big question mark is can the NHS address the social factors behind CHD and provide a better environment?[6]

Why included in QOF

➤ CHD is a huge health burden.
➤ Early identification of underlying CV risks and management is very important. Addressing lifestyle modifications such as smoking cessation, blood pressure control, diet and regular exercise can reduce the risks of developing an MI.
➤ Between 7% and 15% of patients who suffer an MI die within one year of hospital discharge. In these patients risk factor identification, drug therapy and lifestyle measures can prevent future cardiac events and reduce the risk of death. All of these can be done in the primary care setting.

➤ Putting primary care in the front line of patient education, with emphasis on prevention and control of symptoms, can improve the quality of life after a cardiac event, allowing the patient to return to normal or near-normal daily activities.

➤ Improving early diagnosis and maximising secondary prevention can reduce hospital admissions.

➤ CHD plus depression is a dangerous combination. It triples the risk of death. Early detection and effective treatment, such as structured group physical activity, may improve the outcome. GPs are ideally placed to manage this.

The facts

➤ Although fewer people are developing angina, its prevalence remains high as people live longer.

➤ Heart disease is a major cause of hospital admission.[7]

➤ Women in the UK are three times more likely to die from heart disease than from breast cancer.[8]

➤ Women are more likely to have angina. The reason may be that, although atherosclerosis is less common in women, their smaller arteries are at greater risk of calcification.

➤ The cost of angina was estimated to be £700 million in 2000, 1.3% of the total NHS expenditure – a substantial cost to the NHS.

➤ Pharmacotherapy in secondary prevention has been the key factor in reducing the mortality due to CHD and costs to the NHS.[3]

➤ Weekend MI linked is with increased mortality. Patients admitted over the weekend with an MI do less well than those admitted on weekdays because of poor provision of invasive cardiac procedures at the weekend.[9]

QOF: CHD indicators

Indicators and points: total points 87

Records

CHD1

The practice can produce a register of patients with CHD.

Points 4

The register makes it possible for call and recall. It is a prerequisite for good primary care service delivery.

Diagnosis and initial management

CHD2

The percentage of patients with newly diagnosed angina (diagnosed after 1 April 2003) who are referred for exercise testing and/or specialist assessment.

Points 7   Payment stages 40–90%

Patients with chest pains usually present to primary care. The diagnosis is mainly clinical, but investigations such as exercise testing and angiography provide the confirmation. Most areas have a rapid access chest pain clinic. All patients with suspected angina should be referred to the rapid access clinic for confirmation of diagnosis.

Ongoing management

CHD5

The percentage of patients with CHD whose notes have a record of blood pressure in the previous 15 months.

Points 7   **Payment stages 40–90%**

Heart rate and blood pressure should be recorded at every opportunity and routinely. There are no QOF points for checking heart rate but elevated heart rate is an independent risk factor for increased mortality in CHD patients.[10]

CHD6

The percentage of patients with CHD in whom the last blood pressure reading (measured in the previous 15 months) is 150/90 or less.

Points 17   **Payment stages 40–70%**

The QOF awards points for blood pressure readings of 150/90 mm Hg or less, but, consistent with the advice from the British Hypertension Society, NICE and SIGN, blood pressure should be controlled at ≤ 140/85 mm Hg. A review of randomised trials showed that a reduction of 5–6 mm Hg in blood pressure sustained over five years reduces coronary events by 20–25% in patients with CHD.[11] The target value for blood pressure is < 130/80 mm Hg.[10]

CHD7

The percentage of patients with CHD whose notes have a record of total cholesterol within the previous 15 months.

Points 7   **Payment stages 40–90%**

These seven points are easily achievable. There should be no excuse of not doing a cholesterol measurement in a CHD patient even if he or she is housebound.

CHD 8

The percentage of patients with CHD whose last measured cholesterol (measured in the previous 15 months) is 5 mmol/L or less.

Points 17   **Payment stages 40–70%**

Statins should always be given to all patients with CHD irrespective of their measured cholesterol reading.[12]

The Heart Protection Study demonstrated large and significant reductions in the rate of vascular deaths (41% of those who had suffered a prior MI) with Simvastatin versus a placebo.[13] SIGN advocates statin therapy for all patients who have suffered an MI regardless of their baseline cholesterol level. NICE recommends statin but emphasises that other co-morbidities and life expectancy should be taken into account.

Five statins are currently available for prescription in the UK. Simvastatin and atorvastatin are currently the most widely used. Simvastatin 40 mg is the most cost-effective statin and is recommended as first line statin treatment in most cases in the UK. All statins can cause side-effects. Simvastatin is more likely to cause muscular side-effects than the other statins, particularly at high doses. Other side-effects include weakness, tiredness, sleep disturbance and bad dreams. Rhabdomyolysis refers to muscle damage creatine kinase (CK) > 10 times the upper limit of the normal range with evidence of renal involvement.

The British National Formulary (BNF) advises the following.
➤ Liver function tests (LFT) – check before commencing statin.
➤ LFT – check 1–3 months after starting statin, and then yearly.
➤ If the patient develops muscle pains, tenderness or weakness, check CK.

The following options can be used if the patient is not able to tolerate statins.
➤ Diet and lifestyle.
➤ Ezetimibe. This is recommended as an option by NICE only for the treatment of adults with primary (heterozygous – familial or non-familial) hypercholesterolemia.
➤ Fibrates.
➤ Nicotinic acid preparations.
➤ Omega 3 fatty acids.
➤ Bile acid sequestrants.

Omega 3 has been shown to reduce mortality following MI.[14]

CHD 9
The percentage of patients with CHD with a record in the previous 15 months that aspirin, an alternative anti-platelet therapy or an anti-coagulant is being taken (unless a contraindication or side-effects are recorded).

Points 7   **Payment stages 40–90%**

➤ Aspirin should be used in all patients with IHD.
➤ Low dose aspirin (75–150 mg) reduces the risk of MI.[15]
➤ Aspirin's beneficial effect in secondary prevention far outweighs the risk of major bleeding.[16]
➤ Aspirin should be continued indefinitely at a dose of 75–150 mg. Higher doses are associated with greater incidence of gastrointestinal side-effects and are no more effective.[16]
➤ NICE recommends adding proton pump inhibitor (PPI) with aspirin.
➤ Aspirin should be avoided in patients who are anti-coagulated.
➤ If aspirin is not tolerated or contraindicated, clopidogrel 75 mg should be used.[17] This is as effective as aspirin.
➤ Following an acute coronary syndrome (ACS) clopidogrel should be used for one year in addition to aspirin.[17]

➤ Insertion of a drug eluting stent necessitates both aspirin and clopidogrel for 12 months.

➤ With insertion of a bare metal stent, the combined aspirin and clopidogrel should be for one month.

CHD 10

The percentage of patients with CHD who are currently treated with a beta blocker (unless a contraindication or side-effects are recorded).

Points 7   **Payment stages 40–60%**

➤ Long-term effects of beta blockers have shown that their use post MI can improve survival rates by 20–25%.[18]

➤ Both SIGN and NICE advocate that all patients who have had an MI should be treated with beta blockers as early as possible, provided there are no contra-indications and the patient is haemodynamically stable.

➤ The GP Research Database has shown a low beta blocker use in IHD patients.[19] A recent study has shown that 67% of patients receiving elective percutaneous coronary interventions (PCI) had a resting heart rate of 80 beats per minute or above.[20]

➤ Cardio-selective beta blockers with associated vasodilator properties, such as Bisoprolol, Metoprolol or Carvedilol, should be used if there is associated heart failure.

➤ Asthma is an absolute contraindication.

➤ Usually well tolerated, but can cause tiredness, cold hands and feet, bradycardia and atrio-ventricular block.

➤ The target dose of beta blockade should achieve a lowering of the heart rate to between 55 and 60 beats per minute.

➤ Consider Ivabradin for patients who can not take beta blockers or in addition to a beta blocker if the heart rate is not adequately controlled.

➤ Sudden withdrawal of beta blockers should be avoided as this may cause hypertension, tachycardia and exacerbation of angina.

CHD 11

The percentage of patients with a history of MI (diagnosed after 1 April 2003) who are currently treated with angiotensin-converting enzyme (ACE) inhibitor or Angi-otensin 2 antagonists.

Points 7   **Payment stages 40–80%**

➤ Current guidance is that ACE inhibitors should be started in all patients after an MI and continued indefinitely.

➤ The Heart Outcome Prevention Evaluation study (HOPE) provided evidence for their use in post-MI patients regardless of left ventricular function.[21]

➤ They should be slowly titrated up to a maximum tolerated dose to achieve the benefit.[21]

➤ Contraindications of ACE therapy include pregnancy and renovascular disease, and caution is advised in renal impairment.

➤ They should also be used cautiously in patients with aortic stenosis.

➤ Dry cough can be a side-effect in 15% of patients due to accumulation of bradykinin.

➤ Angiotensin 2 receptor blockers do not cause accumulation of bradykinin; therefore cough and angioedema are very rare side-effects. In these situations they provide a suitable alternative.

➤ There is little benefit in prescribing ANG2 over ACE and this is not recommended.

CHD12

The percentage of patients with CHD who have a record of influenza immunisation in the preceding 1 September to 31 March.

Points 7   **Payment stages 40–90%**

Involve your district nurse or community matron in the influenza vaccination of housebound patients.

Maximising quality points

➤ The register should include all patients with a past history of MI, newly diagnosed MI, angina pectoris stable or acute coronary syndrome, and patients who have had coronary bypass grafting.

➤ Cardiac X syndrome should not be included in the register.

➤ Make sure all patients have OMT (optimal medical therapy)-beta blockers, statin, ACE/ANG 2 and antiplatelet.

➤ Know the targets for blood pressure (< 130/80 mm Hg) and cholesterol (< 4 mmol/L). Carry out more frequent follow-ups on those where the targets are not met.

➤ 24-hour blood pressure monitoring could be useful in people with white coat syndrome.

➤ Chase all DNA.

➤ Add a note to the repeat prescription with an appointment – this will save money on posting.

➤ Do opportunistic screening.

➤ Prescribe cost-effective drugs:
   — ACE – Ramipril
   — ANG 2 – Candesartan
   — Statin – Simvastatin.

➤ Ensuring influenza and one-off pneumococcal immunisation will earn extra points.

➤ Exception reporting criteria are the same – patients who refuse to attend and have been invited on three occasions during the preceding 12 months.

➤ Patients who are terminally ill or those who are on maximum tolerated therapy can be excluded.

➤ Do not forget to update smoking history, alcohol consumption and BMI. This will help you achieve smoking, alcohol DES and obesity targets.

Template GMS: CHD (V16)

Prompt	Code	Date	Coded subsets
Exception report: CHD quality indicator	(9h0)		Except CHD QI: Pt unsuit. (9h01) Except CHD QI: inf. dis. (9h02)
Ethnic category – 2001 census	(9i)		See ethnicity template, Chapter 17
CHD annual review	(6A2)		
CHD monitoring	(662N)		
Systolic blood pressure	(2469)		Target < 130/80
Diastolic blood pressure	(246A)		
BP refused (will be difficult to justify)	(8I3Y)		
24-hr BP MONITOR	(662L)		
AVE DAY SYSTOLIC	(246Y)		
AVE DAY DIASTOLIC	(246X)		
AVE NIGHT SYSTOLIC	(246b)		
AVE NIGHT DIASTOLIC	(246a)		
O/E-weight	(22A)		
O/E-height	(229)		
BODY MASS INDEX	(22K)		Target < 25 k/m^2
*WAIST CIRCUMFERENCE	(22N0)		(see below)
WAIST CIRCUMFERENCE DECLINED	(81Af)		
WAIST HIP RATIO	(22N7)		
Smoking status			See smoking status template, Chapter 25
Alcohol consumption			See Alcohol, Chapter 27
O/E PULSE RATE (aim < 70 bpm)	(242)		
PATIENT ADVISED REG. DIET	(8CA4)		
PATIENT ADVISED REG. EXERCISE	(8CA5)		
PATIENT ADVISED ABOUT ALCOHOL	(8CAM)		
F/H IHD	(ZV173)		
Serum cholesterol	(44P)		Aim < 4 mmol/L
HDL cholesterol	(44P5)		Aim > 1 mmol/L (males) > 1.2 mmol/L (females)
LDL	(44P6)		Aim < 2 mmol/L
LFT	(44D)		
CK	(44H4)		
FBC	(424)		
THYROID FUNCTION	(442J)		
Serum creatinine	(44J3)		
Serum sodium	(44I5)		
Serum potassium	(44I4)		
URINE PROTEIN TEST+	(4674)		Urine protein coded subsets same as in CKD template, Chapter 10
URINE MICROALBUMIN	(46W)		Urine microalbumin coded subsets same as in CKD template, Chapter 10

(continued)

Prompt	Code	Date	Coded subsets
URINE ALBUMIN:CR	(46TC)		
Serum digoxin	(44W9)		
12 Lead ECG	(321B)		ECG normal (3216)
			ECG abnormal (3217)
			ECG equivocal (3219)
			ECG shows LVH (3242)
			ECG shows RVH (3252)
REFER FOR ECG	(8HRI)		
Depression screen	(6896)		
Loss of interest	(1BP)		
Depressed mood	(1BT)		
Exercise ECG normal	(32130)		Exercise ECG abn. (32130)
			Ref. for exercise ECG (8HRA)
Exercise grading	(138)		Exercise physically imposs. (1381)
			Avoids even trivial exercise (1382)
			Enjoys light exercise (1383)
			Enjoys mod. exercise (1384)
			Enjoys heavy exercise (1385)
Exercise tolerance contraindicated	(33BE)		
Isot. heart scan	(5744)		
Maximum tolerated dose	(8BL)		On max. tolerat. antihypert. (8BL0)
			On max. tolerat. lipid lowering (8BL1)
Anticoagulation contraindicated	(8I2R)		Anticoag. declined (8I3d)
			Anticoag. not indic. (8I6N)
			Anticoag. not tolerat. (8I7A)
			Anticoag. pres. by 3rd party (8B2K)
Aspirin prophylaxis (OTC)	(EGTONAS1)		Adv. about taking aspirin (67I8)
			H/O aspirin allergy (14LK)
			OTC aspirin therapy (8B3T)
			Salicylate prophyl. (8B63)
			Aspirin prophyl. contraind. (8I24)
			Aspirin prophyl. ref. (8I38)
			Aspirin not indic. (8I66)
			Aspirin not tolerat. (8I70)
			P/H aspirin allergy (ZV148)
Warfarin contraindicated	(8I25)		H/O warf. allergy (14LP)
			Warf. contrind. (8I25)
			Warf. declined (8I3E)
			Warf. not indic. (8I65)
			Warf. not tolerat. (8I71)
			AR-warf. sod. (TJ421)
			P/H warf. allergy (ZV14A)
AR anticoagulant	(TJ42)		AR-anticoag. (TJ42)
			AR-nicoumalone (TJ422)
			AR-phenindione (TJ423)
			AR-anticoag. NOS (TJ42z)

(continued)

Prompt	Code	Date	Coded subsets
*Beta blocker contraindicated	(8I26)		H/O B blocker Allergy (14LL)
			B blocker contraind. (8I26)
			B blocker refused (8I36)
			B blocker not indicat. (8I62)
IVABRADINE ACE inhibitors contraindicated	(8I28)		H/O ACE allergy (14LM)
			ACE declined (8I3D)
			ACE not indic. (8I64)
			ACE not tolerat. (8I74)
			AR-captopril (TJC77)
			AR-enalapril (TJC78)
			[V]P/H ACE allerg (ZV14D)
			[V]Angiot-conv. enz. inh. adv. eff. (U60C4)
Angioten 2 contraindicated	(8I2H)		H/O ANG2 allergy (14LN)
			ANG2 CI (8I2H)
			ANG2 declined (8I3P)
			ANG2 not indic. (8I6C)
			ANG2 not tolerat. (8I75)
			P/H ANG2 allergy (ZV14E)
			Prophyl. ANG2 ther. (EMISQPR5)
			[X]ANG2 adv. eff. (U60CB)
Clopidogrel contraindicated	(8I2K)		H/O clop. allergy (14LQ)
			Clop. prophyl. (8B6P)
			Clop. contraind. (8I2K)
			Clop. declined (8I3R)
			Clop. not indic. (8I6B)
			Clop. not tolerat. (8I72)
			P/H clop. allergy (ZV14B)
H/O Dipyridamol allergy	(14LX)		Dipyrid. contraind. (8I2b)
			Dipyrid. declined (8I3n)
			Dipyrid. not indic. (8I6a)
			Dipyrid. not tolerat. (8I7J)
			AR-dipyridamole (TJC44)
Statin prophylaxis	(8B6A)		Statins contraind. (8I27)
			Statin declined (8I3C)
			Statin not indic. (8I63)
			Statin not tolerat. (8I76)
			Adv. reaction to simvas (TJC24)
			Adverse reaction to Pravas (TJC25)
			[X]Statin cause adv. eff. ther. (U60CA)
ON OMACOR	(6D)		
Diabetes mellitus screen	(6872)		
HBA1C	(42W4)		(aim < 6.5%)
Standard chest X-ray	(535)		Standard chest X-ray requested (5351)
			Standard chest X-ray normal (5352)
			Standard chest X-ray abnormal (5353)

(continued)

Prompt	Code	Date	Coded subsets
Influenza vaccination	(65E)		Influenza vaccination contraind. (8I2F)
			Influenza vaccination not indicat. (8I6D)
			Influenza vaccination declined (9OX5)
			No consent – influenza imm. (68NE)
			First pandemic flu vaccination (65E0)
			Second pandemic flu vaccination (65E1)
Pneumococcal vaccination	(6572)		Pneumococcal vaccination (6572)
			Pneumococcal vaccination given (65720)
			Pneumococcal vaccination contraind. (8I2E)
			Pneumococcal vaccination Declined (8I3Q)
Fill medical review	(8B3V)		
CHD monitoring	(662N)		
FIT TO FLY (if recent admission)	(13ZI[22])		
Cardiological referral	(8H44)		
EMERGENCY HOSPITAL ADMISSION	(8H2)		
CARDIAC REHABILITATION	(8F9)		
CARDIAC REHABILITATION DECLINED	(8I3a)		
CHD MONITORING TELEPHONE INVITE	(9Ob9)		
CHD MONITORING VERBAL INVITE	(9Ob6)		
CHD MONITORING 1st INVITE	(9Ob3)		
CHD MONITORING 2nd INVITE	(9Ob4)		
CHD MONITORING 3rd INVITE	(9Ob5)		

*   Waist circumference targets
        Europeans: Male < 94 cm; Females < 80 cm
        South Asians and Chinese: Males < 90 cm, Females < 80 cm

(Add the capitalised prompts to your template to maximise points and quality care)

Do something extra

➤ Women with heart disease suffer from severe symptoms, and may respond differently to some treatments for CHD. They need a gender-specific treatment. Chase all your female patients with CHD, especially the non-attenders.

➤ A combination of CHD and depression is potentially lethal. CES-D is a sensitive screening tool.[23] It has a low positive predicative value at the standard cut-off point of 16. There is some evidence that patients with sub-threshold depression may also be at increased risk of death.[24]

➤ Calcium supplements without co-administered vitamin D are associated with an increased risk (by nearly one-third) of MI.[25] Run a computer search of patients either at risk or with established osteoporosis who are prescribed calcium supplements – many of these could be elderly women who may also be at high risk of cardiovascular disease.

➤ Consider reducing LDL-cholesterol below 2.0 mmol/L in high-risk patients. The key findings of two meta-analyses published[26] showed that all-cause mortality was reduced by 10% per 1.0 mmol/L LDL reduction and deaths from CHD were reduced by 11% per 1.0 mmol/L LDL reduction. That means more intensive regimes such as 80 mg Simvastatin or 80 mg atorvastatin. For vast majority of patients, 40 mg Simvastatin is appropriate as there is a threefold higher rate of myopathy in patients on Simvastatin 80 mg.

References

1 Atherosclerosis: Mitchell R, Sheppard K, Vinay A, *et al. Robbins Basic Pathology.* 8th ed. Philadelphia: Saunders; 2009. Available at: www.docstoc.com/docs/6465186/Atherosclerosis

2 Mallinson T. Myocardial infarction. *Focus on First Aid.* 2010; **15**: 15. Available at: www.focusonfirstaid.co.uk/Magazine/issue15/ index.aspx (accessed 8 June 2010).

3 Lang N, Fox K. Current drug therapies used in the secondary prevention of MI. *Prescriber.* 2010; **21**: 22–45. Available at: www.onlinelibrary.wiley.com/…/Journal Home/Volume 21/issue 19

4 CAPRIE Steering Committee. A randomised, blinded, trial of clopidogrel versus aspirin in patients at risk of ischaemic events (CAPRIE). *Lancet.* 1996; **348**(9038): 1329–39.

5 Lang N, Fox K. Angina: current approaches to prevention and treatment. *Prescriber.* 2005; 26–41.

6 Glare J. Primary care-related factors affecting CHD mortality variation in England. *JAMA.* 2010; **304**: 2028–34.

7 World Health Organization, Department of Health Statistics and Informatics in the information. *The Global Burden of Disease: 2004 Update.* Geneva: World Health Organization; 2008.

8 Kirby M. Long live the difference? Why women lose out in heart health. *Women's Health Journal.* 2011; **3**(1): 4–6. Available at: www.pcwhj.com/issue/current?sid=481f24fbe97ad55c

9 Kostis WJ, Demissie K, Marcella SW, *et al.* Weekend versus weekday admission and mortality from myocardial infarction. *N. Engl. J Med.* 2007; **356**: 1099–109.

10 Fox K, Ferrari R, Tendera M, *et al.* Risks of cardiovascular events and effects of routine blood pressure lowering among patients. *Eur. Heart J.* 2009; **30**: 2337–45. Available at: www.eurheartj.oxfordjournals.org/letters?first-index=91&hits=10

11 Collins R, Peto R, MacMahon S, *et al.* Pressure sustained over 5 years reduces coronary events by 20–25% in patients with coronary heart disease. *Lancet.* 1990; **335**: 827–38.

12 The Scandinavian Simvastatin Survival Study Group. Randomised trial of cholesterol lowering in 4444 patients with coronary heart disease: the Scandinavian Simvastatin Survival Study (4S). *Lancet.* 1994; **344**: 1383–9. Available at: www.thelancet.com/journals/lancet/…/P11so140-6736(94)90566-5

13 Heart Protection Study Collaborative Group. MRC/BHF heart protection study of cholesterol lowering with Simvastatin in 20,536 high-risk individuals: a randomised placebo-controlled trial. *Lancet.* 2002; **360**(9326): 7–22.

14 Dietary supplementation with n-3 polyunsaturated fatty acids and vitamin E after myocardial infarction: results of the GISSI-Prevenzione trial. Gruppo Italiano per lo Studio della Sopravvivenza nell'Infarto miocardico. *Lancet.* 1999; **354**: 447–55.

15 Ridker PM, Cooke NR, Lee IM, *et al.* A randomised trial of low-dose aspirin in the primary prevention. *N. Engl. J Med.* 2005; **352**: 1293–304. Available at: www.abc. net.au/health/thepulse/stories/2005/.../1515899.htm

16 Antithrombotic Trialists Collaboration. Collaborative meta-analysis of randomised trials of antiplatelet therapy for prevention of death, myocardial infarction and stroke in high risk patients. *BMJ.* 2002; **324**(7329): 71–86. Available at: www.bmj. com/content/324/7329/71.full

17 Yusuf S, Phil D, Zhao F, *et al.* Effects of clopidogrel in addition to aspirin in patients with acute coronary syndromes without ST-segment elevation. *N. Engl. J Med.* 2001; **345**: 494–502.

18 Beta-blocker Heart Attack Study Group. The beta-blocker heart attack trial. *JAMA.* 1981; **246**(18): 2073–4. Available at: www.ncbi.nlm.nih.gov/pubmed/7026815

19 Setakis E, Morley C, Cockle S, *et al.* Beta blocker doses in coronary heart disease patients treated in UK primary care. *European Society of Cardiology Congress 2009.* Abstract 84186.

20 Elder DH, Pauriah M, Lang CC, *et al.* Is there a failure to optimize therapy in angina pectoris (FORGET) study. *QJM.* 2010; **103**: 305–10.

21 Yusuf S, Sleight P, Pogue J, *et al.* The heart outcomes prevention evaluation study investigators. *N. Engl. J Med.* 2000; **342**(3): 145–53. Available at: www.joplink.net/ prev/200107/ref/02-40.html

22 Smith D, Toff W, Joy M, *et al.* Fitness to fly for passengers with cardiovascular disease. *Heart.* 2010; **96**: ii1–ii16.

23 Nabi H, Shipley MJ, Vahtera J, *et al.* Effects of depressive symptoms and coronary heart disease and their interactive associations on mortality in middle aged adults: the Whitehall 11 cohort study. *Heart.* 2010; **20**: 1645–50. Available at: www.heart. bmj.com/content/early/2010/08/20/hrt.2010.198507

24 Seymour J, Benning TB. Depression, cardiac mortality and all-cause mortality. *Adv. Psych. Treat.* 2009; **15**: 107–13.

25 Bolland MJ, Avenell A, Baron JA, *et al.* Effect of calcium supplements on risk of myocardial infarction and cardiovascular events: meta-analysis. *BMJ.* 2010; **341**: c3691.

26 Baigent C. Lower LDL is better even at very low levels. Meta analysis. *The Lancet.* Epub 2010; Nov 9.

Useful reading

For health professionals

➤ Sign Guideline 96. Available at: www.sign.ac.uk/guidelines/fulltext/96/index.html

➤ Sign Guideline 97. Available at: www.sign.ac.uk/guidelines/fulltext/97/index.html

➤ National Institute for Health and Clinical Excellence. *Clopidogrel in the Treatment of Non-ST-segment-elevation Acute Coronary Syndrome*: NICE *technology appraisal TA80.* London: NHICE; 2010. Available at: www.nice.org.uk/Guidance/TA80

➤ www.nice.org.uk/Guidance/TA90

➤ BHS Guidelines. Available at: www.bhsoc.org/NICE_BHS_Guidelines.stm

➤ www.lipidsonline.org/

For patients

➤ www.bhf.org.uk

CHAPTER 10

Chronic kidney disease

Definition

Chronic kidney disease (CKD) is defined as a pathological state of permanent kidney damage (haematuria, proteinuria or anatomical abnormality) or reduction in function (glomerular filtration rate (GFR) < 60 mL/min/1.73 m² present on at least three consecutive occasions within a period of no less than 90 days). It is characterised by irreversible renal scarring.

The stages of CKD are based upon the GFR, as shown in Table 10.1.

Table 10.1 KDOQI classification of chronic kidney disease

Stage	GFR mL/min/1.73 m²
1	> 90
2	60–89
3a	45–59
3b	30–44
4	15–29
5 Kidney failure	< 15 or dialysis

(NICE guidance recommends adding the suffix **p** to patients with significant proteinuria.[1])

CKD stage 3 has been subdivided into 3a and 3b as longitudinal population studies have shown an increased risk associated with GFR 30–44 (stage 3b). Previously the criteria did not take into account the presence of proteinuria. It is well established that proteinuria is a significant prognostic and therapeutic indicator of the disease. Proteinuria is defined as an albumin:creatinine ratio (ACR) of > 30 or protein:creatinine ratio (PCR) of > 50.

Prevalence

CKD is a common long-term condition. Its true prevalence has only been recognised since the widespread use of estimated GFR to measure renal function – a far more sensitive indicator than the serum creatinine level. The prevalence of CKD stages 3–5 in the UK has been estimated at 8.5% (5.8% in males and 10.6% in females aged 18 years and older).[2] The prevalence increases with age and is thought to be increasing year by year. The prevalence of established renal failure is assessed based on the number of patients requiring renal replacement therapy (RRT). The incidence of patients requiring RRT in 2007 was 109 per 1 000 000 population.[1] Kidney transplantation accounted for 46.6%, followed by haemodialysis at 42.1%.[2]

Why included in QOF

The increasing prevalence means increasing demands of renal services. For the majority of patients, CKD management can be community-based services provided by the GP. CKD was added to the QOF in 2006 with indicators CKD 1–4. CKD 4 was replaced by CKD5 in 2008 with the addition of proteinuria to hypertension for patients requiring treatment with an angiotensin converting enzyme inhibitor (ACE) or angiotensin receptor blocker (ARB).

➤ Traditionally, CKD has been under-diagnosed, mainly as a result of the asymptomatic nature of the disease. Its inclusion in the QOF means early detection by GPs.

➤ There is a steady rise in the number of people requiring dialysis. It is hoped that CKD's inclusion in the QOF and active management by GPs will slow the numbers progressing to dialysis.

➤ There is significant excess morbidity and mortality associated with late-presenting patients and an increased length of stay in hospital. Early identification and effective management in its early stages, delivered by the GP, can reduce morbidity and mortality. The incidence of late presentation in 2007 was 21%. The late presenters were defined as those requiring dialysis within three months of referral.[2]

➤ The presence of CKD is associated with increased cardiovascular risk.[3] The primary care has a scope to integrate CKD care pathway with coronary heart disease (CHD).

➤ Early detection of CKD will reduce heart disease risk.[4] It is hoped that the QOF incentive will help to reduce heart disease.

➤ The risk factors associated with an increased rate of decline in renal function include hypertension, diabetes, smoking, chronic use of NSAID, proteinuria and urinary outflow tract obstruction. Targeting the risk factors slows down the disease's progression.[5] CKD fits in well with the NHS health check programme. GPs, with the help of the primary care team, can integrate preventive strategies and early interventions.

➤ Early detection and timely referral to a renal specialist is important to prevent further progression. NICE defines progressive CKD as a decline of eGFR > 5 mL/min/1.73 m^2 within one year or > 10 mL/min/1.73m^2 within five years.[5]

Approximately 1.85 million people have been diagnosed with CKD since the introduction of QOF indicators, based on the latest QOF data for 2007/08, creating an opportunity to provide potentially life-saving advice and timely treatment to a large number of people who would previously have been overlooked. Primary care is where the action is happening.[6]

The facts

➤ In diabetics, the prevalence of CKD is around 31% compared with non-diabetics in whom the prevalence is 6.9%.[5]

➤ Cardiovascular co-morbidities are common in CKD. Approximately three-quarters of CKD patients are co-morbid for one or more circulatory diseases.[7]

➤ Acute coronary syndrome may present atypically with silent ischaemia, collapse and breathlessness in advanced CKD. Measuring troponin is not always helpful as it is often elevated in CKD, leading to poor diagnosis of acute coronary syndrome.

➤ High use of NSAIDs is associated with deterioration of renal function.[8]

➤ Age-related decline in renal function is associated with hypertension.[9] Hypertension can be a cause or consequence of CKD.

➤ There has been a rise in end-stage renal disease – 7% per annum.[10] Renal service accounts for 2% of the NHS budget.

➤ CKD is higher in women compared with men, with a 2:1 women:men ratio. One reason could be that women live longer.[3]

QOF indicators: chronic kidney disease

Indicators and points: total points 38

The QOF indicators set out below apply to people with stages 3, 4 and 5 CKD (eGFR less than 60 mL/min).

Records

CKD1

The practice can produce a register of patients aged 18 years and over with CKD (stages 3–5).

Points 6

The register is a prerequisite for the organisation of good primary care to identify the patients with CKD, so that they receive timely appropriate treatment to prevent further progression of the disease. Having a CKD register ensures an annual assessment of kidney function for people in 'high risk' – with diabetes, hypertension, cerebrovascular disease, stroke, coronary heart disease and peripheral vascular disease.

A register is essential for structured CKD care.

Initial management

CKD2

The percentage of patients on the CKD register whose notes have a record of blood pressure in the previous 15 months.

Points 6   Payment stages 40–90%

Reducing blood pressure delays the progression of CKD. Early detection and early management is cost-effective.

Ongoing management

CKD3

The percentage of patients on the CKD register in whom the last blood pressure reading, measured in the previous 15 months, is 140/85 mm Hg or less.

Points 11   **Payment stages 40–70%**

The NICE draft guidance blood pressure target range is 120–140/70–90 mm Hg.

The QOF target is 140/85 mm Hg or less.

The Renal Association guidance for target blood pressure is:

➤ 130/80 mm Hg with no proteinuria

➤ 125/75 mm Hg with proteinuria.

In patients with diabetes and CKD and an ACR > 70mg/mmol, the aim for systolic blood pressure is < 130 mm Hg (120–129 mm Hg) and the diastolic < 80 mm Hg.

Because the prevalence is higher in older patients it can be challenging to target blood pressure, but active blood pressure management can improve outcome (see www.renal.org/eGFR/eguide.html).

CKD5

The percentage of patients on the CKD register with hypertension and proteinuria who are treated with an angiotensin converting enzyme inhibitor (ACE) or angiotensin receptor blocker (ARB) (unless a contraindication or side-effects are recorded).

Points 9   **Payment stages 40–80%**

These drugs are considered to be more effective than other anti-hypertensive drugs in reducing progression of CKD. When using ACE inhibitors or ARBs, titrate to the maximum tolerated therapeutic dose before adding a second line agent. Measure serum potassium level and eGFR before starting an ACE inhibitor or ARB and repeat these measurements between one and two weeks after starting an ACE inhibitor and after each dose increase.

NICE recommends checking eGFR in stages 3A and 3B every six months. Frequency of monitoring should be adjusted according to the underlying clinical condition and risk factors. CKD 3B (*p*) requires more frequent monitoring than stable CKD 3A with no proteinuria or albuminuria.

Current NICE recommendations for use of ACE inhibitors and ARBs in patients with CKD are as follows.

➤ CKD without diabetes and ACR ≥ 70 mg/mmol, irrespective of presence of hypertension or CVD.

➤ CKD and hypertension without diabetes and ACR > 30 mg/mmol should be regarded as clinically significant proteinuria.

➤ Diabetes and an ACR > 2.5 mg/mmol in men and > 3.5 mg/mmol in women, irrespective of presence of CKD or hypertension.[1]

CKD6

The percentage of patients on CKD register whose notes have a record of a urine albumin:creatinine ratio (or protein:creatinine ratio) test in the previous 15 months.

points 6   **Payment stages 40–80%**

NICE has recommended that ACR be used as the method of choice for screening for proteinuria in all patients.[1]

NICE has defined that in people without diabetes an ACR > 30 mg/mmol or PCR > 50 mg/mmol constitutes CKD.

Results from the QOF for 2006/07 indicated that 99% of general practices had a register of CKD, 3% of the population had been identified with stages 3–5 disease, 98% of identified patients had had their blood pressure measured in the past 15 months and 86% had a blood pressure of 140/85 mm Hg or less, excluding non-excepted patients.[11] Indicators were revised for 2008/09 so that treatment with ACE or ARB is indicated in patients who have CKD and hypertension and proteinuria.[12]

Overlap of QOF points

The overlap of QOF points is shown in Table 10.2.

Table 10.2 Overlap of QOF points

	CKD	CHD	Hypertension	Diabetes
BP record	6	7	18	3
BP target	11	17	57	18
ACE/ARB	9	7		3

Maximising quality points

➤ The vast majority of patients will already be known to you and will be on another CVD register, but some could be unrecognised. Pick up those not known as having CKD. Do an audit to identify gaps against QOF guidance. For example, blood pressure target, initiating patients on ACE or ANG2 therapy as per current recommendations on the level of ACR.[1]

➤ There is a higher prevalence of hypertension in patients with CKD stages 3–5,[13] and these patients will already be a part of a register – call and review them.

➤ Do not enter into the CKD register those with a single reading of eGFR below 60. Remember, eGFR can fluctuate. It is important to reduce these fluctuations by asking patients to abstain from meat for 12 hours and to maintain hydration with clear fluids. Do not test patients if they attend for fasting blood tests as patients often think they should have 'nil by mouth'. NICE recommends checking eGFR 3A and 3B every six months. Frequency of monitoring should be adjusted according to the underlying clinical condition and risk of factors.

➤ For CKD5 the proteinuria code needs to be added to the template. The codes define the patient as being proteinuric for CKD (see the template).

➤ Enquire as to history of smoking and encourage patients to stop smoking. Check eGFR and ACR in smokers and pick up early CKD. This would not only help towards early detection, increasing prevalence and disease progression but also towards maximising smoking targets.

➤ Obesity and blood pressure go hand in hand. Record body mass index (BMI) and waist circumference and give health promotion advice. This would also improve obesity and hypertension quality points.

➤ Testing the urine of the at-risk population can help detect CKD, as the presence of proteinuria is an early marker of CKD. Enter the read code for urine test in the CKD template. If protein is present, request ACR.

➤ All diabetics, hypertensives, CVDs, people with a family history of kidney disease and those with haematuria or proteinuria should be tested for CKD – eGFR and ACR. This would increase your prevalence.

➤ CKD is more common in south Asian, black and Hispanic populations. If your practice has more patients belonging to these groups, actively screen for CKD.

➤ Do a medication review of patients and if they are on NSAID and COX-2, check for CKD, discontinue from repeat prescribing and recheck. Antibiotics, mesalazine, diuretics, lithium, ACE/ARB, cyclosporine and metformin are other drugs which can affect kidney function. Enter an alert message on the prescribing screen of the patients on these drugs and check eGFR every 12 months.

➤ If the ACR is ≥ 30 (or ≥ 2.5 if the patient has diabetes), add a proteinuria code:
  — type 1 diabetes mellitus with persistent proteinuria (C10EK)
  — type 2 diabetes mellitus with persistent proteinuria (C10FL)
  — persistent proteinuria unspecified (K190X)
  — [X]Persistent proteinuria unspecified (Kyu5G).
    If the patient is hypertensive, start ACE/ARB:
  — [D]Proteinuria (R110)
  — [D]Albuminuria (R1100)
  — [D]Proteinuria NOS (R110z).

➤ With CKD ≥ grade 3 with or without diabetes, do a urine microalbumin and ACR test annually (or every two years if done between January and March).

➤ Exception reporting of ACE/ARB use is of course clinically legitimate.

➤ Chase DNA – sending appointments by post, phoning if the patient misses appointment, opportunistically or when the patient requests repeat prescriptions. Enter read code 9Ni9 (DNA monitoring clinic).

➤ Increase you prevalence by actively screening patients who may have donated a kidney (7B0F0, live kidney donor screening). (*I have two such patients in my practice.*)

➤ Ensure influenza and pneumococcal vaccination of patients over 65 years will earn extra points.

Template GMS: CKD (V16)

Prompt	Code	Date	Coded subsets
Exception report: CHD dis. quality indicator	(9hE)		Patient unsuit. (9hE0) Inf. dis. (9hE1)
Ethnic category – 2001 census	(9i)		See ethnicity template, Chapter 17
CKD stages	(1Z1)		CKD stage 1 (1Z10) CKD stage 2 (1Z11) CKD stage 3 (1Z12) CKD stage 4 (1Z13) CKD stage 5 (1Z14) CKD stage 3A (1Z15) CKD stage 3B (1Z16) CKD1 with protein (1Z17) CKD1 without protein (1Z18) CKD2 with protein (1Z19) CKD2 without protein (1Z1A) CKD3 with protein (1Z1B) CKD3 without protein (1Z1C) CKD3A with protein (1Z1D) CKD3A without protein (1Z1E) CKD3B with protein (1Z1F) CKD3B without protein (1Z1G) CKD4 with protein (1Z1H) CKD4 without protein (1Z1J) CKD5 with protein (1Z1K) CKD5 without protein (1Z1L)
F/H POLYCYSTIC DIS.	(12F1)		
O/E WEIGHT	(22A)		
O/E HEIGHT	(229)		
BMI	(22K)		(Aim < 25 kg/m^2)
WAIST CIRCUMFERENCE	(22N0)		
WAIST CIRCUMFERENCE DECLINED	(81F)		
WAIST HIP RATIO	(22N7)		
SMOKING STATUS			See smoking status template, Chapter 25
ALCOHOLCONSUMPTION			See Alcohol, Chapter 27
PATIENT ADVISED REG. DIET	(8CA4)		Restriction of salt, potassium-rich food and low protein
PATIENT ADVISED REG. EXERCISE	(8CA5)		
PATIENT ADVISED ABOUT ALCOHOL	(8CAM)		
Systolic blood pressure	(2469)		(Aim 140/85 mm Hg or less)
Diastolic blood pressure	(246A)		
Blood pressure refused	(8I3Y)		
Maximum tolerance antihypert.	(8BL0)		
Urine protein test +	(4674)		[D]Proteinuria (R110) [D]Albuminuria (R1100) [D]Proteinuria NOS (R110z)

(continued)

Prompt	Code	Date	Coded subsets
Urine microalbumin	(46W)		Urine microalb. +ve (46W0) Urine microalb. -ve (46W1) [D]Microalb. (R1103) Urine microalb. profile (46N8)
Urine protein/creatinine ratio	(441D)		
Urine albumin/creatinine ratio	(46TC)		
URINE BLOOD TEST	(469)		(If +ve screen for CKD)
Serum creatinine	(44J3)		
Plasma creatinine	(44JF)		
Calculated GFR	(451E)		
FBC	(424)		
PLASMA RANDOM GLUCOSE	(44g0)		
PLASMA FASTING GLUCOSE	(44g1)		
ULTRA SOUND SCAN KIDNEY	(7P093)		
ACE inhibitor prophyl.	(8B6B)		
ACE inhibitor contraindicated	(8I28)		ACE declined (8I3D) ACE not tolerat. (8I74) ACE not indic. (8I64) ACE allergy (14LM)
ANG 2 indicated	(EMISQPR5)		
ANG 2 not indicated	(816C)		ANG 2 CI (8I2H) P/H ANG 2 allergy (ZV14E) H/O ANG 2 allergy (14LN) ANG 2 decline (8I3P) ANG2 not tolerat. (8I75)
Renal function tests normal	(4511)		Renal function tests abn. (4512) Renal function tests borderline (4516)
Renal function monitoring	(8A6)		
CHRONIC KIDNEY DIS. MONITORING 1st LETTER	(90t0)		
CHRONIC KIDNET DIS. MONITORING 2nd LETTER	(90t1)		
CHRONIC KIDNEY DIS. MONITORING 3rd LETTER	(90t2)		
CHRONIC KIDNEY DIS. VERBAL INVITE	(90t3)		
CHRONIC KIDNEY DIS. TELEPHONE INVITE	(90t4)		
DNA MONITORING CLINIC	(9Ni9)		
INFLUENZA VACCINATION	(65E)		*Influenza vaccination coded subsets same as in CHD template, Chapter 9*
PNEUMOCOCCAL VACCINATION	(6572)		*Pneumococcal vaccination coded subsets same as in CHD template, Chapter 9*

(Add the capitalised prompts to your template to maximise points and quality care)

Ultrasound scan

NICE recommends an ultrasound scan for all people with CKD who have:
➤ visible or persistent invisible haematuria
➤ symptoms of urinary tract obstruction
➤ stage 4 or 5 CKD
➤ a family history of polycystic kidney disease and are over the age of 20 years
➤ progressive CKD – an eGFR decline of more than 5 mL/min/1.73 m² within one year or 10 mL/min/1.73 m² within five years.

References

1 National Institute for Health and Clinical Excellence. *Chronic Kidney Disease: early identification and management of chronic kidney disease in adults in primary and secondary care: guideline CG73*. London: NHICE; 2008. www.nice.org.uk/guidance/GC73

2 Ansell D, Feehally J, Fogarty D, *et al. UK Renal Registry Report 2008*. Bristol: UK Renal Registry; 2008.

3 Go AS, Chertow GM, Fan D, *et al.* Chronic kidney disease and the risks of death, cardiovascular events, and hospitalization. *N. Engl J Med.* 2004; **351**(13): 1296–1305.

4 Sangala N. Early detection of CKD will reduce heart disease risk. *The Practitioner.* 2009; **253**(1717): 24–7.

5 New JP, Middleton RJ, Klebe B, *et al.* Assessing the prevalence, monitoring and management of chronic kidney disease in patients with diabetes compared with those without diabetes in general practice. *Diabet. Med.* 2007; **24**(4): 364–9.

6 Department of Health. *The National Service Framework for Renal Services. Second progress report*. London: Department of Health; 2007.

7 de Lusignan S, Chan T, Stevens P, *et al.* Identifying patients with chronic kidney disease from general practice computer records. *Fam. Pract.* 2005; **22**(3): 234–41.

8 Gooch K, Culleton BF, Manns BJ, *et al.* NSAID use and progression of chronic kidney disease. *Am. J Med.* 2007; **120**(3): 280.e1–7.

9 Lindeman R, Tobin J, Shock NW, *et al.* Association between blood pressure and the rate of decline in renal function with age. *Kidney Int.* 1984; **26**: 861–8.

10 Department of Health. *National Service Framework for Renal Services– Part two: chronic kidney disease, acute renal failure and end of life care*. London: Department of Health, 2005.

11 Information Centre. *National Quality and Outcomes Framework Statistics for England 2007/8*. London: IC, 2007.

12 NHS Employers. *Quality and outcomes framework*. 2008. Available at: www.nhsemployers.org/pay-conditions/primary-809.cmf

13 Stevens P. Successes and gaps: what is working, what's not? UK experience. *Chronic Kidney Disease Summit*. 2007 Available at: www.bckidneysummit.com/download/DrStevens

Useful websites

For health professionals
➤ Department of Health: www.dh.gov.uk
➤ British Renal Society: www.britishrenal.org

➤ UK CKD guidelines. Available at: www.renal.org/CKDguide/ckd.html
➤ NICE Guidelines. Available at: www.nice.org.uk/Guidance/CG73/NiceGuidance/pdf/English

For patients
➤ National Kidney Federation (NKF): www.kidney.org.uk
➤ Kidney Research UK: www.kidneyresearchuk.org
➤ NICE CKD: www.nice.org.uk/media/9B8/.../CKDQualityStandardPatient Information.pdf

Useful information
➤ Renal Association: www.renal.org
➤ Kidney care: www.kidneycare.nhs.uk
➤ UK Renal Registry: www.renalreg.com
➤ Kidney Research UK: www.kidneyresearchuk.org

CHAPTER 11

Chronic obstructive pulmonary disease

Definition

Chronic obstructive pulmonary disease (COPD) is a chronic inflammatory condition of the airways and lung parenchyma, characterised by airflow obstruction, which is usually progressive and irreversible.[1] It has an insidious onset and generally occurs in people over the age of 50 and is predominantly caused by smoking, although it does occur occasionally in non-smokers.

In COPD the inflammation primarily affects the small airways and lung parenchyma.

Prevalence

COPD incidence appears to have peaked and high prevalence of the disease remains a cause for concern.

Researchers found that between 2001 and 2004 the incidence of COPD rose for both men and women. For women it rose from two cases per 1000 patient-years to 2.4, while for men it rose from 2.1 to 2.7 cases per 1000 patient-years.

By 2005, the prevalence remained at 1.7% with particularly high levels in the north-east of the UK.[2]

In the UK, 3.7 million people are estimated to have COPD, of whom roughly 900 000 are actually diagnosed – the missing millions highlighted by the British Lung Foundation (BLF).[3]

Why included in QOF

➤ Primary care with improved knowledge and understanding of COPD management can provide a better and more cost-effective service.
➤ An average UK general practice of 7000 patients will have up to 200 patients with COPD. An increasing number of these are elderly.
➤ Early identification leads to better outcome.

➤ By 2020, COPD will be responsible for the third highest number of deaths.[4]
➤ Of the people who develop COPD, 95% are smokers and their lung function declines faster than that of non-smokers.[5] The most effective intervention is to stop smoking, preferably at an early stage.[6]
➤ The economic toll of COPD is set to soar. An international survey questioning 2426 COPD patients of working age (45–68 years), combined with available standard UK healthcare provider costs, showed that the monthly impact to healthcare on governments is over £875 000, for those patients alone. This represents an average cost of £362 per patient per month.[7]
➤ COPD exacerbations resulting in hospital admissions are the major contributor to the economic burden associated with the disease; one in every eight emergency medical admissions in the UK is due to COPD.[8] Preventing, recognising an exacerbation and early intervention by a GP can avert a hospital admission thus reducing financial burden.

The facts

The long-awaited National Clinical Strategy (NCS) for COPD,[9] consultation for which closed in April 2010, is an exciting development to raise the profile of COPD, the updated NICE guidelines and the new oxygen guidelines,[10] all of which aim to reduce the prevalence and improve the care and outcomes of COPD patients.
➤ In 1999, there were approximately 30 000 deaths due to COPD in the UK.[11] This represented 5.1% of all deaths (5.9% of all male deaths and 4.3% of all female deaths).
➤ In women, there has been a small but progressive increase over the last 20 years because of an increase in cigarette smoking among women.[12]
➤ NICE has announced that the performance of GP commissioners will be judged on improved quality indicators delivery in COPD.[13] Quality standards will be used by the National Commissioning Board to judge the performance of GP consortiums. Achievements of quality standards will also feed into the calculation of payment of quality premiums.

QOF: COPD indicators

Indicators and points: total points 30

Records
COPD1
The practice can produce a register of patients with COPD.

Points 3

Producing an accurate register for a computerised practice should be easy. It is worth checking your prevalence against the QOF average. A provisional diagnosis can be made on the basis of history and examination. Clinical COPD questionnaires can give you an idea of the severity; symptom-based questionnaires can help you differentiate between asthma and COPD.[14]

Any newly registered patient with wheezy bronchitis will be classified as COPD – get rid of that code.

Any A&E letter arriving with a diagnosis of acute exacerbation of COPD does not automatically mean entry on the register. **Do not** enter on the register without post-dilator spirometry.

The register makes call and recall possible.

Initial diagnosis

COPD12

The percentage of all patients with COPD diagnosed after 1 April 2008 in whom the diagnosis has been confirmed by post-bronchodilator spirometry.

Points 5   **Payment stages 40–80%**

NICE has issued updated COPD guidance to improve the diagnosis.[7]
➤ Consider a diagnosis of COPD in patients aged over 35 years who have a risk factor (smoking) and present with chronic cough, sputum, frequent winter bronchitis and exertional wheeze.
➤ A diagnosis of COPD should be made in the presence of characteristic signs and symptoms and an obstructive spirometry characterised by a post-bronchodilator FEV1/FVC ratio of 0.7.[7]
➤ Assess the severity of airflow obstruction – mild, moderate, severe and very severe according to FEV1 – this matches with GOLD (Global Initiative for Chronic Obstructive Lung Disease). This is not the clinical severity for COPD.
➤ Severity assessment includes BODE index-BMI, airflow obstruction, dyspnoea and exercise capacity.
➤ Consider alternative diagnosis in younger people with symptoms of COPD where the FEV1/FVC ratio is ≥ 0.7, and older people without typical symptoms of COPD where the ratio is < 0.7.

Ongoing management

COPD10

The percentage of patients with COPD with a record of FEV1 in the previous 15 months.

Points 7   **Payment stages 40–70%**

The QOF suggests checking every 15 months but as a clinician you should check every six months to assess the progress of moderate to severe COPD. FEV1 does not vary markedly with an acute exacerbation of COPD and is not a useful indicator in this situation.

Patients with symptoms that are worse than would be expected on the basis of the reduction in FEV1 should be investigated with full lung function tests, including high resolution CT scanning.

COPD13

The percentage of patients with COPD who have had a review, undertaken by a healthcare professional, including an assessment of breathlessness using the MRC dyspnoea score in the preceding 15 months.

Points 9   **Payment stages 50–90%**

The primary aims of treatment are to improve symptoms such as breathlessness, exercise capacity, activity and sleep quality and reduce exacerbations.

The review should cover the following.

➤ Symptom control.
➤ Run a Medical Research Council (MRC) dyspnoea score.[15]
➤ Smoking status and desire to stop.
➤ Encourage and offer help to smokers to stop smoking. Smoking cessation is a key intervention.[7]
➤ Effects of each drug and compliance.
➤ Inhaler technique. Use long-acting bronchodilator at an early stage.
➤ Nutritional status.
➤ Self-management plan – to enable interventions in patients with an exacerbation.
➤ Need for long-term oxygen therapy.
➤ Presence of depression.
➤ Need for pulmonary rehabilitation. Pulmonary rehabilitation should be offered to all patients who are limited by COPD.[7]
➤ Is osteoporosis screening indicated?

COPD8

The percentage of patients with COPD who have had influenza immunisation in the preceding 1 September to 31 March.

Points 6   **Payment stages 40–85%**

There is no excuse for losing these six points.

Maximising quality points

➤ There are about 40 codes for COPD. Use the following codes:
— H36 Mild COPD
— H37 Moderate COPD
— H38 Severe COPD.
The following codes should not be used:
— H34 Bronchiectasis
— H35 Alveolitis.
➤ Get rid of the asthma code (H33 stem) once a diagnosis of COPD is confirmed.
➤ If patient has both asthma and COPD, keep both on the register.
➤ The QOF gives an incentive to identify patients. Screen smokers, ex-smokers and those who have had two or more chest infections in the previous year.

➤ Primary care-based screening questionnaires can be easily done by a healthcare assistant. This would identify the disease at an early stage.

➤ Spirometry is fundamental to the screening, diagnosis and monitoring of COPD.

➤ Adequate training and familiarity with the equipment is vital.

➤ The following criteria have been agreed for exception reporting:
— Unsuitable (bedridden) 9H51
— Patient refusing three invitations 9H52
— Spirometry contraindicated 812M.

➤ Provide pneumococcal vaccination for all patients with COPD.

➤ Ensure influenza immunisation for all patients with COPD.

➤ Enter read code 679V, self-management plan.

➤ Enter all acute admissions read coded as 8H2.
This will help you to improve the management of these patients.

➤ Chase all DNA.

➤ The most important single intervention is smoking cessation.

Template GMS: COPD (V16)

Prompt	Code	Date	Coded subsets
Exception report: COPD quality indicator	(9h5)		Except. COPD QI: Pt unsuit. (9h51) Except. COPD QI: inf. dis. (9h52)
Ethnic category – 2001 census	(9i)		*See ethnicity template, Chapter 17*
Spiro screening	(68M)		
COPD excluded	(1I70)		
COPD monitoring	(66YB)		
COPD annual review	(66YM)		
Systolic blood pressure	(2469)		
Diastolic blood pressure	(246A)		
O/E – weight	(22A)		
O/E – height	(229)		
Body Mass Index	(22K)		
WAIST IN CM	(22N0)		
Smoking status			*See smoking status template, Chapter 25*
ALCOHOL CONSUMPTION			*See Alcohol, Chapter 28*
PATIENT ADVISED REG. DIET	(8CA4)		
PATIENT ADVISED REG. EXERCISE	(8CA5)		
PATIENT ADVISED ABOUT ALCOHOL	(8CAM)		
FBC	(424)		
PLASMA RANDOM GLUCOSE	(44g0)		
PLASMA FASTING GLUCOSE	(44g1)		
Peak exp. flow rate: PEFR/PFR	(3395)		
Forced expiratory volume in 1 second	(3390)		
% predicted	(339S)		
COPD severity	(H3)		
FVC	(3396)		

(continued)

Prompt	Code	Date	Coded subsets
FEV1/FVC percent	(339R)		
Spirometry screening	(68M)		Negative reversibility test salbutamol (33H0) Positive reversibility test salbutamol (33H1) Referral for spirometry (8HRC) Spirometry declined (8I3b) Spirometry not indic. (8I6L)
Airway obstruction reversible	(663J)		Airway obstruction reversible (663J) Air way obstruction irreversible (663K)
Inhaler technique – good	(663H)		Inhaler technique good (663H) Inhaler technique poor (663I)
USING SPACER	(6631)		
MRC Breathlessness Scale	(173H)		MRC b/less. scale grade 1 (173H) MRC b/less. scale grade 2 (173I) MRC b/less. scale grade 3 (173J) MRC b/less. scale grade 4 (173K) MRC b/less. scale grade 5 (173L)
PULSE OXIMETRY	(8A44-1)		
12 LEAD ECG	(321B)		
ECHO	(58531)		
PLASMA B NATRIURETIC			(Do if available in your area)
PEPTIDE LEVEL	(44AR)		
DEXA SCAN (to exclude osteoporosis)	(58E-1)		
Home nebuliser	(6638)		
Oxygenator therapy	(8774)		
DEPRESSION SCREEN	(6896)		
LOSS OF INTEREST	(1BP)		
DEPRESSED MOOD	(1BT)		
Influenza vaccination	(65E)		Influenza vaccination coded subsets same as in CHD template, Chapter 9
Pneumococcal vaccination	(6572)		Pneumococcal vaccination coded subsets same as in CHD template, Chapter 9
Medication review done	(8B3V)		
HEALTH EDUCATION – COPD	(679V)		
FIT TO FLY	(13ZI)		
ACUTE EXACERBATION COPD	(H3122)		
EMERGENCY HOSPITAL ADMISSION	(8H2)		
COPD monitoring FU	(66YB)		
COPD Annual FU	(66YM)		
COPD MONITOR 1st LETTER	(90i0)		
COPD MONITOR 2nd LETTER	(90i1)		
COPD MONITOR 3rd LETTER	(90i2)		

(Add the capitalised prompts to your template to maximise points and quality care)

Do something extra

➤ Pulse oximetry to assess need for oxygen therapy, if cyanosis or cor-pulmonale is present or if FEV1 is < 50% predicted.

➤ Chest X-ray to exclude other pathologies.

➤ CT scan to investigate chest X-ray abnormalities.

➤ Full blood count (FBC) to identify anaemia or polycythaemia.

➤ Investigate other co-morbidities – diabetes, hypertension, osteoporosis, vitamin D deficiency.

➤ ECG, ECHO to exclude other causes of breathlessness.

➤ Offer pulmonary rehabilitation.

➤ Screen for anxiety and depression.

➤ Deliver COPD care through a multidisciplinary approach – involve the healthcare assistant and community matron.

➤ Death is a common outcome for patients with severe COPD and the majority wish to die at home. Make sure you are up to date with end-of-life care. Put patients on the palliative care register when you start to provide end-of-life care for them.

References

1 Global Initiative for Chronic Obstructive Pulmonary Disease (GOLD). *Global Strategy for the Diagnosis, Management and Prevention of COPD.* Available at: www. goldcopd.com

2 Simpson CR, Hippisley-Cox J, Sheikh A. Trends in the epidemiology of chronic obstructive pulmonary disease in England: a national study of 51 804 patients. *Br J Gen. Prac.* 2010; **60**: 483–8.

3 Jarrold I, Eiser N, Morrel J. Who and where are the 'missing millions' of COPD patients in the UK? *Thorax.* 2009; **64**(Suppl. 4): A155.

4 Lopez AD, Murray CC. The global burden of disease, 1990–2020. *Nat. Med.* 1998; **4**: 1241–3.

5 Fletcher C, Peto R. The natural history of chronic airflow obstruction. *BMJ.* 1977; **1**: 1645–8.

6 Anthonissen NR, Connett JE, Kiley JP, *et al.* Effects of smoking intervention and the use of an inhaled anticholinergic bronchodilator on the rate of decline of FEV1: the lung health study. *JAMA.* 1995; **273**: 1497–505.

7 National Clinical Guideline Centre. *Chronic Obstructive Pulmonary Disease: management of chronic obstructive pulmonary disease in adults in primary and secondary care.* London: National Clinical Guideline Centre 2010. Available at: http://guidance.nice. org.uk/CG101 (accessed September 2010).

8 Lung and Asthma Information Agency. *Trends in Emergency Hospital Admissions for Lung Disease.* London: Lung and Asthma Information Agency; 2001.

9 Rupert J, Kevin G-J, Hilary P, *et al. Summary of the Consultation on a Strategy for Services for Chronic Obstructive Pulmonary Disease (COPD) in England.* Available at: www. dh.gov.uk/en/Consultations/Liveconsultations/DH_112977 (last accessed 21 April 2010).

10 O'Driscoll BR, Howard LS, Davison AG (British Thoracic Society). BTS guideline for emergency oxygen use in adult patients. *Thorax.* 2008; **63**(Suppl. 6): vi1–vi68.

11 Office for National Statistics. *Mortality Statistics: cause.* 1999, DH2 (No. 26). Ref. ID 19419. London: TSO; 2000.

12 Office for National Statistics. *Health Statistics Quarterly,* 2000; 8. Ref ID 19418. London: TSO; 2000.

13 Pulse. NICE unveils nine more 'quality standards' to judge GP commissioning. www.pulsetoday.co.uk/story.asp?

14 Tinkelman DG, Price DB, Nordyke RJ, *et al.* Symptom based questionnaire for differentiating COPD and asthma. *Respiration.* 2006; **73**:296–305.

15 Fletcher C, Elmes P, Fairbairn A, *et al.* The significance of respiratory symptoms and the diagnosis of chronic bronchitis in a working population. *BMJ.* 1959; **2**(5147): 257–66.

Useful information

➤ www.lunguk.org
➤ The BLF help line offers advice and information to healthcare professionals, patients and carers: 08458 505020.

CHAPTER 12

Long-acting reversible contraception (LARC)

Definition

NICE defines long-acting reversible methods of contraception (LARC) as those methods that require administering less than once per cycle or month.[1] Included in the category of LARC are:

➤ copper intrauterine devices
➤ progesterone only intrauterine system
➤ progesterone only injectable contraceptives
➤ progesterone only sub-dermal implants.

In the UK, at present only 8% of contraceptive users use LARC.[1]

LARC are also referred to as 'Long-lasting reliable contraception'.

The live birth rate for all age groups in England and Wales has increased since 2007, with the greatest increase seen in women aged 40 years and over. The live birth rate was 12.0/1000 women in 2007 and 12.6/1000 in 2008, with the number of live births to mothers aged 40 years and over nearly doubling.[2] There is a growing trend within the UK for women to have children later in life.[2]

Contraceptive choices

At present in the UK the pill and durex remain the most commonly used contraception methods. Office of National Statistics survey data (2008/09) indicated that for 16–19-year-olds who were at risk of pregnancy, 78% were using the pill.[3] LARC (the progesterone only implant, injectable and intrauterine methods) are used by a minority of women, but there is a trend towards its increasing use.[4]

Why included in QOF

➤ Of the prescribed contraception in the UK, 80% is provided by the GPs. It is hoped that its inclusion in the QOF will play a significant role in preventing unplanned pregnancies, especially in young people.

➤ Contraception has proved to be an effective means of preventing pregnancy.[5] There are currently three forms of combined hormonal contraception available in the UK: the combined oral contraceptive pill (COC), the combined transdermal patch and the combined vaginal ring (CVR). An open label randomised study compared the ethinylestradiol from the ring, patch and combined pill and found that NuvaRing is an equally effective low-dose contraceptive method.[5] NICE says it is important that women are helped to make an informed choice about which contraceptive method to use, taking in to account their individual needs and preferences.[6] GPs play a significant role in helping women to make a decision.

➤ This indicator has been included to increase the awareness of women seeking advice of LARC methods and to increase the percentage of women using these methods.

➤ LARC are more cost-effective at one year of use.[1] Intrauterine devices (IUD), the intrauterine system, Mirena (IUS), and implants are more cost-effective than the injectable contraceptives.

➤ The failure rates of LARC are lower than the shorter-acting methods such as the contraceptive pill.[7]

The facts

➤ There is no delay of fertility with LARCs.[8]

➤ Of the LARC methods, injectables are the least cost-effective.

➤ Young women's choice of contraception may be influenced by a number of factors, such as safety, effectiveness, discreetness, ease of use and less likelihood of forgetfulness. LARC fulfils all of these issues.

➤ LARC methods such as the progesterone only implants and injectables are used to a lesser extent amongst those aged over 40 years than younger women, although women over 40 are more likely to report use of intrauterine methods.[3]

QOF: contraception indicators

Indicators and points: total points 10

SH1

The practice can produce a register of women who have been prescribed any method of contraception at least once in the last year or other appropriate interval (e.g. last five years for an intrauterine system).

Points 4

The register should include women who have been prescribed any method of contraception: COC, POP, contraceptive cap, durex, IUD, IUS, implant, contraceptive patch. This indicator is prospective from 1 April 2009.

SH2

The percentage of women prescribed an oral or patch contraceptive method in the last year who have also received information from the practice about long-acting reversible methods of contraception in the previous 15 months.

Points 3   **Payment stages 40–90%**

➤ Run a computerised search on all women prescribed any form of contraception in the last 12 months. Put an alert message on these patients as a reminder to discuss LARC when they attend for repeat prescriptions. (Can be done by healthcare assistant, practice nurse or family planning nurse.)

➤ Make sure your practice nurse/family planning nurse and midwife are aware of this indicator.

➤ Women should be given detailed information, both verbal and written, about LARC contraceptive efficacy, risks and side-effects, duration of use and when to seek help while using the method.

➤ If you or your practice do not provide LARC, there should be an agreed arrangement in place for referring women for LARC to a neighbouring practice, community clinic or Brook's clinic.

➤ Cultural differences and religious beliefs should be taken in to account when discussing LARC.

➤ Have trained interpreters (if required) to encourage their use.

➤ This appears in the QOF box – there is no excuse for not achieving full points.

SH3

The percentage of women prescribed emergency hormonal contraception at least once in the year by the practice who have received information from the practice about long-acting reversible methods of contraception at the time of, or within one month of, the prescription.

Points 3   **Payment stages 40–90%**

➤ Patients prescribed emergency contraception oral tablets must be given a follow-up appointment to discuss future contraception.

➤ Discuss and offer the emergency IUD at the time of emergency contraception. An emergency coil can have a higher efficacy in prevention of pregnancy and provide an ongoing contraception.

➤ Use the 'My contraception' tool. This is a simple tool with the short and long questionnaires which helps patients to decide on the choice of contraception, taking in to account all sorts of preferences, concerns, age and medical history. This tool can be downloaded from www.brook.org.uk/mycontraceptiontool or www.fpa.org.uk/mycontraceptiontool by patients.

➤ As part of good medical practice, give advice on sexually transmitted infections and advise testing when appropriate.

Maximising quality points

➤ Start a dedicated family planning clinic – once a week or a fortnightly clinic depending on your list size.

➤ Optimise access to patients asking for emergency contraception – the best time to discuss the future contraceptive methods, including long-acting reversible contraception.

➤ Appoint a family planning-trained nurse who can take a holistic approach assisting women in making contraceptive choices.

➤ Some family planning nurses are trained to fit Levonorgestrel (LNG) IUS. They are an ideal choice to appoint to maximise your quality points and can earn more money for your practice if it is part of Local Enhanced Services (LES).

➤ Perhaps the trained practice or family planning nurse could increase your list size by seeing patients who do not want to attend community family planning or Brook's clinics.

➤ Setting up a register is the first step – which should not be difficult. There is no dedicated contraception template. (*I made by own template because I run a dedicated family planning clinic.*)

➤ Discuss LARC at the time of post-natal checks.

Template GMS: Contraception (V16)

Prompt	Code	Date	Coded subsets
Ethnic category – 2001 census	(9i)		*See ethnicity template, Chapter 17*
O/E HEIGHT	(229)		
O/E WEIGHT	(22A)		
BODY MASS INDEX	(22K)		
WAIST CIRCUMFERENCE	(22N0)		
PATIENT ADVISED REG. DIET	(8CA4)		
PATIENT ADVISED REG. EXERCISE	(8CA5)		
ALCOHOL CONSUMPTION			*See Alcohol, Chapter 27*
PATIENT ADVISED ABOUT ALCOHOL	(8CAM)		
LIFE STYLE COUNSELLING	(67H)		
SYSTOLIC BLOOD PRESSURE	(2469)		
DIASTOLIC BLOOD PRESSURE	(246A)		
SMOKING STATUS			*See smoking template, Chapter 25*
LMP	(1513)		
PILL CHECK	(614)		
ORAL CONTRACEP. PILL	(614)		Oral contracep. started (6141) Oral contracep. stopped (6142) Oral contracep. rpt. (6144) Oral contracep. changed (6149) Oral contracep. restarted (6143) Oral contracep. prescribed (614D)
PROGESTERONE ONLY	(6148)		POP started (EMISNQPR57)
			POP rpt. (EMISNQPR58)
EMERGENCY CONTRACEP. ADVICE	(614F)		
EMERGENCY CONTRACEP.	(61M)		
DEPO PROVERA INJECTION	(61B1-1)		Depo Provera given (61B1) Depo Provera rpt. (61B2) Depo Provera stopped (61B5) Depo Provera failure (61B6)

(continued)

Prompt	Code	Date	Coded subsets
INTRAUTERINE CONTRACEP. DEVICE	(615)		IUD fitted (6151) IUD removed (6152) IUD checked (6154) IUD change due (6159) IUD check due (615A)
NORPLANT INSERTION	(7G2AA)		
CHECK OF SUBCUT. CONTRAINDICATED	(61KB)		
REMOVAL OF SUBCUT. CONTRAINDICATED	(7G2H7)		
LONG ACTING REVERSIBLE CONTRACEP. LEAFLET GIVEN	(8CEG)		
LARC advice	(8CAw)		
HVS TAKEN	(4JK2)		
POST NATAL EXAM.	(EGTONPO2)		
SMEAR TAKEN	(7E2A2)		
LBC SCREENING	(685R)		
CHLAMYDIA URINE	(68K7)		
CHLAMYDIA -ve	(43U6)		
GONORRHOEA -ve	(4JQ8)		

(Add the capitalised prompts to your template to maximise points and quality care)

Do something extra

➤ A woman's choice of contraception is influenced by many factors that will reflect not only her medical condition but also social circumstances. Develop a decision-making algorithm for women attending for contraception or emergency contraception. (*I use this:* www.ffprhc.org.uk/admin/.../ CEUGuidanceQuickStartingContraception.pdf (accessed 26 Aug 2010)).

➤ Start a dedicated family planning clinic.

➤ Make sure your nurse is trained in family planning and sexual health.

➤ Young people attending for contraception should be encouraged to have regular STI testing, particularly when there has been a new sexual partner.

➤ Inform young people about using condoms with any new or additional partners, where and how to access free condoms and how to use condoms correctly.

➤ Condom demonstration may be appropriate, for first-time users in particular. This is only possible if your nurse is trained and you have a dedicated FP clinic.

➤ Perform STI screen if the individual presents with UPSI. Do STI tests two and 12 weeks after an incident of UPSI.

References

1 National Institute for Health and Clinical Excellence. *Long Acting Reversible Contraception: the effective and appropriate use of long acting reversible contraception 2005.* www. nice.org.uk/nicemedia/pdf/CG030fullguideline.pdf (accessed October 2010).

2 Office for National Statistics. *Statistical Bulletin for Births and Deaths in England and Wales 2008, 2009.* www.statistics.gov.uk/pdfdir/bdths0509.pdf (accessed 14 May 2010).

3 Office for National Statistics. *Contraception and Sexual Health 2008/2009.* www.gserve. nice.org.uk/media/386/cz/ImpUptakeReportCG30.pdf.

4 National Institute for Health and Clinical Excellence. *NICE implementation Uptake Report: long acting reversible contraception (LARC).* 2009. Available at: www.nice.org. uk/media/386/C2/ImpUptakeReportCG30.pdf

5 Van den Heuvel MW, Van Bragt AJ, Alnabawy AK, *et al.* Comparison of ethinylestradiol pharmacokinetics in three hormonal contraceptive formulations : the vaginal ring, the transdermal patch and an oral contraceptive. *Contraception.* 2005; **72**: 168–74.

6 Oddsson K, Leifels B, Wiel-Masson D, *et al.* Contraceptive technology. *Hum. Reprod.* 2005; **20**: 2764–8.

7 Trussell J. Summary table of contraceptive efficacy. In: Hatcher RA, Trussell J, Nelson AL, *et al. Contraceptive Technology.* 19th ed. New York, NY: Ardent Media; 2007.

8 Faculty of Sexual and Reproductive Healthcare. *Intrauterine Contraception 2007.* Available at: www.fsrh.org/admin/uploads/CEUGuidanceIntrauterineContraception Nov07.pdf (accessed 14 May 2010).

Useful reading

➤ Faculty of Sexual and Reproductive Healthcare: www.ffprhc.org.uk
➤ NHS choices: www.nhs.uk/worthtalkingabout
➤ www.contraception.co.uk

CHAPTER 13

Dementia

Definition

Dementia is a progressive neurodegenerative disease that is associated with an ongoing decline of memory, judgement, understanding, language and thinking. People with dementia may have problems controlling their emotions, and may see or hear things that other people do not or have false beliefs. There is no cure for dementia and symptoms get worse with time. Less is known about its prognosis compared with other life-threatening diseases.[1,2]

Prevalence

There are estimated to be over 750 000 people in the UK with dementia and numbers are expected to double in the next 30 years.[3] The prevalence of dementia increases with age and is estimated to be approximately 20% at 80 years of age. There are also a significant number of people (currently around 15 000) who develop dementia earlier in life.[3]

The total number of people with dementia is forecast to increase to just under 1 million in 2021 and 1.74 million by 2051, an increase of 38% over the next 15 years and 154% over the next 45 years.[4]

Alzheimer's disease accounts for 50–75% of cases of dementia. The annual incidence of dementia of the Alzheimer's type rises to 34.3 per 100 person-years at risk in the 90-year age bracket, and is higher in women than in men. Lewy body and fronto-temporal dementia are very rare.

Mortality

A cohort study investigating the survival rate of people with dementia concluded that the median survival rate of people diagnosed with dementia at age 60–69 years was 6.7 years, falling to 1.9 years for those diagnosed at 90 years and over.[5] The mortality was highest in the first year after diagnosis, with relative risk of 3.68, dropping to 2.49 in the second year. The authors concluded that the high death rate in the first year may mean late or missed diagnosis. Late diagnosis means missed opportunities for early disease intervention.[5]

Why included in QOF

➤ It could be challenging, but most dementia patients can be managed in a primary care setting. The National Dementia Strategy *Living Well with Dementia*, published in February 2009, seeks to enhance GPs' diagnostic and management skills in dementia. The three aims of the strategy are to raise awareness, improve assessment and improve services.[3]

➤ Dementia is increasing in prevalence and is the largest cause of disability which affects the ability to carry out domestic tasks and self-care. The number of patients with Alzheimer's disease and related disorders is expected to rise over the next 50 years.

➤ Diagnosis is often delayed in primary care. This could be due to lack of training and skills or difficulty in differentiating the disease with cognitive changes of the normal ageing process. Its inclusion in the QOF means better education and training of primary care physicians, leading to early diagnosis.

➤ Engaging GPs in the assessment process leads to early diagnosis of dementia.[6]

➤ Hypertension and hypercholesterolemia in midlife are risk factors for developing dementia, whereas in later life lower blood pressure and lower cholesterol concentration are associated with dementia.[7] GPs are best placed to target these modifiable risk factors.

➤ Early diagnosis enables patients and carers to plan for the future and get help from the support services.[3] This can promote independent living at home and delay admission to a care home.

➤ Increased fruit and vegetable consumption can also reduce the incidence of dementia.[8] GPs are best placed to offer this health promotion advice to target people at high risk of dementia, for example, older people, people with depression or diabetes.

The facts

➤ Direct costs of dementia to the NHS and social care are in the region of £8.2 billion annually.[3]

➤ The UK is in the bottom third of countries in Europe for diagnosing and treating dementia.

➤ Forty per cent of people in hospital have dementia and people with dementia stay longer in hospital.

➤ In care homes, two-thirds of people have dementia.

➤ An estimated 180 000 people with dementia are on anti-psychotic drugs. Drugs have a beneficial effect in only one-third of cases. Behavioural disturbances are often treated poorly in nursing homes.

➤ NICE guidance restricts treatment to patients who have Mini-mental State Examination (MMSE) scores between 10 and 20.

➤ Drug-related deaths account for 1800 deaths per year.

➤ Dementia has a higher association with suicidal ideation. Mild dementia has been shown to be associated with increased suicide in comparison with advanced dementia.[9]

➤ Diversion of resources from secondary care to primary care would be needed to address the challenges faced by primary care for early diagnosis and delivery of care.[10]

➤ A collaborative care model between primary and secondary care, the patient's family/carer and the social services is the only way these patients can be managed in a primary care setting.

➤ The National Dementia Strategy began the first effort in February 2009 to transform services for dementia patients. This has already shown some demonstrable results.

QOF: dementia indicators

Indicators and points: total points 20

Records
DEM1

The practice can produce a register of patients diagnosed with dementia.

Points 5

Patients must be put on the register after a proper diagnosis. Diagnosis should be made only after a comprehensive assessment, including history-taking, physical examination, routine blood tests and cognitive and mental state examination.

History

Ask people assessed for dementia whether they wish to know the diagnosis and with whom they would like to share it.

Ask the history of:
➤ difficulty in performing familiar tasks
➤ memory loss causing problems in daily functioning
➤ misplacing things
➤ putting things in odd places, for example, clothes in the freezer
➤ confusion, suspicion or paranoia
➤ poor judgement
➤ not recognising numbers
➤ changes in mood or behaviour
➤ disorientation in time and place
➤ forgetting words, speech problems.

Taking a thorough patient's history is the best way to establish a diagnosis. It is useful to ask relatives and colleagues if they have noticed a change in the patient's personality.

Clinical cognitive assessment

When conducting the formal cognitive tests, take into account patients educational level, psychiatric illness, sensory impairment and physical or neurological factors.
➤ Examine orientation, language, attention and concentration, praxis.
➤ Conduct tests such as MMSE, 6-item cognitive impairment test (6-CIT), GP assessment of cognition (GPCOG).

➤ Seven-minute screen.

MMSE can be accessed on www.aaa-online.org.uk/Pages/Delerium/Mini-Mental%20State%20Exam.htm

MMSE does not take account of function, behaviour or personality. These should be taken into account before deciding the severity of dementia.

If you have not got the time or capacity to make a diagnosis, refer the patient to memory clinic for assessment.

➤ CT or MRI scanning should be undertaken to assist with early diagnosis. Cerebral atrophy is seen on brain scanning.

Ongoing management

DEM2

The percentage of patients diagnosed with dementia whose care has been reviewed in the previous 15 months.

Points 15   **Payment stages 25–60%**

GPs are best placed to provide continuity of care across the whole trajectory of the disease, acting as advocates and problem-solvers when other agencies fail to do so. The NICE guidelines emphasise the importance of an integrated and coordinated approach to manage patients with dementia.

At every review allow people with dementia to give information with confidence.

Dementia patients should be followed-up, in the surgery or at home, for the following.

➤ Medication review as per the national service framework shared care protocol.
➤ Check for any behavioural and psychological symptoms of dementia (BPSD):
    — pain
    — behavioural changes, for example, walking a lot
    — depression
    — delusion.
➤ Depression occurs in at least 20% of patients with Alzheimer's disease[11] and an even higher proportion of patients with vascular dementia or dementia with Lewy bodies. Selective serotonin re-uptake inhibitors (SSRIs) are probably the treatment of choice for severe depression in these patients. Tricyclic anti-depressants should be avoided.
➤ Make separate time for carers. Address the health of the carer, identify needs and provide support.
➤ If new problems are emerging, do the analysis and treat or refer.
➤ Let the carer know who to contact if an acute crisis (confusion or extreme changes in behaviour) occurs out of hours or at the weekend when you are not available.

Maximising quality points

➤ Identify and treat the risk factors for dementia such as smoking, excessive alcohol use, obesity, diabetes, hypertension and high cholesterol. If diabetes or hypertension is picked up you will increase the prevalence in these disease areas.

➤ Enter the diagnosis read coded once the hospital letter confirms the diagnosis.
➤ Make sure care homes registering patients with a diagnosis of dementia with the practice are read coded. (*With recent changes in electronic data transfer this should not be difficult.*)
➤ Providing influenza vaccination every year and one-off pneumococcal vaccination will earn extra points.
➤ Use the read code Dementia (E00-97).
  — [X]Vascular dementia (Eu01)
  — Senile dementia (E00-1)
  — H/O dementia (1461)
  — Multi infarct dementia (E004-1)
  — Alcohol dementia (E012-1).
➤ The proposed indicator for next year's QOF includes the percentage of patients with a new dementia diagnosis to have FBC, LFT, TFT, U&E, serum vitamin B12, folate, calcium and glucose level recorded six months before and after entering the register. **Start doing it now. Enter read codes in the template.**
➤ Pain is common in people with dementia and may not be recognised. **Although no points are attached, always have a high level of suspicion that pain might be present.** Your patient and their carer will give you maximum points for early detection and management of pain.

Template GMS: Dementia (V16)

Prompt	Code	Date	Coded subsets
Exception report: dementia quality indicator	(9hD)		Except. dementia QI: Pt unsuit. (9hD0) Except. dementia QI: inf. des. (9hD1)
Ethnic category – 2001 census	(9i)		*See ethnicity template, Chapter 17*
O/E HEIGHT	(229)		
O/E WEIGHT	(22A)		
BODY MASS INDEX	(22K)		
WAIST CIRCUMFERENCE	(22N0)		
WCM DECLINE	(8IAf)		
IDEAL WEIGHT	(66CB)		
SMOKING STATUS			*See smoking template, Chapter 25*
ALCOHOL CONSUMPTION UNITS/ WEEK	(136)		
ALCOHOL SCORE	(9k17)		*See Alcohol, Chapter 27*
PATIENT ADVISED REG. DIET	(8CA4)		
PATIENT ADVISED REG. EXERCISE	(8CA5)		
PATIENT ADVISED ABOUT ALCOHOL	(8CAM)		
LIFE STYLE COUNSELLING	(67H)		
6 item cognitive impairment test	(3AD3)		
Mini mental state score	(388V)		
SYSTOLIC BP	(2469)		
DIASTOLIC BP	(246A)		
O/E PULSE RATE	(242)		
FULL BLOOD COUNT	(424)		

(continued)

Prompt	Code	Date	Coded subsets
SERUM FERRITIN	(42R4)		
SERUM B12	(42T)		
BONE PROFILE	(44Z2)		
LFT	(44D)		
TFT	(442J)		
SERUM SODIUM	(44I5)		
SERUM POTASSIUM	(44I4)		
SERUM UREA LEVEL	(44J9)		
SERUM CREATININE	(44J3)		
eGFR	(451E)		
URINE PROTEIN TEST +ve	(4674)		*See urine protein test coded subsets in CKD template, Chapter 10*
SERUM TOTAL CHOLESTEROL	(44PJ)		
SERUM HDL – CHOLESTEROL	(44P5)		
SERUM LDL – CHOLESTEROL	(44P6)		
SERUM TRIGLYCERIDES	(44Q)		
SERUM CHOLESTEROL:HDL RATIO	(441F)		
PLASMA RANDOM GLUCOSE	(44g0)		
PLASMA FASTING GLUCOSE	(44g1)		
MRI SCAN BRAIN	(569K0)		MRI scan normal (569F) Refer for MRI scan (8HQ3-1) MRI scan abnormal (5694)
CT SCAN BRAIN – NORMAL	(5C00)		
CT BRAIN SCAN DECLINED	(56F0)		
DEPRESSION SCREEN USING QUESTIONNAIRE	(6896)		
HAD ANXIETY	(388N)		
HAD DEPRESSION	(388P)		
PHQ-9	(388f)		
SUICIDE RISK	(1BD4)		
SUICIDE ATTEMPT	(TK)		
Psychiatry care plan	(8CM2)		
MH medication review	(8BM0)		
MH health personal health plan	(8CR7)		
ADVISED REGARDING DRIVING	(8CAJ)		
CARER'S DETAILS	(9180)		*Carer's coded subsets same as in mental health template, Chapter 22*
Disability assessment – mental	(3A)		
WORK STATUS	(13J)		*Work status coded subsets same as in mental health template, Chapter 22*
HOUSING DEPENDENCY SCALE	(13F)		*Housing dependency coded subsets same as in mental health template, Chapter 22*
Dementia annual review	(6AB)		
Mental health review	(6A6)		
INFLUENZA VACCINATION	(65E)		*Influenza vaccination coded subsets same as in CHD template, Chapter 9*

(continued)

Prompt	Code	Date	Coded subsets
PNEUMOCOCCAL VACCINATION	(6572)		Pneumococcal vaccination subsets same as in CHD template, Chapter 9
DEMENTIA MONITORING 1st LETTER	(90u1)		
DEMENTIA MONITORING 2nd LETTER	(90u2)		
DEMENTIA MONITORING 3rd LETTER	(90u3)		
DEMENTIA MONITORING VERBAL INVITE	(90u4)		

(Add the capitalised prompts to your template to maximise points and quality care)

Do something extra

➤ Early assessment or a referral to the memory clinic with suspected mild cognitive impairment benefits the patient and the carer.

➤ Carry out FBC, ESR, TFT, B12, folate levels, urine check and chest X-ray. Routine serology for syphilis is no longer recommended.

➤ Always seek valid consent from people with dementia. Use the Mental Capacity Act 2005 if the person lacks the capacity.

➤ Discuss with the person with dementia while he or she still has the capacity to make decisions about a preferred place of care plan, lasting power of attorney and advanced decisions to refuse treatment. Enter all these in the computer.

➤ If alcohol abuse is suspected, run an alcohol screen and offer help from an alcohol counsellor. Excessive alcohol consumption can cause significant cognitive impairment.

➤ Enter the name of the social worker and the carer, with the contact numbers, in the records.

➤ Do a medication review. Can the behavioural changes be due to the prescribed medication, for example, diuretic given for hypertension/heart failure causing electrolyte imbalance and confusion?

➤ Remember, vascular dementia is less treatable – do not prescribe cholinesterase inhibitors unnecessarily.

➤ Advise all patients with dementia to stop driving immediately. Not advising a driver regarding driving after diagnosing dementia may be seen as a clinical negligence.

➤ Refer the patient to structured group cognitive stimulation programme – recommended by NICE.

➤ There is good evidence that simple exercises do confer a significant benefit to dementia patients with depression.

➤ Give information to the carers about the available resources. For information and support, give them the address of Alzheimer's Society (see Useful reading below).

➤ Find out whether and how the National Dementia Strategy objectives have been implemented in your area. In some areas dementia cafes, a valued expenditure, have been set up, where patients with dementia can form relationships with other people with problems.

➤ Provide influenza vaccination to the carers.

➤ Offer referral to genetic counselling to unaffected relatives of those thought to have a genetic cause of dementia.
➤ Do not advise or prescribe statins, hormone replacement therapy (HRT), vitamin E (over-the-counter (OTC)) for the primary prevention of dementia.

References

1 Wolfson C, Wolfson DB, Asgharian M, *et al.* A reevaluation of the duration of survival after the onset of dementia. *N. Engl. J Med.* 2001; **344**: 111–16.
2 Neale R, Brayne C, Johnson AL. Cognition and survival: an exploration in a large multicentre study of the population aged 65 years and over. *Int. J Epidemiol.* 2000; **30**: 1383–8.
3 Department of Health. *Living Well with Dementia: a national dementia strategy.* 2009. www.dh.gov.uk/en/SocialCare/Deliveringadultsocialcare/olderpeople/National DementiaStrategy/index.htm
4 Knapp M, Prince M, Albanese E, *et al.* (2007) *Dementia UK: Report to the Alzheimer's Society, Kings College London and London School of Economics and Political Science.* London: Alzheimer's Society; 2007.
5 Rait G, Walters K, Bottomley C, *et al.* Survival of people with a clinical diagnosis of dementia in primary care: cohort study. *BMJ.* 2010; **341**: c3584.
6 Curran S, Wattis J. *Practical Management of Dementia: a multi-professional approach.* London: Radcliffe Publishing; 2004, p. 895.
7 Van Vliet P, Westendorp R, van Heemst D, *et al.* Cognitive decline precedes late-life longitudinal changes in vascular risk factors. *J Neurol. Neurosurg. Psychiatry.* Epub. 2010. June 11.
8 Ritchie K, Carriere I, Ritchie CW, *et al.* Designing prevention programmes to reduce incidence of dementia: prospective cohort study of modifiable risk factors. *BMJ.* 2010; **341**: c3885.
9 Osvath P, Kovacs A, Voros V, *et al.* Risk factors of attempted suicide in the elderly: the role of cognitive impairment. *Int. J Psychiatry Clin. Pract.* 2005; **9**: 221–5.
10 Callahan CM, Boustani M, Sachs GA, *et al.* Integrating care for older adults with cognitive impairment. *Curr. Alzheimer Res.* 2009; **6**: 368–74.
11 Burns A, Jacoby R, Levy R. Psychiatric phenomena in Alzheimer's disease. Disorders of mood. *Br J Psychiatry.* 1990; **157**: 81–6, 92–4.

Useful reading

➤ www.dementiaweb.org.uk/driving-and-dementia.pdf
➤ National Institute for Health and Clinical Excellence, Social Care Institute for Excellence. *Dementia: supporting people with dementia and their carers in health and social care NICE guideline CG42.* London: NHICE; 2006. Available at: www.nice.org.uk/.../CG042
➤ Read the UK Mental Capacity Act 2005, five principles and legal frameworks.
➤ Social Care Institute for Excellence. *Assessing the Mental Health Needs of Older People: SCIE practice guide 2.* 2006. Available at: www.scie.org.uk/publications/practiceguides/practiceguide02
➤ Social Care Institute for Excellence. *Implementing the Carers (Equal Opportunities).* Available at: www.scie-socialcareonline.org.uk/profile.asp?guid=004cd7db
➤ Alzheimer's Society: www.alzheimers.org.uk

CHAPTER 14

Depression

Depression is the most common and costly mental health problem seen in general practice.[1] By 2020 it will be second only to ischaemic heart disease as the leading cause of morbidity and mortality worldwide.[2]

It is the third most common cause of consultation in a primary care setting, but there is a controversy as to whether this increase reflects a real increase in incidence or a greater awareness and identification of the condition.

Definition

Depression is a change in mood and behaviour characterised by feelings of sadness, loss of enjoyment of life, low energy, poor motivation and low self-worth.

Prevalence

Depression affects 121 million people worldwide and is one of the leading causes of disability in the world.[3]

➤ The UK prevalence of major depression is around 1.7% in men and 2.5% in women aged 16–65 years.[4]
➤ Mixed anxiety and depression is more common, at 7.1% in men and 12.4% in women.[4]
➤ The prevalence of major depression among community-dwelling older adults ranges from 8% to 16%.[5,6] It is substantially higher in older women than men.[7]
➤ In residential homes the prevalence is up to 40%.[8]
➤ In nursing homes it is about 33%.[9]
➤ One in four women and one in 10 men suffer a major depression requiring treatment.
➤ Prevalence in acutely ill patients is about 46%.[10]

Why included in QOF

➤ Depression increases the risk for both social and physical disability. The socio-economic burden of this illness is increasing. An even greater strain on the

NHS arises from the cost of undiagnosed and untreated depression. The World Health Organization (WHO) predicts that by 2030 depression will be the second leading cause of disability worldwide, behind only HIV/AIDS.

➤ An early diagnosis and early treatment can lessen the burden on the NHS. A comprehensive assessment, including the use of validated tools, can be carried out easily by a GP.

➤ The GP can explore any suicidal ideas and negotiate drug treatment with the patient.

➤ Initiating the prescription and monitoring progress on anti-depressants can be carried out by a primary care physician. This collaborative care, along with well-structured disease management, has been shown to be cost-effective and hence its inclusion in the QOF.

➤ The prescription of anti-depressant drugs has continued to rise in England, reaching 33.6 million items in 2007,[11] which has prompted concerns that this largely reflects over-treatment of patients with sub-threshold depression. On the other hand, only a minority of patients with major depression receive effective treatment.[12] Its inclusion in QOF would correct this ambiguity.

➤ The aim of the QOF is to improve the targeting of anti-depressants by incentivising GPs to use a validated measure of severity tool.

The facts

➤ Depression is an independent risk factor for both cardiovascular disease and myocardial infarction, associated with a three- to fourfold increase in cardiovascular mortality and morbidity.[13]

➤ The probability of recurrence of depression at five years is as high as 60% and increases to 74% in people with a history of two or more episodes.[14]

➤ Up to 75% of older people who committed suicide had visited a physician in the month before death.[15]

QOF: depression indicators

Indicators and points: total points 33

DEPRESSION 1

The percentage of patients on the diabetes register and/or the CHD register for whom case finding for depression has been undertaken on one occasion during the previous 15 months using two standard screening questions.

Points 8   **Payment stages 40–90%**

NICE guidelines recommend the following two questions for depression screening.

➤ During the past month, have you often been bothered by feeling down, depressed or hopeless?

➤ During the past month, have you often been bothered by having little interest or pleasure in doing things?

If the patient answers 'No' to the above two questions, depression can be excluded from the register. If the patient answers 'Yes' to either question, further assessment must be undertaken. The QOF recommends using either the patient health questionnaire (PHQ) or the hospital anxiety and depression scale (HADS).

Assessment

Characteristic features of depression are as follows.[16]

➤ Emotional symptoms:
  — low mood
  — loss of enjoyment
  — sad feeling
  — shame
  — anger
  — guilt
  — anxiety.
➤ Somatic symptoms:
  — tiredness
  — insomnia or hypersomnia
  — appetite change, weight loss or gain
  — poor concentration
  — low energy
  — increased pain
  — loss of libido.
➤ Cognitive symptoms:
  — lack of motivation
  — hopelessness/negative view of the future, recurrent thoughts of death or suicide
  — negative thoughts.
➤ Behavioural symptoms:
  — social withdrawal
  — excessive rest
  — reduction in enjoyable activities
  — self-harm/suicidal behaviour.
➤ Older patients with depression may present with:
  — poor grooming
  — crying
  — dressed in sombre colours
  — a dishevelled appearance
  — not engaging with consultation
  — restless, agitated
  — hunched posture
  — slowness of movements.

For older people, use the geriatric depression scale (GDS) (available at: www. stanford.edu/-yesavage/GDS.html).

The ICD-10 symptom list for depression is another tool for identifying depression and establishing severity.[17]

DEPRESSION 2

In those patients with a new diagnosis of depression, recorded between the preceding 1 April to 31 March, the percentage of patients who have had an assessment of severity at the outset of treatment using a validated tool in primary care.

Points 25   **Payment stages 40–90%**

HADS is a validated tool for measurement of severity of anxiety and depression. The questionnaire can be loaded on the computer and given to the patients at the time of consultation.

DEPRESSION 3

This is a new indicator introduced in 2009/10. In those patients with a new diagnosis of depression and assessment of severity recorded between the preceding 1 April to 31 March, the percentage of patients who have had a further assessment of severity 5–12 weeks (inclusive) after the initial recording of the assessment of severity. Both assessments should be completed using an assessment tool validated for use in primary care.

(New) Points 20   **Payment stages 40–90%**

For the purpose of QOF measurement 'at the outset of treatment' is defined as within 28 days of the initial diagnosis.

Maximising quality points

➤ For patients who have been diagnosed with anxiety and depression, use read code E2003 and enter as an active problem.
➤ Make sure assessment of severity is undertaken using either the HADS or PHQ questionnaire:
  — Depression screen (6896)
  — HAD anxiety (388N)
  — HAD depression (388P)
  — PHQ-9 (388f).
➤ You can use some other acceptable read codes for this disease which will not trigger the mental health disease register:
  — Agitated depression (E135)
  — Reactive depression (Eu32z)
  — Depressive disorder (E2B)
  — Mild/moderate/severe depression (Eu320/Eu321/Eu322).
➤ The following codes are not depression codes:
  — Bereavement (13Hc)
  — Grief reaction (E2900)
  — Depressed mood (1BT).
➤ Once the patient is recovered and off the medication, enter the depression resolved read code 212S.
➤ Patients with a record of depression require a second assessment of depression between five and 12 weeks after the first. To score this:

— enter an alert message on the screen – due assessment with a date
— do not enter the medication on repeats until the second assessment score has been done
— enter a diary date for a follow-up appointment in 8–10 weeks
— build up the template by entering the depression medication review read code (9H9I)
— add the 5–12 week review read code (9H92) to the template.

➤ If unsure of the diagnosis or waiting for blood test results to exclude medical causes of the symptoms, use safe codes such as:
— Depressed mood (IBT) or
— Loss of interest (IBP).

➤ There are other safe codes which can be used – choose from the following:
— General nervous symptoms (1B1...)
— Nerves – nervousness (1B11)
— Anxiousness (1B13)
— Inadequate (1B18)
— Depressed (1B17)
— Emotional problems (1B1J)
— Crying, excessive (1B1I).

➤ Never use these codes:
— H/O depression (1465)
— [X]Depression NOS (Eu32z-1)
— Chronic depression (E2B1)
— On depression register (9HAO)
— Recurrent depression (E1137)
— [X]Reactive depression NOS (Eu32z-4).

➤ Remember, there are nine depression codes that will put the patient in the mental health group. Do not use any depression code which includes 'psychosis'. Beware of the following:
— Reactive depression psychosis (E130)
— Recurrent major depression with psychosis (E1134)
— Single episode major depression with psychosis (E1124)
— [X]Severe depressive +psychotic (Eu323)
— [X]Post schizophrenic depression (Eu204)
— [X]Schizophrenic psychotic depression (Eu251)
— [X]Recurrent psychotic depression (Eu333)
— [X]Major depression, severe with psychotic symp. (Eu328)
— [X]Endogenous depression+psychotic symptoms (Eu333...).

➤ If a patient does not attend the follow-up appointment for review of their condition, you must send three letters and must document:
— Depression monitoring first letter (90V0)
— Depression monitoring second letter (90VI)
— Depression monitoring third letter (90V2).

➤ If patient fails to attend the third booked appointment use the following code:
— Removed from depression register (9HAI).

Template GMS: Depression (V16)

Prompt	Code	Date	Coded subsets
Exception reporting: depression quality indicator	(9hC)		Except. depress. QI: Pt unsuit. (9hC0) Except. depress. QI: inf. dis. (9hC1)
Ethnic category – 2001 census	(9i)		See ethnicity template, Chapter 17
O/E WEIGHT	(22A)		
O/E HEIGHT	(229)		
BMI	(22K)		
WAIST CIRCUMF.	(22N0)		
WCM DECLINE	(8IAf)		
SYSTOLIC BLOOD PRESSURE	(2469)		
DIASTOLIC BLOOD PRESSURE	(246A)		
URINE PROTEIN TEST +	(4674)		Proteinuria (R110) Albuminuria (R1100) Microalbumin (R1103)
SMOKING STATUS			See smoking status template, Chapter 25
ALCOHOL CONSUMPTION			See Alcohol, Chapter 27
PT ADV REG DIET	(8CA4)		
PT ADV REG EXERCISE	(8CA5)		
PT ADV ABOUT ALCOHOL	(8CAM)		
LIFE STYLE COUNSELLING	(67H)		
HISTORY POST NATAL DEPRESSION	(E204-1)		
H/O RECREATIONAL DRUGS	(146E)		
CURRENT DRUG USER	(13c7)		
HISTORY OF SUICIDE	(TK)		
SUICIDE RISK	(1BD4)		
SERUM CHOLESTEROL	(44P)		
SERUM HDL	(44P5)		
SERUM LDL	(44P6)		
SERUM TRIGLYCERIDE	(44Q)		
PLASMA RANDOM GLUCOSE	(44g0)		
PLASMA FASTING GLUCOSE	(44g1)		
JBS CARDIOVASCULAR RISK <10% 10 YEARS	(662k)		JBS risk 10–20% 10 years (662l) JBS risk > 20–30% 10 years (662m) JBS risk > 30% 10 years (662n)
TFT	(442J)		
FBC	(424)		
FERRITIN-SERUM	(42R4-1)		
SERUM VITAMIN B12	(42T)		
Depression resolved	(212S)		
Removed from depression register	((9HA1)		
Depression annual review	(9H90)		
Depression screen using questionnaire	(6896)		

(continued)

Prompt	Code	Date	Coded subsets
PHQ-9 score	(388f)		
HAD anxiety	(388N)		
HAD depression	(388P)		
5–12 week review	(9H92)		
DEPRESSION MONITORING 1st LETTER	(90v0)		
DEPRESSION MONITORING 2nd LETTER	(90v1)		
DEPRESSION MONITORING 3rd LETTER	(90v2)		
DEPRESSION MONITORING VERBAL INVITE	(90v3)		
DEPRESSION MONITORING TELEPHONIC INVITE	(90v4)		
INFLUENZA VACCINATION	(65E)		Influenza vaccination coded subsets same as in CHD template, Chapter 9
PNEUMOCOCCAL	(6572)		Pneumococcal vaccination coded subsets same as in CHD template, Chapter 9

(Add the capitalised prompts to your template to maximise points and quality care)

Do something extra

➤ Assess the severity. This can be done in a primary care setting. It is important to distinguish between sub-threshold, mild, moderate and severe depression.
   See www.nice.org.uk/CGgoniceguidelines for details.
➤ If depression is suspected check the following:
   — TFT-hypothyroidism can present with low mood and lethargy
   — FBC, ferritin, vitamin B12 level. Deficiency of vitamin B12, folate and ferritin may be associated with depression
   — chronic fatigue syndrome, which can be differentiated from depression by the presence of characteristic cognitive dysfunction.[18]
➤ Depressive symptoms are risk factors for CHD. Women with recurrent major depression are at a greater risk of coronary atherosclerosis than women with single or no episodes.
   Screen patients for cardiovascular risk assessment:
   — check blood pressure, blood sugar, fasting cholesterol and calculate the Joint British Societies Guidelines (JBS 2).[19]
➤ Ask history of drug or alcohol abuse. Give advice or refer these patients to a drug or alcohol counsellor.
➤ Vitamin D deficiency in older people can be associated with depression. Correcting the problem could be an effective public health measure. Check serum 25-hydroxy vitamin D level.
➤ Ask about past history of post-natal depression. Screen, refer or treat these patients early.

➤ Ask about history of suicide attempts. Present or past history of suicide attempts needs urgent attention. Patients with this history must be fitted in the same day if they ask for an appointment.

➤ Update yourself by reading the NICE stepped-care model for the management of depression.[20]

➤ Make sure that you taper down the anti-depressants gradually before stopping them. Treatment should be continued for at least six months after full remission to reduce the risk of relapse. Move the prescription from the repeat to the acute prescribing screen after six months. This is one way of reminding all the clinicians in a big practice.

➤ Warn the patients of this tapering and stopping when initiating the treatment. Tapering must be done for a period of six to eight weeks before stopping treatment.

References

1 Katon W, Schulberg H. Epidemiology of depression in primary care. *Gen. Hosp. Psychiatry*. 1992; **14**: 237–47.

2 Murray C, Lopez A. Alternative projections of mortality and disability by cause 1990–2020. Global Burden of Disease Study. *Lancet*. 1997; **349**: 1498–1504.

3 See www.who.int/mental_health/management/depression/definition/en/ (accessed 1 May 2009).

4 National Institute for Health and Clinical Excellence. *Depression: Management of Depression in Primary and Secondary Care: clinical guideline 23*. London: NHICE; 2004.

5 Berkman LF, Berkman CS, Kasl S, *et al*. Depressive symptoms in relation to physical health and functioning in the elderly. *Am. J Epidemiol*. 1986; **124**: 372–88. Available at: www.ncbi.nlm.nih.gov/pubmed/3740038

6 Blazer DG, Burchett B, Service C, *et al*. The association of age and depression among the elderly: an epidemiologic exploration. *J Gerontol. Med. Sci*. 1999; **46**: 201–5.

7 Barry LC, Allore HG, Guo Z, *et al*. Higher burden of depression among older women. The effect of onset, persistence and mortality over time. *Arch. Gen. Psychiatry J Gerontol. Med. Sci*. 2008; **65**(2):172–8.

8 Mann AH, Schneider J, Mozley CG, *et al*. Depression and the response of residential homes to physical health needs. *Int. J Geriatr. Psychiatry*. 2000; **15**: 1105–12.

9 Rovner BW, German PS, Brant C. Depression and mortality in nursing homes. *JAMA*. 1991; **265**: 993–6.

10 Shah A, Herbert R, Lewis S, *et al*. Screening for depression among acutely ill geriatric inpatients with a short geriatric depression scale. *Age and Aging*. 1997; **26**: 217–21.

11 Prescription Pricing Authority. *Prescribing Review Drugs used in Mental Health*. 2007. Available at: www.nhsbsa.nhs.uk/PrescriptionService/250.aspx

12 Kendrick T, King F, Albertella L, *et al*. GP treatment decisions for patients with depression: an observational study. *Br J Gen. Pract*. 2005; **55**: 280–6.

13 Ford D, Mead L, Chang P, *et al*. Depression is a risk factor for coronary artery disease in men: the precursors study. *Arch. Intern. Med*. 1998; **158**: 1422–6.

14 Solomon D, Kellor M, Leon A, *et al*. Multiple recurrences of major depressive disorder. *Am. J Psychiatry*. 2000; **157**: 229–33.

15 Conwell Y. Suicide in later life; a review and recommendations for prevention. *Suicide and Life Threatening Behaviour*. 2001; **31**(Suppl.): 32–47.

16 David L. *Using CBT in General Practice: the 10 minute consultation.* Bloxham: Scion Publishing; 2006.

17 World Health Organization. *The ICD-10 Classification of Mental and Hehavioural Disorders: clinical description and diagnostic guidelines.* Geneva: World Health Organization; 1992.

18 Moss-Morris R, Pitrie KJ. Discriminating between chronic fatigue syndrome and depression; a cognitive analysis. *Psychological Medicine.* 2001; **31**: 469–79.

19 www.heart.bmj.co/content/91/suppl_5/vi.extract

20 www.nice.org.uk/nicemedia/pdf/CG90NICEguideline.pdf

Useful reading

➤ National Institute for Health and Clinical Excellence. *Depression: the treatment and management of depression in adults: NICE guideline 23.* London: NHICE; 2006. www.nice.org.uk/guidance/CG23 (accessed 17 July 2010).

➤ www.nice.org.uk/nicemedia/pdf/CG90NICEguideline.pdf An online educational tool is also available on the website.

CHAPTER 15

Diabetes mellitus

Diabetes is a major healthcare challenge for both the primary and secondary care sectors. There is a worldwide epidemic of type 2 diabetes.

Diagnosis

Diabetes is a biochemical diagnosis. The diagnosis of diabetes has important implications for driving and insurance. Diagnosis must be made on the blood glucose estimation from a laboratory. Finger prick test results should never be used for diagnosis.

The WHO criteria for diagnosing diabetes[1] were adopted in the UK in 2000:

➤ fasting blood sugar of 7 mmol/L and above
➤ random plasma glucose or a post-75 g glucose challenge of 11.1 mmol/L or above
➤ in asymptomatic patients, two abnormal blood glucose levels must be obtained to diagnose diabetes.

Blood glucose levels are also used to define impaired glucose tolerance (IGT) and impaired fasting glucose (IFG), which together have been labelled as 'pre-diabetics'.[1]

A fasting blood glucose level below 6 mmol/L is classified as normal in IFG and IGT. A level between 6 and 7 mmol/L is classified as IFG.

Diabetes UK recommends carrying out an oral glucose tolerance test (GTT) to confirm diabetes.[2]

Prevalence

The UK prevalence of diabetes in men aged 65–74 years age increased from 5.8% in 1994 to 15.7% in 2006, while that in women increased from 4.8% to 10.4%.[3]

One in 10 people in hospital in the UK have diabetes.[4] An estimated 25% of diabetics require surgery at some point in their lives.[5]

Diabetes UK reports that there is currently a population of 2.8 million known diabetics in the UK.[6]

Type 1 diabetes accounts for more than 90% of diabetes in patients under the age of 25. There is a hereditary element, and 12–15% of young people under the age of 15 will have a first degree relative with the condition. Although type 1 diabetes typically appears during adolescence, it can develop at any age.

Why included in QOF

➤ There is a worldwide epidemic of type 2 diabetes, causing significant morbidity, mortality and cost. Its inclusion means early diagnosis, effective control and early attention to complications, reducing the cost related to management of long-term complications.

➤ Of all deaths among 20–79 year-olds in England, 11.6% can be attributed to diabetes.[4]

➤ Ten per cent of NHS expenditure is spent on diabetes.[7] Its inclusion in the QOF will hopefully reduce the financial burden on the NHS.

➤ Children who developed diabetes in the year 2000 at the age of 10 will lose about 19 years of life and the loss of quality adjusted life years (QALYs) for such children is likely to be 31 for boys and 33 for girls.[8] Its inclusion in the QOF is to prevent premature mortality.

➤ Obesity is implicated in the increasing incidence of type 2 diabetes, and both obesity and diabetes are risk factors for cardiovascular disease. Because of their knowledge and regular contact with patients, GPs and practice nurses are best placed to offer advice on weight and exercise programmes (free gym membership, free Weight Watchers vouchers, exercise on prescription, referral to a health trainer, etc.), hence its inclusion in the QOF.

➤ Diabetes care requires a multi-disciplinary approach, which can be time-consuming. GPs are well placed to organise the structured care plan.

➤ It is well accepted that tight glycaemic control can slow the disease progression and microvascular complications. To achieve this, patient education and good concordance are important elements. Primary care is the best place to provide this. Patients like to see and listen to their GPs.

➤ Diabetic foot disease (DFD) is estimated to affect 15–25% of patients with diabetes at some time in their life. More than one in 10 foot ulcers result in amputation of the foot. Its inclusion in the QOF is intended to reduce the significant morbidity and mortality associated with DFD.

➤ The patient's and carer's education is an integral part of diabetes care. It is hoped that its inclusion will enable GPs to provide structured education to every person and their carer at and around the time of diagnosis.

➤ Primary care, with its resources, is able to provide individualised and ongoing dietician advice from a healthcare professional with expertise in diabetes. Make sure the advice is provided in a form that is sensitive to patient's culture and beliefs. GPs are best placed to provide in-house dietary advice or refer these patients to dietetic services.

The facts

➤ HBA1c looks likely to be recommended as a diagnostic test for diabetes. An international expert committee is recommending that a diagnosis should be made with an HBA1c level of 6.5% or above.[9] This is being considered by the WHO.

➤ HBA1c rises with age and is unreliable in sickle cell disease or thalassaemia.[10] The diagnosis of diabetes during pregnancy, when changes in red cells turnover makes HBA1c measurement problematic, will require glucose measurements.

➤ Improving glycaemic control early on in the disease has sustained benefits for cardiovascular outcomes.

➤ The lowest risk of mortality was noted in patients with an HBA1c of around 7.5% in a study of 50 000 patients from the UK general practice research database.[11] For patients on insulin or sulphonylureas, an HBA1c of 7.5% is optimum and driving HBA1c levels lower increases the mortality.[11] The NICE guideline recommends a target of 6.5% for newly diagnosed and those on an oral therapy of one or two agents. For those diabetics who are on the maximum tolerated dose of two oral agents, the recommended HBA1c target for adding the third oral agent is 7.5%.

➤ Men diagnosed with type 2 diabetes over the age of 65 years have no excess mortality compared with their non-diabetic counterparts, a finding that was not replicated for women. Women diagnosed with type 2 diabetes at an older age had an increased risk of mortality compared with older non-diabetic women.[12]

➤ A 10-year follow-up of patients confirmed a 15% reduction in the risk of MI and a 13% reduction in death rates with intensive treatment.[13]

➤ Microalbuminuria is an independent risk factor for cardiovascular disease.

➤ Insulin resistance is closely associated with type 2 diabetes and, in turn, with abdominal obesity. Ninety-two per cent of patients with type 2 diabetes are insulin resistant.

➤ In the UK, maculopathy is a more common and more significant sight-threatening complication of diabetes. Although type 2 diabetics are 10 times more likely to have maculopathy than type 1 diabetics, 14% of type 1 patients who become blind do so as a result of maculopathy.

➤ Metformin causes lactic acidosis, a rare but serious complication – about 0.03 cases per 1000 patient-years, with a greater risk in elderly patients. Reduce the dose of metformin if the eGFR drops below 45 and stop metformin if it drops below 30.

➤ Glitazones should not be used in people with heart failure.

➤ The new SIGN guidelines state that low-dose aspirin is not recommended for diabetes.[14]

➤ NICE recommends intensifying the cholesterol-lowering treatment if there is associated CVD or associated microalbuminuria to achieve a level of cholesterol < 4 mmol/L and low-density lipoprotein (LDL) < 2 mmol/L.[15]

➤ A remarkable rate of resolution of diabetes is seen in 80–90% of patients who have undergone bariatric surgery, with 60% experiencing complete resolution two years after surgery.

➤ Patients should notify the DVLA if they are treated with insulin.[16]
➤ An open parallel group randomised trial showed that there is no convincing evidence of an effect of self-monitoring blood glucose with or without instructions of self-care.[17]
➤ All members of the practice team should be familiar with the NICE guidelines so that the patient gets a consistent advice.

QOF: diabetes mellitus indicators

Indicators and points: total points 100

DM19

The practice can produce a register of all patients aged 17 years and over with diabetes mellitus, which specifies whether the patient has type 1 or type 2 diabetes.

Points: 6

An accurate disease register underpins high-quality primary care provision. An efficient call and recall system for annual checks is only possible if there is a register.

The UK is going to adopt the approach of the American Diabetic Association (ADA) of using an HBA1c of 6.5% on a single reading as a better diagnostic test.

The newly introduced health check programme uses HBA1c as a diagnostic test. The diagnostic groups of impaired fasting glucose and impaired glucose tolerance will be soon put to rest.

Improve your prevalence by running a routine HBA1c test during adult health checks in patients aged 40–75 years.

DM2

The percentage of patients with diabetes whose notes record body mass index (BMI) in the previous 15 months.

Points 3   Payment stages 40–90%

➤ Diabetic patients are often on treatment that causes weight gain.
➤ Many diabetics are already overweight.
➤ Referral to a dietician, diabetes support group, health trainer, free gym (if available in your area) or treatment with orlistat should be considered in obese or overweight people.
➤ NICE has published guidance on bariatric surgery as part of its clinical guideline on obesity. Adults with a BMI $\geq$ 35 kg/m^2 accompanied by co-existing disease that could be improved by weight loss.[18]

DM5

The percentage of patients with diabetes who have a record of glycated haemoglobin (HBA1c) or equivalent in the previous 15 months.

Points 3   Payment stages 40–90%

There is a lot of evidence that tight control of blood sugar reduces the risks of renal and retinal damage (microvascular complications).

DM23

The percentage of patients with diabetes in whom the last HBA1c is 7 or less (or equivalent test/reference range depending on local laboratory) in the previous 15 months.

Points 17   **Payment stages 40–50%**

Although debatable, this is certainly an ambitious goal. If a patient does not achieve his or her HBA1c target through lifestyle changes, NICE recommends that metformin should be the first choice. If metformin titrated to its maximally tolerated dose does not achieve the target, sulfonylurea should be added. If this combination does not achieve the glycaemic target, there are several possible alternatives.

The NICE guideline focuses on the oral DPP-4 inhibitors, GLP-1 analogues, thiazolidinediones and insulin analogues.[19] Only consider exenatide as an option if the patient has a BMI > 35 and meets the criteria outlined by NICE.

Undoubtedly the incidence of hypoglycaemia is likely to rise as the HBA1c threshold gets lower. This has clinical and cost implications with regard to hospital admissions.

The risk of hypoglycaemia with sulphonylureas in type 2 diabetes mellitus has been reported to be as high as 39%.[20] Newer agents are less likely to cause the problem of hypoglycaemia. The latest incretin-based therapies enable the possibility of blood glucose lowering with a low risk of hypoglycaemia and either weight neutrality (DPP-4 inhibitors) or weight loss (GLP-1 receptor agonists). The increments in QALYs gained by reductions in HBA1c can be offset by the decrements in QALYs as a result of hypoglycaemia in the context of blood glucose lowering therapies as per revised the NICE guidelines. It is important to individualise the treatment strategies.

DM 24

The percentage of patients with diabetes in whom the last HBA1c is 8 or less (or equivalent test/reference range depending on local laboratory) in the previous 15 months.

Points 8   **Payment stages 40–70%**

NICE recommends giving as much information as possible to diabetics and encouraging them to get involved with their control, with the aim of achieving the individualised targets.[15]

DM25

The percentage of patients with diabetes in whom the last HBA1c is 9 or less (or equivalent test/reference range depending on local laboratory) in the previous 15 months.

Points 10   **Payment stages 40–90%**

➤ Insulin is a third line therapy if metformin as a first line and sulphonylurea as a second line do not control the HBA1c level.

➤ Hypoglycaemia is a potential problem with insulin.

➤ Minimise hypoglycaemia risk by choice of regimen[21] and patient education, and stress the need to test blood sugar before driving.

➤ Insulin therapy may be inappropriate in a patient with a BMI of 35 kg/m² or more.

➤ Give proper advice to those who do shift work and those who fast (e.g. during Ramadan).

➤ When insulin is added to oral therapy, a long-acting human insulin is appropriate and should be injected before going to bed or twice daily as necessary.

➤ Start with 10 units, titrating upwards.

➤ The 4-T trial used an algorithm which predicted the dose of insulin.[22]

DM21

The percentage of patients with diabetes who have a record of retinal screening in the previous 15 months.

Points 5   **Payment stages 40–90%**

Diabetic retinopathy remains the commonest cause of blindness. The prevalence of diabetic retinopathy depends on the duration of diabetes and glycaemic and blood pressure control. Diabetic retinopathy is more common in the ethnic minorities than in Caucasians.

An eye-screening programme should be available in each primary care trust and all diabetic patients should be referred to the local scheme. Most areas have static or mobile units that visit surgeries. The screening is performed by a trained staff using the quality assured digital photography programme.

For housebound diabetics, arrange a home visit by an approved optician. You should have a list of these trained and approved staff.

DM9

The percentage of patients with diabetes with a record of the presence or absence of peripheral pulses in the previous 15 months.

Points 3   **Payment stages 40–90%**

➤ Peripheral vascular disease is seen in up to 10% of patients.

➤ Microvascular circulatory disease leads to local ischaemia, thus increasing the potential for ulcer formation, and can delay wound-healing when ulceration occurs.

➤ NICE recommends visual inspection of the patient's feet and assessment of foot sensation.

➤ Use palpation of foot pulses for detection of risk factors for ulceration.

➤ Consider doing a Doppler test if in doubt.

➤ An ankle: Brachial Pressure Index of 1–1.3 indicates normal arterial blood flow.

➤ The presence of other microvascular complications such as nephropathy and retinopathy is also a risk factor for foot ulcer development.
➤ If patient has suspected or documented osteomyelitis, antibiotic therapy should be continued for at least 4–6 weeks.
➤ Previous foot ulceration is a risk factor and deserves careful and frequent follow-up.
➤ If an ulcer develops, reduction of oedema, optimising diabetic control, infection control and an urgent referral to the hospital clinic is needed. The risk of leg amputation is more than 15 times higher in diabetics.
➤ Infected ulcers should be treated following the culture and sensitivity result of a swab test. Antibiotics should be continued until the wound appears clean and the surrounding cellulitis has disappeared.

DM10

The percentage of patients with diabetes with a record of neuropathy testing in the previous 15 months.

Points 3   **Payment stages 40–90%**

➤ Mandatory at diagnosis and at least yearly even though the QOF asks for a check within 15 months.
➤ Test vibration, fine touch (with a 10 g monofilament) and reflexes as a minimum.
➤ Using a neurothesiometer or biothesiometer gives a more quantitative measure of vibration than a 128 Hz tuning fork.
➤ Inability to feel the vibrating head at > 25 v in the toes is associated with a significant risk of neuropathic ulceration and should be considered as 'at risk' feet.

DM11

The percentage of patients with diabetes who have a record of blood pressure in the previous 15 months.

Points 3   **Payment stages 40–90%**

There is simply no excuse for losing these three points.

DM12

The percentage of patients with diabetes in whom the last blood pressure is ≤ 145/85 mm Hg.

Points 18   **Payment stages 40–60%**

NICE recommends the following.[15]
➤ In the absence of kidney, cerebrovascular or eye damage, the blood pressure target is 140/80 mm Hg.
➤ In the presence of kidney, cerebrovascular or eye damage, the blood pressure target is 130/80 mm Hg.

➤ Blood pressure should be measured at diagnosis and annually if it is at or below these targets.

➤ If blood pressure is above these targets it should be measured sooner – depending upon the reading, in one or two months.

➤ Raised blood pressure should be treated with ACE inhibitors or ARB if the ACE is not tolerated. If the target blood pressure is not reached, add a thiazide diuretic or calcium channel blocker as a second line. Add an alpha or beta blocker next if the blood pressure has not reached the target.

➤ A potassium sparing diuretic should be used with caution if a patient is already taking an ACE inhibitor or ARB.

➤ Lifestyle advice aiming to lower the BP should be given to all patients.

DM13

The percentage of patients with diabetes who have a record of microalbuminuria testing in the previous 15 months (exception reporting for patients with proteinuria).

Points 3   **Payment stages 40–90%**

➤ NICE recommends an annual check for microalbuminuria.[15]

➤ Microalbuminuria is detected by sending a urine sample to a laboratory for measurement of the albumin:creatinine ratio (ACR). An ACR > 2.5 mg/mmol for males and 3.5 mg/mmol for females indicates microalbuminuria.

➤ If the ACR is abnormal, NICE recommends that the test must be repeated within one month.[15]

➤ If microalbuminuria is present, NICE recommends a target blood pressure of < 130/80 mm Hg.[15] If the ACR is normal, do a repeat check in one year.

DM22

The percentage of patients with diabetes who have a record of estimated glomerular filtration rate (eGFR) or serum creatinine testing in the previous 15 months.

Points 3   **Payment stages 40–90%**

The aim is to assess kidney damage. Again, this is an easily achievable three points. Most laboratories routinely carry out eGFR with urea and electrolyte tests.

DM15

The percentage of patients with diabetes with a diagnosis of proteinuria or micro-albuminuria who are treated with ACE inhibitors (or angiotensin II receptor blockers).

Points 3   **Payment stages 40–80%**

➤ NICE recommends treating patients with an ACE inhibitor, with dose titration to maximum dose, if microalbuminuria, or an ARB if intolerant to ACE.

➤ Microalbuminuria can occur after exercise or during a febrile illness.

➤ Always check microalbuminuria using the first morning urine sample because it can occur in healthy people after they have been standing for a while.

➤ ACE inhibitors are the first line rennin angiotensin system drugs of choice.

➤ The only one major benefit of ARB is a lower rate of cough.
➤ Both ACE and ARB can cause hyperkalaemia.
➤ There is no clinically significant difference between these groups of drugs.

DM16

The percentage of patients with diabetes who have a record of total cholesterol in the previous 15 months.

Points 3   **Payment stages 40–90%**

Again not difficult to achieve these three points.

DM17

The percentage of patients with diabetes whose last measured total cholesterol with in the previous 15 months is ≤ 5 mmol/L.

Points 6   **Payment stages 40–70%**

➤ The SIGN guideline recommends Simvastatin 40 mg or atorvastatin 10 mg for primary prevention in patients with type 2 diabetes aged 40 years, regardless of baseline cholesterol.[14]
➤ Diabetics under 40 years and other risk factors such as microalbuminuria should be considered for Simvastatin 40 mg daily.
➤ NICE also recommends that in a patient who is 40 years old or over, Simvastatin 40 mg should be given as a more cost-effective statin.
➤ If the QOF target of 5 mmol/L is not achieved, change to a more effective statin or increase the dose.

DM18

The percentage of patients with diabetes who have had influenza immunisation in the preceding 1 September to 31 March.

Points 3   **Payment stages 40–85%**

An easily achievable three points if you have an accurate disease register and an efficient recall system in place. Advertise on JX board, insert a message on repeat prescriptions, do opportunistic vaccination and involve the district nurse or community matron to achieve this target.

Maximising quality points

➤ Improve your prevalence by improving the disease register. Your low prevalence could be because of poor coding.
  — Run a search to identify miscoded patients. Search for people with diabetes using the C10 code, but who do not have C10E or C10F – the type 1 and type 2 codes recognised by the QOF.
  — Search for people with type 1 diabetes who are not prescribed insulin or who are prescribed insulin plus oral agents.

— If you have a large numbers of Asian patients, who have a genetic predisposition to diabetes, your prevalence should be higher compared with other practices.

➤ Use the correct coding. One common error is a person being coded as having type 1 diabetes when they actually have type 2 diabetes. The type 2 diabetics who require insulin on top of oral agents remain as type 2 diabetics.

➤ All patients with cystic fibrosis should be screened for diabetes annually from the age of 10 years. Twenty per cent of cystic fibrosis patients will develop diabetes by the age of 35 years.

➤ Use the WHO criteria for diagnosis before putting patients on the disease register. Misdiagnosis may result in medical harm and can result in wastage of NHS resources.

➤ Make sure 50% of your patients have an HBA1c at or below 7%, 70% have an HBA1c at or below 8% and 90% have an HBA1c at or below 9%. If you are struggling to meet the targets, add another agent but watch out for the risk of hypoglycaemia. Try adding newer agents.

➤ In discussion with the patient, develop a care plan, agree the targets for weight loss, HBA1c and blood pressure. Patients are more likely to stick to lifestyle interventions and compliance with medication if they are told the targets and why achieving the targets is beneficial. Spending an extra five minutes could make all the difference.

➤ For a blood pressure target of 145/85 mm Hg or less, you may have to use multiple drug regimes. Use the maximum tolerated therapy code if a patient is unable to tolerate the lipid lowering, anti-hypertensives or anti-diabetic drugs, **but** be prepared to explain at the time of the QOF visit. Document clearly.

➤ Recording BMI and identifying obesity will earn you 3 points on the diabetes indicator and another 1 point on the obesity register.

➤ Lifestyle intervention – Look AHEAD (Action for health in Diabetes)[23] will help you achieve the targets. It is best delivered by GPs because patients trust and listen to their GPs.

➤ Exercise and sport should be encouraged. (*Give an example of the Olympic rower Sir Steve Redgrave.*)

➤ Self-monitoring of blood glucose (SMBG) does help in diabetic control and should be given to those on insulin treatment, those on oral agents to provide information on hypoglycaemia, to monitor changes during inter-current illness and to ensure safety including, driving bearing in mind the cost-effectiveness when issuing the strips. Discuss its purpose and agree how it should be interpreted and acted upon.

➤ If people are not willing to engage in education, offer an alternative such as the *Diabetes Manual*, available from Warwick Medical School. A one-to-one diabetes education model could be useful.

➤ Make sure you provide the eye-screening practitioner in your area with an updated register and list of newly diagnosed diabetics. You will loose points if the newly diagnosed are not invited for retinal screening.

➤ If you are fortunate enough to have a unit coming to your premises, take advantage of that. (*In my area the screening unit comes to my health centre each*

November – perfect timing to offer flu vaccination and also to catch up with non-attenders. This helps me achieve maximum on my influenza immunisation points.)

➤ Check all DNA for retinal screening. Chase them actively and make sure they get an alternative appointment (delegate this task to reception staff). This is easy if the unit visits your surgery.

➤ DM 9 and DM10 – foot pulses and neuropathy testing – are easy to achieve. Simply enter read coded in the template. If you are fortunate enough to have a podiatrist, refer these patients to him or her. The podiatrist could test your housebound diabetic patients too, which will save your practice nurse time.

➤ Diabetes carries a twofold risk of suffering depression. Test using HADS/PHQ-9 – both give a more comprehensive assessment.

➤ Carry out an audit of coding, classification and correct diagnosis at least once a year.

➤ Finally, capitalise any opportunity that would draw in diabetic non-attenders. Even if the target is worth only a few points, the aim should be to improve the clinical outcome and prevent complications.

➤ Exception reporting can be done for those patients who refuse to attend for review and have been invited on three occasions during the preceding 12 months.

➤ Patients who are on maximum tolerated treatment or when the medication is not clinically appropriate or those who are terminally ill can be excluded. Make sure you are able to give a valid reason at the time of the QOF visit.

➤ Make sure the patient leaves the surgery with a follow-up appointment for the next diabetic review.

Template GMS: Diabetes mellitus (V16)

Prompt	Code	Date	Coded subsets
Exception report: diabetes quality indicator	(9h4)		Except. diabetes QI: Pt unsuit. (9h41) Except. diabetes QI: inf. dis. (9h42) Except. diabetes QI: sv una (9h43)
Ethnic category – 2001 census	(9i)		*See ethnicity template, Chapter 17*
Diabetic monitoring	(66A)		
Diabetes resolved	(212H)		
Diabetic annual review	(66AS)		
Smoking status			*See smoking template, Chapter 25*
O/E weight	(22A)		
O/E height	(229)		
Body Mass Index	(22K)		
Waist circumference	(22N0)		
Ideal weight	(66CB)		
Alcohol consumption			*See Alcohol, Chapter 27*
Diabetic monitoring	(66A)		Diabetic on diet only (66A3) Diabetic on oral treatment (66A4) Diabetic on insulin (66A5)
Patient advised reg. diet	(8CA4)		
Patient adv reg. exercise	(8CA5)		

(continued)

Prompt	Code	Date	Coded subsets
Patient advised about alcohol	(8CAM)		
Systolic blood pressure	(2469)		
Diastolic blood pressure	(246A)		
Blood pressure refused	(8I3Y)		
24-HR BP MONITOR	(662L)		
AVERAGE DAY SYSTOLIC	(246Y)		
AVERAGE DAY DIASTOLIC	(246X)		
AVERAGE NIGHT SYSTOLIC	(246b)		
AVERAGE NIGHT DIASTOLIC	(246a)		
12 LEAD ECG	(321B)		*ECG coded subsets same as in CHD template, Chapter 9*
STANDARD CHEST X-RAY	(535)		*Standard chest X-ray coded subsets same as in CHD template, Chapter 9*
Depression screen using questionnaire	(6896)		Loss of interest (1BP) Depressed mood (1BT)
Impotence	(E2273)		
Last hypo attack	(66A6)		
Metabolic monitoring	(8A1)		Self-monitoring of blood glucose (8A17) Self-monitoring of urine glucose (8A18) Self-monitoring of blood + urine glucose (8A19)
Hb A1c < 7%	(42W1)		
Patient on max. tolerated dose	(8BL)		Pt on max. tolerat. lipid low ther. (8BL1) Pt on max tolerat. ther. for diabetes (8BL2)
Urine protein test-trace	(4673)		Urine protein test = -ve (4672) Urine protein test = + (4674) Urine protein test = ++ (4675) Urine protein test = +++ (4676) Urine protein test = ++++ (4677) Proteinuria (4678)
Serum creatinine	(44J3)		
Urine albumin:creatinine ratio	(46TC)		
Serum cholesterol	(44P)		
Serum HDL cholesterol	(44P5)		
Serum LDL cholesterol	(44P6)		
Serum triglycerides	(44Q)		
Plasma glucose level	(44g)		
Plasma fasting glucose	(44g1)		
ACE inhibitor declined	(8I3D)		*ACE coded subsets same as in CHD template, Chapter 9*
ANG2 recpt. ant. contraindicated	(8I2H)		*ANG2 coded subsets same as in CHD template, Chapter 9*
Statin prophylaxis	(8B6A)		*Statin coded subsets same as in CHD template, Chapter 9*
Aspirin prophylaxis (over the counter) (EGTONAS1)			*Aspirin coded subsets same as in CHD template, Chapter 9*

(continued)

Prompt	Code	Date	Coded subsets
Influenza vaccination	(65E)		*Influenza vaccination coded subsets same as in CHD template, Chapter 9*
Pneumococcal vaccination	(6572)		*Pneumococcal vaccination coded subsets same as in CHD template, Chapter 9*
Medication review done	(8B3V)		
Medication review	(8B314)		
Diabetic monitoring	(66A)		
Diabetic annual review	(66AS)		
*Diabetic retinopathy screen	(68A7)		DNA diabetic retinopathy clin. (9N4p) Diabetic retinopathy screen refused (8I3X) Diabetic pt unsuit. dig. ret. photo (9OLD) Seen in diabetic eye clinic (9N1v) Seen by optician (9N2U) Seen by ophthalmologist (9N2e) Seen by retinal screener (9N2f)
O/E Right retina not seen	(2BBB)		H/O retinal detachment (1481) O/E Rt retina not seen (2BBB) O/E no Rt diabetic retinopathy (2BBJ) O/E Rt eye back diabetic retinopathy (2BBP) Rt non-proliferative diabetic retinopathy (EMISQR18) Diabetic retinopathy (F420) O/E Rt cataract present (2BT0)
O/E Left retina not seen	(2BBC)		H/O retinal detachment (1481) O/E Lt retina not seen (2BBC) O/E no Lt diabetic retinopathy (2BBK) O/E Lt eye back diabetic retinopathy (2BBQ) Left non-proliferative diabetic retinopathy (EMISQLE8) Diabetic retinopathy (F420) Hypertensive retinopathy (F4213) O/E Lt cataract present (2BT1)
Diabetic foot examination declined	(8I3W)		
Monofilament foot sensation test	(311A)		10 g monofilament sensation present (29B7) 10 g monofilament sensation absent (29B8) 10 g monofilament Rt foot normal (29BB) 10 g monofilament Rt foot abnormal (29B9) 10 g monofilament Lt foot normal (29BC) 10 g monofilament Lt foot abnormal (29BA)
O/E Vibr. sens. Rt foot normal	(29H5)		
O/E Vibr. sens. Rt foot abnormal	(29H4)		
O/E Vibr. sens. Rt foot reduced	(29H9)		
O/E Vibr. sens. Rt foot absent	(29HA)		
O/E Vibr. sens. Lt foot normal	(29H7)		
O/E Vibr. sens. Lt foot abnormal	(29H6)		
O/E Vibr. sens. Lt foot reduced	(29H8)		

(continued)

Prompt	Code	Date	Coded subsets
O/E Vibr. sens. Lt foot absent	(29HB)		
O/E Rt leg pulses all present	(24E1)		
O/E absent Rt foot pulses	(24EA)		
O/E Lt leg pulses all present	(24F1)		
O/E absent Lt foot pulses	(24FA)		
O/E Rt femoral pulse present	(24E2)		
O/E Rt femoral pulse absent	(24E3)		
O/E Lt femoral pulse present	(24F2)		
O/E Lt femoral pulse absent	(24F3)		
O/E Rt popliteal pulse present	(24E4)		
O/E Rt popliteal pulse absent	(24E5)		
O/E Lt popliteal pulse present	(24F4)		
O/E Lt popliteal pulse absent	(24F5)		
O/E Rt post. tib. pulse present	(24E6)		
O/E Rt post. tib. pulse absent	(24E7)		
O/E Lt post. tib. pulse present	(24F6)		
O/E Lt post. tib. pulse absent	(24F7)		
O/E Rt dorsalis pedis. present	(24E8)		
O/E Rt dorsalis pedis. absent	(24E9)		
O/E Lt dorsalis pedis. present	(24F8)		
O/E Lt dorsalis pedis. absent	(24E9)		
O/E Rt diabetic foot at risk	(2G5A)		O/E Rt diabetic foot at low risk (2G5E) O/E Rt diabetic foot at mod. risk (2G5F) O/E Rt diabetic foot at high risk (2G5G) O/E Rt diabetic foot ulcerated (2G5H)
O/E Lt diabetic foot at risk	(2G5B)		O/E Lt diabetic foot at low risk (2G5I) O/E Lt diabetic foot at mod. risk (2G5J) O/E Lt diabetic foot at high risk (2G5K) O/E Lt diabetic foot ulcerated (2G5L)
O/E – amputated Rt leg	(2G42)		O/E amputated Rt above knee (2G44) O/E amputated Rt below knee (2G46)
O/E – amputated Lt leg	(2G43)		O/E amputated Lt above knee (2G45) O/E amputated Lt below knee (2G47)
Refer to diabetic foot screener	(8H7r)		
DIABETES MONITORING 1st LETTER	(9OL4)		
DIABETES MONITORING 2nd LETTER	(9OL5)		
DIABETES MONITORING 3rd LETTER	(9OL6)		
DIABETES MONITORING VERBAL INVITE	(9OL7)		
DIABETES MONITORING TELEPHONE INVITE	(9OL8)		

(Add the capitalised prompts to your template to maximise points and quality care)

Do something extra

➤ Smoking is probably the single most important risk factor for heart disease and when a smoker has diabetes the risk is much greater. Record and offer smoking cessation advice and support to diabetics who smoke.

➤ Keeping a record of obesity will earn you points **but** do something more than that. Offer help. Provide individualised and ongoing advice from a healthcare professional with specific expertise and competencies in nutrition. A referral to health trainer if available in your area could be beneficial too.

➤ At a time when diabetes is taking up 10% of the UK's healthcare budget, costing an estimated £1 million per hour,[24] be firm and persistent with patients who do not engage in a diet and exercise programme. Maybe they need more than just handing out another diet sheet. A referral to a dietician and free gym membership (if this scheme is available in your area) could be helpful.

➤ There is a well-proven benefit of tighter glycaemic control in a type 2 diabetics diagnosed aged 50 years. If not properly controlled they end up losing 10 years of their life.[21] See them more often.

➤ The blood pressure target for the contract is set at 145/85 mm Hg or less but the UK Prospective Diabetes Study Group (UKPDS)[25] and the Hypertension Optimal Treatment (HOT) study[26] suggest an optimum blood pressure of 140/80 mm Hg, with greater reductions bringing further benefits in diabetic patients.

➤ Do not neglect patients with HBA1c ≥ 10% because there are no incentives. They should be given equal consideration to reduce complications and prolong life.

➤ Follow the quick reference guide (NICE[27]) – a four-step approach to dealing with the full range of depression, from subclinical symptoms to major depression, in diabetics with depression.

➤ Try not to use sulphonyl urea with elderly patients because of the hypoglycaemia risk. A Swedish study looked at all patients over 70 years admitted to hospital with sulphonylurea-induced hypoglycaemia.[28] One-third of them died or had a permanent neurological deficit. Look at the whole patient and decide where the priorities lie. For example, control the blood pressure rather than getting the HBa1c down from 7.5 to the 7 target.

➤ Buy a Doppler. This will pick up early peripheral vascular disease (PVD).

➤ Assess for autonomic neuropathy – postural hypotension, gustatory sweating, anhidrosis, urinary retention or overflow incontinence and impotence.

References

1 World Health Organization. *Definition, Diagnosis and Classification of Diabetes Mellitus and its Complications. Report of a WHO Consultation.* Geneva: World Health Organization; 1999.

2 Diabetes UK. www.diabetes.org.uk

3 *Health Survey for England 2006.* Volume 1, cardiovascular disease and risk factors in adults. The Information Centre, NHS; 2008.

4 Yorkshire and Humber Public health Observatory. *Diabetes Attributable Deaths: estimating the excess deaths among people with diabetes.* Available at: www.yhpho.org.uk/diabetes.aspx (accessed 3 September 2010).

5 *Emedicine. Perioperative Management of the Diabetic Patient.* http://emedicine.medscape.com/article/284451-overview (accessed 19 May 2010).

6 www.diabetes.org.uk/Reports. Statistics and case studies/Reports and Statistics/Diabetes prevalence 2010 (last accessed 2010).

7 Statistics taken from *Diabetes. Beware the Silent Assassin,* October 2008. www.diabetes.org.uk/Get.../Silent-Assassin-campaign/ (accessed 3 September 2010).

8 Narayan KM, Boyle JP, Thompson TJ, *et al.* Lifetime risk for diabetes mellitus in the United States. *JAMA.* 2003; **290**:1884–90.

9 International Expert Committee. The role of HBA1c assay in the diagnosis of diabetes. *Diab Care.* 2009; **32**: 1327–34.

10 Owens D, Horrocks J, House A, *et al.* HBA1c as a screening tool for detection of type 2 diabetes: a systematic review. *Diabet. Med.* 2007; **24**: 333–43.

11 Currie CJ, Peters JR, Tynan A, *et al.* Survival as a function of HBA1c in people with type 2 diabetes. *Lancet.* 2010; **375**: 481–9.

12 Panzram G. Mortality and survival in type 2 (non-insulin dependent) diabetes mellitus. *Diabetologia.* 1987; **30**(3): 123–31.

13 Holman RR, Paul SK, Bethel MA, *et al.* Ten year follow up of intensive glucose control in type 2 diabetes. *NEJM.* 2008; **359**: 1577–89.

14 Scottish Intercollegiate Guideline Network. *Management of diabetes: SIGN guideline 116.* Edinburgh. SIGN: 2010. www.sign.ac.uk

15 National Institute for Health and Clinical Excellence. *The Management of Type 2 Diabetes.* 2008. www.nice.org.uk

16 DVLA. www.dvla.gov.uk

17 www.bmj.com/content/335/7611/132

18 National Institute for Health and Clinical Excellence. *Obesity: guidance on the prevention, identification, assessment and management of overweight and obesity in adults and children: NICE guideline CG43.* London: NHICE; 2006. www.nice.org.uk/guidance/CG43

19 National Institute for Health and Clinical Excellence. *Type 2 Diabetes: newer agents (practical update of CG66): NICE guideline CG87.* London: NHICE; 2009. www.nice.org.uk/guidance/CG87

20 Fisher M. Hypoglycaemia in patients with type 2 diabetes: minimising the risk. *Br J Diabetes Vasc. Dis.* 2010; **10**: 35–41. Available at: www.dvd.sagepub.com/content/10/1/35

21 British National Formulary. Drugs used in diabetes. March 2010. www.bnf.org/bnf/bnf/current/4080.htm

22 Holman RR, Farmer AJ, Davies MJ, *et al.* and 4T Study Group. Three-year efficacy of complex insulin regimens in type 2 diabetes. *NEJM.* 2009; **361**: 1736–47.

23 Win RR, Bahnson BA, Bray GA. Long term effects of a lifestyle intervention on weight and cardiovascular risk factors in individuals with type 2 diabetes mellitus. *Arch. Intern. Med.* 2010; **170**(17): 1566–75.

24 Diabetes UK. 2010. Available at: www.diabetes.org.uk/Documents/.../Diabetes_in_the_UK_2010.pdf

25 UK Prospective Diabetes Study Group. Tight blood pressure control and risk of microvascular and macrovascular complications in type 2 diabetes. UKPDS 38. *BMJ.* 1998; **317**: 703–13.

26 Hansson I, Zanchetti A, Carruthers SG, *et al.* Effects of intensive blood-pressure lowering and low dose aspirin in patients with hypertension: principal results of the Hypertension Optimal Treatment (HOT) randomised trial. HOT Study Group. *Lancet.* 1998; **351**: 1755–62.

27 National Institute for Health and Clinical Excellence. 2009. Available at: www.goodmedicine.org.uk/.../2009/.../updated-nice-guidelines-treating-depression

28 Asplund K, Wiholm BE, Lithner F. Glibenclamide-associated hypoglycaemia: a report on 57 cases. *Diabetologica.* 1983; **24**(6): 412–17.

Useful information

Diabetes UK is committed to ensuring people with diabetes have a voice. It works alongside healthcare professionals to raise awareness about the benefits of a healthy lifestyle while lobbying the government for better standards of care and best quality of life for people with diabetes. The charity launched GP Surgery Network (GPSN) in June 2009 and provides regular updates and information to assist the diagnosis and management of people with diabetes. See www.diabetes.org.uk/professionals

Useful reading

➤ National Institute for Health and Clinical Excellence. *Type 2 Diabetes – newer agents (partial update of CG66): NICE guideline GC87.* London: NHICE; 2006. www.nice. org.uk/guidance/CG87 (accessed 1 September 2010).

➤ SIGN. *Management of diabetes.* Available at: www.sign.ac.uk/pdf/sign116.pdf (accessed 1 September 2010).

CHAPTER 16

Epilepsy

Epilepsy is the most common chronic, disabling neurological condition in the UK. It is a challenging disease to diagnose and manage and can have a huge impact on patients and their families.

Definition

Epilepsy is defined as a tendency to have recurring, unprovoked seizures.

Prevalence

Between five and 10 people per 1000 have active epilepsy.[1,2] It affects all age groups with varied severity. The incidence of epilepsy is high in older people.[3] Most epilepsy in older people is a consequence of cerebrovascular disease.[4]

Why included in QOF

➤ The Chief Medical Officer's attention[5] to the findings of the audit in 2002 of the large number of deaths due to epilepsy led to its inclusion in the QOF.[6]

➤ It is believed that epilepsy can be managed by a structured, goal-orientated regime in the primary care sector as there are better-defined indicators for secondary care referrals as per NICE guidelines.

➤ To reduce the emergency admissions where epilepsy was defined as the reason for admission. The QOF financial incentive may lessen the admission and hence the financial strain on the NHS.

➤ Epilepsy has the potential for stigmatisation and psychological consequences.[7] GPs know their patients well and all concerns and anxieties related to the misunderstanding of this disease can be managed well in a primary care setting.

➤ It is well established that patients prefer to see their GPs if they have a chronic illness.

➤ Symptoms of anxiety and depression are common in epileptic patients. This can be picked up and treated early in the primary care.

➤ The most important aspect of management of status epilepticus is early treatment in the community.[8,9]

The facts

➤ Every year approximately 1000 people in England die of epilepsy-related causes, of which 400 deaths are avoidable.[10]

➤ Seventy-four thousand people are taking medications they do not need to take.[10]

➤ £189 million is wasted every year.[10]

➤ Sixty-nine thousand people are living with unnecessary seizures.[10]

➤ Suicide accounts for 12–22% of epilepsy deaths – five times that of the normal population.[11]

➤ About 10% of people are incorrectly diagnosed as having epilepsy.

➤ The risk to the foetus with anti-epileptic drugs (AED)[12,13] is:
— carbamazepine 2.2%
— lamotrigine 3% (depending on dose)
— sodium valproate 5–9% (depending on the dose).

➤ The newer generation of medication has increased clinicians' and patients' choices, especially in women of child-bearing age.

➤ There is an increased risk of seizures in the children of parents with epilepsy, but the probability that a child will be affected is very low.[12,13]

QOF: epilepsy indicators

Indicators and points: total points 15

Records

EPILEPSY 5

The practice can produce a register of patients aged 18 and over receiving drug treatment for epilepsy.

Points 1

The primary care physician is responsible for the care of adults with epilepsy. Children with diagnosed epilepsy should be seen, treated and followed up in the secondary care sector.

It is important that a diagnosis is established before the patient is placed on the register. Following a suspected first seizure, the patient should be seen by a specialist within two weeks to confirm the diagnosis as per the NICE guidelines.[12] The patient should not be entered on the register without confirmation of the diagnosis. Use the code suspected epilepsy in those who are waiting for EEG or CT brain scan for confirmation of diagnosis. There has been considerable concern over misdiagnosis as many conditions may mimic epilepsy. Some surveys have shown that 20% of people in the primary care sector have a wrong diagnosis.[14]

A wrong diagnosis can lead to unnecessary loss of driving licence, loss of job and relationship problems.

Ongoing management

EPILEPSY 6

The percentage of patients age 18 and over on drug treatment for epilepsy who have a record of seizure frequency in the previous 15 months.

Points 4   **Payment stages 40–90%**

The role of a GP is to have a face-to-face consultation with the patient. Phone consultation is not appropriate. Face-to-face consultation gives an opportunity to assess the patient as a whole and to make sure that any support or information, if needed, is provided. This reduces anxiety and encourages the patient to adapt to the illness.[15] Each patient's care plan is different. Care should be provided as per the Scottish Intercollegiate Guidelines Network (SIGN)[13] and NICE.[12]

EPILEPSY 7

The percentage of patients aged 18 and over on drug treatment for epilepsy who have a record of medication review involving the patient and/or carer in the previous 15 months.

Points 4   **Payment stages 40–90%**

During medication review enquiry should be made about drug side-effects and patient's concerns. The newer generation of drugs, such as Levitiracetam, pregabalin, topiramate and zonisamide, has increased the clinician's choice. This is of particular importance in women of child-bearing age, those with continued seizures and patients concerned about side-effects.

EPILEPSY 8

The percentage of patients age 18 and over on drug treatment for epilepsy who have been seizure free for the past 12 months recorded in the previous 15 months.

Points 6   **Payment stages 40–70%**

The management goal should be complete seizure control. Patients with frequent seizures or refractory seizures should be referred back to specialist care. It is important to check drug compliance because it is well known that up to 50% of patients do not comply with the prescribed medication.[16] Taking an extra five minutes to explain to the patient about the dangers associated with seizures – falls, fractures, injuries – can make all the difference. Between 1.8 and 10% of epilepsy deaths are due to drowning in the bath.[17] Providing such information and advice may encourage patients to comply with their medication regime.

Enquire and give advice about lifestyle modifications to control the seizure frequency including the use of alcohol, recreational drugs and oral contraceptives as these may all decrease the effectiveness of AEDs.

Maximising quality points

➤ Epilepsy should be coded as F25.
➤ The register should include only patients aged 18 and over.

➤ Run a regular audit on repeat anti-epileptic medication every month and pick up patients who are not on the register.

➤ Patients referred to the hospital for confirmation of diagnosis, for example, EEG, brain scan, can be coded as:
— refer for EEG (8HR5)
— refer for imaging (8HQ) while waiting for the results.

➤ Do not code until the diagnosis is proven.

➤ Do not use an epilepsy code if patient has been diagnosed with 'Fits' due to alcohol.

➤ Patients with a past history of epilepsy who are not on any medication should be removed from the register.

➤ Patients who are not seizure-free should be followed up more often – every two to three months. Remember, with the epilepsy 8 indicator you only get points if your patient has been seizure-free for 12 months. Make sure your practice nurse knows this indicator and brings it to your attention for action if she is reviewing a patient who continues to have seizures on their current AEDs.

➤ Refer the patient to secondary care for other treatment options if they continue to have seizures. They may require poly therapy to control seizures.

➤ Exception reporting can be done on those patients who refuse to attend review and have been invited on at least three occasions during the preceding 12 months. Patients who are on maximum tolerated treatment, patients in whom anti-epileptic medication is not appropriate, patients who have clinically experienced an adverse reaction and those who are terminally ill can also be exception reported. The code should only be used if there are very clear reasons for not stepping up or altering the treatment and you as the patient's physician are able to explain the reasons at the time of the QOF visit. Use the code 8BL3.

➤ If a patient does not agree to investigation to confirm the diagnosis or refuses the treatment, enter a code of informed dissent. This should be recorded clearly in the medical notes.

➤ Record BMI at every review. This is not only a good clinical practice but also financially attractive for your obesity indicator achievement.

➤ Ensuring influenza immunisation for patients over the age of 65 will earn extra points.

➤ It is easy to make mistakes while recording the data. Small errors can make you loose money.

➤ Getting the coding right will be financially beneficial to the practice.

➤ It is a good idea always to use the template. While updating epilepsy indicators some other data can be collected which could help you maximise the QOF.

Template GMS: Epilepsy (V16)

Prompt	Code	Date	Coded subsets
Exception report: epilepsy quality indicator	(9h6)		Except. epilepsy QI: Pt unsuit. (9h61) Except. epilepsy QI: inf. dis. (9h62)
Ethnic category – 2001 census	(9i)		See ethnicity template, Chapter 17
Epilepsy monitoring	(667)		
Epilepsy resolved	(212J)		
Seizures free > 12 months	(667F)		Fit frequency (6675) Seizure free > 12 months (667F) No seizure on treatment (667P) 1–12 seizures a year (667Q) 2–4 seizures a month (667R) 1–7 seizures a week (667S) Daily seizures (667T) Many seizures a day (667V)
Last fit	(6676)		
O/E WEIGHT	(22A)		
O/E HEIGHT	(229)		
BODY MASS INDEX	(22K)		
SMOKING STATUS			See smoking template, Chapter 25
ALCOHOL CONSUMPTION			See Alcohol, Chapter 27
PATIENT ADVISED REG. DIET	(8CA4)		
PATIENT ADVISED REG. EXERCISE	(8CA5)		
PATIENT ADVISED ABOUT ALCOHOL	(8CAM)		
WEIGHT PROGRAMME	(8HHH)		
Contraception counselling	(6777)		
Pre-pregnancy counselling	(676)		
Epilepsy drug side-effects	(6677)		Epilepsy drug side-effects (6677) Epilepsy treatment changed (6678) Epilepsy treatment started (6679) Epilepsy treatment stopped (667A) No epilepsy drug side-effects (667X) Pt on max. tolerat. anticonvuls. ther. (8BL3)
SUICIDE RISK	(1BD4)		Suicide risk coded subsets same as in mental health template, Chapter 22
SUICIDE ATTEMPT	(TK)		
Patient Advised to inform DVLA	(8CA9)		
Neurological referral	(8H46)		
SUSPECTED EPILEPSY	(1JA0)		
REFER FOR EEG	(8HR5)		
REFER FOR IMAGING	(8HQ)		
CAT SCAN – BRAIN	(5675)		
CAT SCAN BRAIN NORMAL	(5C00)		
CAT SCAN BRAIN ABNORMAL	(5C12-1)		
Epilepsy medication review	(8BIF)		
Medication review done	(8B3V)		

(continued)

Prompt	Code	Date	Coded subsets
Epilepsy monitoring	(667)		
OCCUPATION	(915A)		
WORK STATUS	(13J)		Work status coded subsets same as in mental health template, Chapter 22
EPILEPSY RESTRICTS EMPLOYMENT	(667G)		
EPILEPSY PREVENTS EMPLOYEMENT	(667H)		
EPILEPSY INVITE1	(90F0)		
EPILEPSY INVITE2	(90f1)		
EPILEPSY INVITE3	(90f2)		
MAXIMUM TOLERARED DOSE	(8BL3)		
EPILEPSY CONTROL POOR	(667D)		
NEUROLOGICAL REFERRAL	(8H46)		
STATUS EPILEPTICUS	(F253-1)		
EPILEPSY SCREEN INVITE 1	(90f0)		
EPILEPSY SCREEN INVITE 2	(90f1)		
EPILEPSY SCREEN INVITE 3	(90f2)		
INFLUENZA VACCINATION	(65E)		Influenza vaccination coded subsets same as in CHD template, Chapter 9
PNEUMOCOCCAL VACCINATION	(6572)		Pneumococcal vaccination coded subsets same as in CHD template, Chapter 9

(Add the capitalised prompts to your template to maximise points and quality care)

Do something extra

➤ Depression and anxiety are more common in people with epilepsy. It is essential to recognise and treat this at an early stage.[18,19]

➤ Contraception. Advise women to continue using effective contraception until they consider getting pregnant.

➤ Pre-conception planning. Prescribe folic acid to reduce the incidence of neural tube defects.

➤ Once pregnant, refer women urgently for review by an epilepsy specialist. Encourage them to notify the pregnancy to the UK Epilepsy and Pregnancy Register (www.epilepsyandpregnancy.co.uk).

➤ Address issues related to driving, including informing the DVLA.

➤ Give general advice about protective measures in a seizure and when to call an ambulance must be given to the carer.

➤ Look for any past history of status epilepticus. This is associated with significant morbidity and mortality.

➤ Provide information to the patient and their carer by drawing up an appropriate personal care plan.

➤ Introduce the patient to various support groups and 'Expert Patient Programmes'.

➤ Address occupational issues such as notification to employers.

➤ Advice about alcohol and recreational drugs must be given at every review.
➤ Record and offer smoking cessation support to epileptics who smoke.

References

1 Foregren L, Beghi E, Oun A, *et al.* The epidemiology of epilepsy in Europe: a systematic review. *Eur. J Neurol.* 2005; **12**: 245–53.
2 Sander JW. The epidemiology of epilepsy revisited. *Curr. Opin. Neurol.* 2003; **16**: 165–70.
3 Wallace H, Shorvon S, Tallis R. Age-specific incidence and prevalence rates of treated epilepsy in an unselected population and age-specific fertility rates of women with epilepsy. *Lancet.* 1998; **352**: 1790–3.
4 Pryor FM, Ramsey RE, Rowan AJ, *et al.* Epilepsy in older adults: update from VA co-operative study (VACS) no. 428. *Epilepsia.* 2001; **43**(Suppl. 7): S165–6.
5 Chief Medical Officer (England). *Annual Report.* London: HMSO; 2001.
6 Amos P. *New GMS Contract QOF Implementation Dataset and Business Rules.* Available at: www.pcc.nhs.uk/.../QOF/Business%20PRules%z0v14/epilepsy_ruleset_r4_v14_0.pdf (accessed 22 September 2009).
7 Couldridge L, Kendall S, March A. A systematic overview – a decade of research. The information and counselling needs of people with epilepsy. *Seizure.* 2001; **10**: 605–14.
8 Raspall-Chaure M, Chin RFM, Neville BGR, *et al.* Childhood convulsive status epilepticus: epidemiology, management and outcome. *Lancet Neurol.* 2006; **5**: 769–79.
9 Chin RF, Neville BGR, Scott RC. Treatment of community-onset, childhood convulsive status epilepticus: a prospective, population-based study. *Lancet.* 2006; **368**: 222–9.
10 All Party Parliamentary Group. *The Human and Economic Cost of Epilepsy in England 2007.* Available at: www.epilepsy.org.uk/compaign/lobbying/appg/ (accessed 9 April 2011).
11 Zielinski JS. Epilepsy and mortality rate and cause of death. *Epilepsia.* 1974; **15**: 191–201.
12 National Institute for Health and Clinical Excellence. *The Epilepsies: the diagnosis and management of the epilepsies in adults and children in primary and secondary care: NICE guideline CG20.* London: NHICE; 2004. www.nice.org.uk/guidance/CG20 (accessed 22 September 2009).
13 *SIGN. Diagnosis and management of epilepsy in adults: No 70.* Edinburgh: Scottish Intercollegiate Guidelines Network, 2003 (updated 2005). Available at: www.sign.ac.uk/guidelines/fulltext/70/index.html
14 Chadwick DW, Smith D. The misdiagnosis of epilepsy. *BMJ.* 2002; **324**: 495–6.
15 Upton D, Thompson PJ. Effectiveness of coping strategies employed by people with chronic epilepsy. *J Epilepsy.* 1992; **5**: 119–27.
16 National Institute for Health and Clinical Excellence. *Medicines Adherence: involving patients in decisions about prescribed medicines and supporting adherence: NICE guideline CG76.* London: NHICE; 2006. www.nice.org.uk/guidance/CG76 (accessed 22 September 2009).
17 Nashef L, Sander JWAS, Shorvon SD, *et al. Mortality in Epilepsy. Recent Advances in Epilepsy.* Edinburgh: Churchill Livingstone; 1995, pp. 271–87. www.epilepsysociety.org.uk/FileStorage/.../main.../Chapter39Sander.pdf

18 Mensah SA, Beavis JM, Thapar AK, *et al*. A community study of the presence of anxiety disorder in people with epilepsy. *Epilepsy Behav*. 2007; **11**: 118–24.

19 Mensah SA, Beavis JM, Thapar AK, *et al*. The presence and clinical implications of depression in a community population of adults with epilepsy. *Epilepsy Behav*. 2006; **8**: 231–9.

Useful reading

For health professionals

➤ NICE Guidelines October 2004: www.nice.org.uk
➤ SIGN Guidelines 2005: www.sign.ac.uk

For patients

➤ The National Society for Epilepsy: www.epillepsynse.org.uk
➤ British epilepsy association: www.epilepsy.org.uk

CHAPTER 17

Ethnicity

Under the QOF, ethnic origin must be recorded for **all** newly registered patients. Only one point is awarded to this record indicator 21.

The NHS has a legal responsibility to promote race equality and tackle discrimination, both as an employer and as a provider or commissioner of healthcare. Ethnicity is a major factor affecting the health of individuals and communities. Studies show that black and minority ethnic (BME) groups have worse health than the overall population, have more difficulties accessing healthcare and when they do the outcome is not as good as for other people. NHS evidence on ethnicity and health gives information about specific healthcare needs of minority ethnic groups.[1]

According to the 2001 census, 92% of the UK population is white, which includes significant non-British white minorities such as Irish, 2% is black or black British, 4% is Asian or Asian British and 1.5% is mixed. The UK is likely to become multi-ethnic in the future. BME groups account for 73% of the UK's total population growth.[2]

There are nationally used ethnic categories[3] acceptable to the majority of the population and these should be used in the NHS and social care. This data can be used for public health purposes to compare patients accessing and being treated by the NHS. It can also be used for clinical purposes. It is well known that Pakistani men are more at risk of IHD. Bangladeshi and Irish men are more likely to smoke. Bangladeshi, Pakistani, Indian and African-Caribbean women are more likely to suffer from type 2 diabetes.

Why included in QOF

➤ At present there is a lack of regular, accurate data to monitor ethnic variations in the use of NHS services.[2] It is hoped that its inclusion in the QOF will make GPs record the ethnicity data on their patient's profile, which should help in tackling ethnic health inequalities.

➤ BME groups as a whole are more likely to report ill health and that ill health starts at a younger age compared with white British.[4] It is hoped that recording the data will help the NHS Plan 2000 which is committed to two national public service agreement (PSA) targets to reduce health inequalities.[2]

➤ Patterns of ethnic health inequality vary. BME groups tend to have higher rates of CVD but lower rates of cancer. Asians have a genetic predisposition to diabetes. A small financial incentive may encourage GPs to provide a structured primary prevention screening of heart disease and diabetes in this group.

How to maximise the quality point

There should be no excuse of losing this one point. Simply enter the ethnicity categories, not only in the new patient registration health check but also in all the clinical indicators templates.

Template GMS: Ethnicity (V16)

Prompt	Code	Date	Coded subsets
Ethnic category – 2001 census	(9i)		British/mixed British 2001 census (9i0)
			White British ethnic cat. 2001 census (9i00)
			Irish ethnic cat. 2001 census (9i1)
			White Irish ethnic cat. 2001 census (9i10)
			Other white ethnic cat. 2001 census (9i2)
			White and black Carribbean ethnic cat. 2001 census (9i3)
			White and black African ethnic cat. 2001 census (9i4)
			White and Asian ethnic cat. 2001 census (9i5)
			Other mixed ethnic cat. 2001 census (9i6)
			Indian/British Indian ethnic cat. 2001 census (9i7)
			Pakistani/British Pakistani ethnic cat. 2001 census (9i8)
			Bangladeshi/British Bangladeshi ethnic cat. 2001 census (9i9)
			Other Asian ethnic cat. 2001 census (9iA)
			Carribbean ethnic cat. 2001 census (9iB)
			African ethnic cat. 2001 census (9iC)
			Other black ethnic cat. 2001 census (9iD)
			Chinese ethnic cat. 2001 census (9iE)
			Other ethnic cat. 2001 census (9iF)
			Ethnic cat. not stated 2001 census (9iG)

References

1 www.evidence.nhs.uk
2 Parliamentary Office of Science and Technology. Postnote. *Ethnicity and Health.* 2007; 276. Available at: www.parliament.uk/documents/post/postpn276.pdf
3 Practical guide to ethnic monitoring in the NHS and social care. 29 July 2005. www.dh.gov.uk
4 Bhopal R. *Race, Ethnicity and Health in Multicultural Societies.* Oxford: Oxford University Press; 2007.

Useful reading

➤ NHS Evidence. A service supplied to the NHS evidence by CEEHD (Centre for Evidence in Ethnicity, Health and Diversity). *Ethnicity and Health Newsletter.* (For free subscription email sleh@dmu.ac.uk and ask to be put on the mailing list.)

CHAPTER 18

Heart failure

Definition

Heart failure is a clinical syndrome comprising reduced cardiac output, tissue hypoperfusion and congestion[1] resulting in breathlessness, fatigue and ankle oedema. These symptoms are due to persistent cardiac dysfunction.

In a GP practice, patients often present with less acute symptoms and signs, and as a result the diagnosis can be missed.

Prevalence

Heart failure is common and disabling. It affects roughly 2–3% of the population in many industrialised countries. In the UK, 900 000 people are affected with this serious condition.[2] Increasing prevalence is due to an ageing population and improved diagnosis of ischaemic heart disease.[3]

Community prevalence varies from 1.6 to 4.6 cases per 1000 in men aged 45–74 years and from 0.9 to 2.2 cases per 1000 in women. In 2003 NICE acknowledged that the increasing prevalence is not only due to the ageing population but also a result of the more effective treatment available for coronary heart disease.[1]

About 1% of men develop heart failure after the age of 75 years and 2% after 80 years.[4]

Why included in QOF

➤ Heart failure has high mortality rate and poor prognosis if not treated aggressively. Numerous co-morbidities such as chronic anaemia, renal dysfunction, depression, COPD and arthritis may co-exist. There is emerging evidence that appropriate management of these co-morbidities influences the progression of heart failure and improves the outcome. Early recognition and management of these co-morbidities by the primary care sector can alter the outcome.

➤ Despite advances in management, patients with heart failure are still associated with a high mortality rate, 30% at one year and 60–70% after five years. The aim of its inclusion in the QOF was to reduce the mortality.

➤ Heart failure admissions account for 5% of all UK hospital admissions and 20% of patients with heart failure require two or more hospital admissions per year,[5] costing the NHS almost £1 billion.[6] Early detection, assessment, appropriate and effective treatment and regular follow-up by the GP can prevent a hospital admission.

➤ Heart failure is physically and emotionally disabling and has a major impact on quality of life. Primary care teams with excellent negotiating skills can coordinate input from other agencies, such as social services, housing benefits and mobility benefits.

➤ The term heart failure can cause extreme anxiety to the patient and their carer. GPs are best placed to educate patients and their families about this condition and treatment, making sure there is compliance with the medications.

➤ GPs are best placed to teach patients to recognise the symptoms and signs of deterioration, such as ankle oedema, weight gain and increasing shortness of breath – secondary care has less time for educating patients. Treating the early signs of deterioration can prevent a hospital admission.

➤ GPs are best placed to detect early CKD as this is an independent predictor of poor outcomes in patients with CHF.[7]

➤ Early detection of treatment of anaemia can improve the survival rate. Anaemia is a common co-morbidity associated with CHF, with a prevalence rate of 20–50%. It can be easily managed by a primary care physician.

➤ The prevalence of depression in heart failure is between 13% and 77%.[8] GPs know their patients well and can pick up and manage early depression.

➤ Cognitive dysfunction exists in between 35 and > 50% of cases.[9] A skilled GP can pick up cognitive dysfunction and provide the necessary care. Cognitive dysfunction is associated with a fivefold increase in overall mortality and a sixfold increase in dependence for daily living activities.[10]

➤ Who better than a GP to address palliative care? A great deal of anxiety related to end-of-life care, wishes and sudden death can be managed well within primary care. A quantitative study of 40 patients with heart failure showed that the palliative care values of a 'good death' from cancer may not apply to elderly patients with heart failure.[11]

The facts

➤ The average life expectancy is only about three years after the diagnosis. This is much worse than other serious conditions such as cancer of the colon or breast.[12]

➤ Heart failure is associated with poor quality of life and frequent admissions to hospital.[13]

➤ GPs can make an earlier diagnosis by testing for elevated levels of natriuretic peptides (BNP) rather than doing an ECG in patients suspected of having heart failure who have not had a myocardial infarction. Testing for natriuretic peptides – b-type natriuretic peptide (BNP) or N-terminal BNP (N-BNP) – levels is the best way of quickly identifying patients who need ECHO or specialist assessment.[14] These tests cost about £15 each and are becoming easily available.

The use of BNP testing will result in earlier diagnosis of heart failure and of left ventricular systolic dysfunction.[14]

➤ The recent development of a highly sensitive test for cardiac protein may improve heart failure risk assessment in elderly patients claimed by researchers. Measurement of cardiac troponin T (cTnT) alongside the NICE recommended test for serum BNP may potentially predict heart failure risk. Researchers found that raised levels of the protein cardiac troponin T were linked to increased risk of heart failure and death.[15]

➤ About 40% of patients with CHF have CKD, defined as eGFR < 60 mL/min and a serum creatinine level of 133 μmol/L.[16] This is usually the result of chronic renal hypo perfusion in combination with other risk factors such as diabetes mellitus and hypertension.

QOF: heart failure indicators

Indicators and points: total points 29

Records
HF1

The practice can produce a register of patients with heart failure.

Points 4

From April 2006, all heart failure patients should be added to the register.

The register makes call and recall easy and is a prerequisite for good delivery of heart failure service provision.

Initial diagnosis
HF2

The percentage of patients with a diagnosis of heart failure diagnosed after 1 April 2006 which has been confirmed by an echocardiography or by specialist assessment.

Points 6   Payment stages 40–90%

It is essential not to rely only on clinical signs and symptoms alone. The presenting symptoms of heart failure are frequently non-specific. Only about one-quarter of patients have shortness of breath symptoms.

For an accurate diagnosis, there must be evidence of cardiac dysfunction. ECHO is a non-invasive method and is necessary to establish the diagnosis of heart failure. Since its introduction into the QOF, rapid access to ECHO is available to most GPs. ECHO also helps to ascertain whether the cause is ventricular, valvular, both or neither. If you are one of the lucky GPs who have BNP testing available in their area, it could be a good reassurance tool, because if the value is normal in someone suspected of having heart failure, the diagnosis is highly unlikely.

Current guidance requires either ECHO or specialist assessment for all patients with suspected heart failure. Patients with worsening symptoms or deteriorating kidney function should be referred to a specialist.

Ongoing management
HF3

The percentage of patients with a current diagnosis of heart failure due to left ventricular dysfunction (LVD) who are currently treated with an ACE inhibitor or angiotensin receptor blocker (ARB),who can tolerate therapy and for whom there is no contraindication.

Points 10   **Payment stages 40–80%**

Once the diagnosis is confirmed, the treatment should be initiated without delay. The aims of treatment are to improve quality of life by addressing symptoms and to prevent hospitalisation. Unless there are specific contraindications, ACE inhibitors should be prescribed to all patients with LVD. ACE inhibitors reduce mortality,[17] slow the progression of ventricular dysfunction[18] and reduce hospitalisation rates and number of days in hospital.[18] The accumulation of bradykinin because of ACE inhibitors can cause cough or angioedema.

ARBs do not cause an increase in bradykinin levels and are as effective as ACE inhibitors – an alternative to ACE.[19]

The most effective ACE is Ramipril 10 mg daily. Available ARBs are Candesartan 32 mg daily, Losartan 50–100 mg daily, Valsartan 160 mg daily. The most cost-effective is Candesartan. Renal functions should be checked before starting the therapy, two weeks after initiating and at every dose increase, as they may cause renal impairment.

Although renal artery stenosis is relatively common in patients with IHD,[20] renal failure caused by ACE is rare.

If a patient remains symptomatic despite optimal treatment with an ACE inhibitor and a beta blocker, an aldosterone antagonist licensed for heart failure should be added. Digoxin should be considered for worsening or severe heart failure.

Referral to specialist

The patient should be referred to a specialist in the following circumstances.
➤ No response to the treatment.
➤ Valvular disease.
➤ For initial diagnosis if ECHO is not available in your area.
➤ Severe heart failure, NYHA class IV.

Table 18.1 sets out the New York Heart Association (NYHA) classification of heart failure symptoms.

Table 18.1 New York Heart Association classification of heart failure symptoms

Class 1	No limitations
Class 11	Slight limitation of physical activity (mild heart failure)
Class 111	Marked limitation of physical activity (moderate heart failure)
Class 1V	Symptoms of heart failure are present even at rest (severe heart failure)

Cardiac synchronisation therapy, CRT and implantable cardioverter defibrillator (ICD) are available for patients with NYHA class III symptoms and should not be denied on the basis of age alone.

HF4

The percentage of patients with a current diagnosis of heart failure due to LVD who are treated with an ACE or ARB, who are additionally treated with a beta blocker licensed for heart failure, or recorded as intolerant to or having a contraindication to beta blocker.

Points 9   **Payment stages 40–60%**

Cardio-selective beta blockers reduce both morbidity and mortality. The benefits of beta blockers on mortality, symptoms and hospitalisation rates in heart failure are well established.[21] One reason for under-prescribing is a great fear of causing bronchospasm. However, most patients with COPD do not have reactive bronchospasm and beta blockers are well tolerated in congestive heart failure patients who have COPD.[22] Patients with COPD and slight wheeze should not be excluded from the benefits obtained from adding beta blockers.[23] Patients should be on a low dose of both beta blocker and ACE inhibitor/ARB rather than a full dose of one or the other. The beta blocker used should be one licensed for heart failure, in line with NICE recommendations. These are bisoprolol 1.25 mg daily, carvedilol 3.125 mg twice daily and nebivolol 1.25 mg once daily. In the case of hypotension, reduce the dose of ACE and continue with the beta blocker. The effect of the beta blocker is dose dependent. Increasing the dose of the beta blocker over the ACE inhibitor leads to a better response in terms of left ventricular function. Start in a 'start low, go slow' manner and assess heart rate, blood pressure and clinical condition after every increase in dose. Titrate slowly over a period of weeks and months to the maximum tolerated dose.

Some argue that beta blockers worsen diabetic control, although carvedilol is as well tolerated in diabetics as in non-diabetics.[24]

Maximising quality points

➤ Once ECHO confirms the diagnosis of left ventricular systolic dysfunction enter the diagnosis, read code (G58) and use the heart failure template:
— ECHO Left ventricular systolic dysfunction (585f)
— ECHO Left ventricular diastolic dysfunction (585g).
➤ Enter the diagnosis once the hospital letter with the result of ECHO confirms the heart failure.
➤ If the patient is referred for ECHO, enter the read code ECHO requested (33BD) or Suspected heart failure (1J60).
➤ A difficult patient may refuse ECHO. Entering the read code ECHO declined (56F1) and forgetting the problem is not a good idea. Do enter the read code and try to persuade the patient at the next visit. Most of us are good at making our patients understand why this particular investigation is important.
➤ Do not forget to put a diary date for a follow-up visit.

➤ Chase all DNAs.
➤ Carry out opportunistic reviews.
➤ Add a note to the repeat prescription of heart failure patients with an appointment. This will save money on posting.
➤ Make sure patients receive an influenza vaccine every year and a one-off pneumococcal vaccine. This will boost your target for influenza vaccination.
➤ Any exception reporting must be documented with a clear recorded reason.

Template GMS: Heart failure (V16)

Prompt	Code	Date	Coded subsets
Exception report: heart failure quality indicator	(9hH)		Except. heart fail. QI: Pt unsuit. (9hH0) Except. heart fail. QI: inf. dis. (9hH1)
NYHA classification	(662f)		NYHA classification Class I (662f) NYHA classification Class II (662g) NYHA classification Class III (662h) NYHA classification Class IV (662i)
Ethnic category – 2001 census	(9i)		See ethnicity template, Chapter 17
O/E WEIGHT	(22A)		
O/E HEIGHT	(229)		
BODY MASS INDEX	(22K)		
WAIST CIRCUMFERENCE	(22N0)		
WCM DECLINE	(8IAf)		
WAIST HIP RATIO	(22N7)		
PATIENT ADVISED REG. DIET	(8CA4)		
PATIENT ADVISED REG. EXERCISE	(8CA5)		
PATIENT ADVISED ABOUT ALCOHOL	(8CAM)		
SYSTOLIC BP	(2469)		
DIASTOLIC BP	(246A)		
24-hr BP MONITOR	(662L)		
AVERAGE DAY SYSTOLIC	(246Y)		
AVERAGE DAY DIASTOLIC	(246X)		
AVERAGE NIGHT SYSTOLIC	(246b)		
AVERAGE NIGHT DIASTOLIC	(246a)		
O/E PULSE RATE	(242)		
Smoking status			See smoking status template, Chapter 25
Alcohol consumption			See Alcohol, Chapter 27
FBC	(424)		
TFT	(442J)		
PLASMA RANDOM GLUCOSE	(44g0)		
PLASMA FASTING GLUCOSE	(44g1)		
PROTEINURIA	(R110)		
MICROALBUMINURIA	(R1103)		
URINE ALBUMIN:CR	(46TC)		
SERUM CREATININE	(44J3)		
eGFR	(451E)		

(continued)

Prompt	Code	Date	Coded subsets
12 LEAD ECG	(321B)		*ECG coded subsets same as in CHD template, Chapter 9*
STANDARD CHEST X-RAY	(535)		*Standard chest X-ray coded subsets same as in CHD template, Chapter 9*
Echocardiogram abnormal	(58531)		Ultrasound heart scan (5853) Echo. abn. (58531) Echo. request (33BD) Echo. decline (56F1) Echo shows LVSDF (585f) Echo. equivocal (5C20) Referral for echo. (8HQ7)
PLASMA B NATRIURETIC PEPTIDE LEVEL	(44AR)		*Enter the read code if available in your area*
Angiocardiography awaited	(5531)		Angio. awaited (5531) Angio. normal (5532) Angio. abnormal (5533) Angio. declined (5534) Angio. equivocal (5538) Angio. Rt & Lt heart (79380) Angio. Lt NEC (79382)
B blocker prophylaxis	(8B69)		B blocker contraind. (8I26) H/O B blocker allergy (14LL) B blocker refused (8I36) B blocker not indic. (8I62) AR B blocker (TJC6) B blocker not tolerat. (8I73)
ACE inhibitor contraindicated	(8I28)		H/O ACE allergy (14LM) ACE declined (8I3D) ACE not indic. (8I64) ACE not tolerat. (8I74) Adverse reaction to Ramip. (TJC79)
ANG 11 receptor ant. contr.	(8I2H)		H/O ANG2 allergy (14LN) ANG2 declined (8I3P) ANG2 not indic. (8I6C) ANG2 not tolerat. (8I75) PH ANG2 allergy (ZV14E)
Cardio referral	(8H44)		Ref. to cardio. GPwSI (8H4R)
			Priv. ref. to cardio. (8HVJ)
INFLUENZA VACCINATION	(65E)		*Influenza vaccination coded subsets same as in CHD template, Chapter 9*
PNEUMOCOCCAL VACCINATION	(6572)		*Pneumococcal vaccination coded subsets same as in CHD template, Chapter 9*
FITNESS TO FLY	(13ZI)		
EMERGENCY HOSPITAL ADMISSION	(8Z2)		
HEART FAILURE MONITORING 1st LETTER	(90r3)		
HEART FAILURE MONITORING 2nd LETTER	(90r4)		
HEART FAILURE MONITORING 3rd LETTER	(90r5)		

(continued)

Prompt	Code	Date	Coded subsets
HEART FAILURE TELEPHONE INVITE	(90r1)		
HEART FAILURE VERBAL INVITE	(90r2)		

* Beta blockers used should be licensed for heart failure, in line with NICE recommendations. The only such agents are carvedilol, bisoprolol and nebivolol. You can add the name-specific read codes on the template under the pick list.

(Add the capitalised prompts to your template to maximise points and quality care)

Do something extra

➤ Although not included in the QOF, run simple tests like FBC and TFT because both anaemia and thyroid dysfunction can cause or exacerbate heart failure.

➤ 12 lead ECG. A completely normal ECG indicates significant heart failure is unlikely.[25]

➤ Renal function test – serum creatinine levels.

➤ Around 25–30% of patients with heart failure meet the diagnostic criteria for COPD.[26] Smoking and ageing are the main cause in both. Perform a spirometry test as there could be overlapping of symptoms.

➤ Check the heart rate. High heart rate is an independent risk factor for heart failure and lowering the heart rate should be an important target of therapy. In patients with coronary artery disease and LVD, a heart rate of 70 beats per minute or higher is associated with a 34% increased risk of cardiovascular death and 53% increase in admission to hospital for heart failure compared with heart rate lower than 70 beats per minute[27] and heart rate reduction is associated with improved outcomes.[28] Reduction of heart rate with Ivabradine results in the improvement of clinical outcomes in heart failure.[29]

➤ Make sure your team is up to date with high risk features in chronic heart failure. If yours is a high locum-user practice, incorporate these in the template.

High risk features

There will be patients at much higher risk. They should be picked up early and receive a high level of care to prevent a hospital admission. These high risk markers **should be added as read codes** in the already-existing template of heart failure.

➤ Anaemia: add **FBC read code 424** in the template

➤ Renal impairment: add **U&E read code 44J-2 or 44J** – check with your local pathology laboratory.

➤ Check blood sugar: Add **read code Random blood sugar 44T1, fasting blood sugar 44T2**.

➤ ECG: add **ECG read code 321**.

➤ Heart rate: in a randomised controlled trial,[30] researchers found that raised heart rate is a risk factor. Patients with a heart rate of ≥ 87 beats per minute were more than twofold higher risk than were patients with the lowest heart rate (70 to < 72 beats per minute). The risk increases by 3% with every beat increase from baseline heart rate and 16% for every five beats per minute.

➤ New or established left bundle branch block: add **read code 329A**.

➤ Recent hospitalisation: add **Admission to hospital read code 8Hd, Emergency hospital admission read code 8HZ.**

➤ NYHA classification: classes III, IV.

➤ Hypotension: < 90 mm Hg systolic blood pressure, **read code Hypotension G87.**

➤ Fitness to fly. Most patients will need guidance regarding fitness to fly. The usual advice is that flying after 6 weeks if stabilised for acute heart failure is acceptable and no restrictions for chronic heart failure.[31] Add read code **13ZI.**

References

1 Chronic congestive heart failure. *BMJ Best Practice.* Available at: http://bestpractice. bmj.com/best-practice/monograph/61.html

2 Hogg K, Swedberg K, McMurray J. Heart failure with preserved left ventricular systolic function; epidemiology, clinical characteristics and prognosis. *J Am. Coll. Cardiol.* 2004; **43**: 317–27.

3 Bhatia RS, Tu JV, Lee DS, *et al.* Outcome of heart failure with preserved ejection fraction in a population-based study. *N. Engl. J Med.* 2006; **355**: 260–9.

4 Mant J, Doust J, Roalfe A, *et al.* Systematic review and individual patient data meta-analysis of diagnosis of heart failure, with modelling of implications of different diagnostic strategies in primary care. *Health Technol. Assess.* 2009; **13**: 932. Available at: www.hta.ac.uk/project/1509.asp

5 McMurray J, McDonagh T, Morrison CE, *et al.* Trends in hospitalisation for heart failure in Scotland 1980–1990. *Eur. Heart J.* 1993; **14**: 1158–62.

6 Khand AU, Gemmell I, Rankin AC, *et al.* Clinical events leading to the progression of heart failure: insights from a national database of hospital discharges. *Eur. Heart J.* 2001; **22**: 153–64.

7 Kearney MT, Fox KA, Lee AJ, *et al.* Predicting death due to progressive heart failure in patients with mild to moderate chronic heart failure. *J Am. Coll. Cardiol.* 2002; **40**: 1801–8.

8 Konstam V, Moser DK, De Jong MJ. Depression and anxiety in heart failure. *J Cardiac Failure.* 2005; **11**: 455–63.

9 Almeida OP, Flicker L. The mind of a failing heart: a systematic review of the association between congestive heart failure and cognitive functioning. *Internal Medicine J.* 2001; **31**: 290–95.

10 Gluseppe ZI. The effects of cognitive impairment on mortality among hospitalised patients with heart failure. *Am. J Med.* 2003; **115**: 97–103.

11 Gott M, Small N, Barnes S, *et al.* Older people views of a good death in heart failure. Implications for palliative care provision. *Soc. Sci. Med.* 2008; **67**: 1113–21.

12 National Institute for Health and Clinical Excellence. *Chronic heart failure: NICE guideline CG5.* London: NHICE; 2006. www.nice.org.uk/guidance/CCG5

13 Ho KK, Anderson KM, Kannel WB, *et al.* Survival after the onset of congestive heart failure in Framingham Heart Study subjects. *Circulation.* 1993; **88**: 107–15.

14 National Institute for Health and Clinical Excellence. *Chronic Heart Failure: management of chronic heart failure in adults in primary and secondary care: NICE guideline GC108.* London: NHICE; 2006. www.nice.org.uk/guidance/GC108

15 Christopher R, deFilippi MD, James A. Association of serial measures of cardiac troponin T using a sensitive assay with incident heart failure and cardiovascular mortality in older adults. *JAMA.* 2010; **304**(22): 2494–502. www.jama.ama-assn.org/content/304/22/2494full.pdf

16 Ezekowitz J, McAlister FA. The association among renal insufficiency, pharmacotherapy, and outcomes in 6,427 patients with heart failure and coronary artery disease. *J Am. Coll. Cardiol.* 2004; **44**: 1587–92.

17 Effects of Enalapril on mortality in severe congestive heart failure. Results of the Cooperative North Scandinavian Enalapril Survival Study CONSENSUS *N. Engl J Med.* 1987; **316**: 1429–35.

18 Jong P, Yusuf S. Effects of Enalapril on 12 year survival and life expectancy in patients with left ventricular systolic dysfunction; a follow up study. *Lancet.* 2003; **361**: 1843–8.

19 Granger CB, McMurray JJV, Yusuf S, *et al.* (for the CHARM Investigators and Committees). Effects of candesartan in patients with chronic heart failure and reduced left ventricular systolic function intolerant to angiotensin converting enzyme inhibitors: the CHARM-Alternative trial. *Lancet.* 2003; **362**: 772–6.

20 De Silva R, Loh H, Rigby AS, *et al.* Epidemiology, associated factors and prognostic outcomes of renal artery stenosis in chronic heart failure assessed by magnetic resonance angiography. *Am. J Cardiol.* 2007; **100**: 273–9.

21 Cleland JGF, Freemantle N, McGowan J, *et al.* The evidence for beta blockers equals or surpasses that for ACE inhibitors in heart failure. *BMJ.* 1999; **318**: 824–5.

22 Shelton RJ, Rigby AS, Cleland JG, *et al.* Effect of a community heart failure clinic on uptake of beta blockers by patients with obstructive airway disease and heart failure. *Heart.* 2006; **92**: 331–6.

23 Witte KK, Clark AL. Beta blockers and inspiratory pulmonary function in chronic heart failure. *J Cardiac Failure.* 2005; **11**: 112–16.

24 Nodari S, Metra M. Efficacy and tolerability of the long term administration of carvedilol in patients with chronic heart failure with and without concomitant diabetes mellitus. *Eur. J Heart Fail.* 2003; **5**: 803–9

25 Khan NK, Goode KM, Cleland JG, *et al.* EuroHeart failure survey investigators. Prevalence of ECG abnormalities in an international survey of patients with suspected or confirmed heart failure at death or discharge. *Eur. J Heart Fail.* 2007; **9**: 491–501.

26 Braunstein JB, Anderson GF, Gerstenblith G, *et al.* Noncardiac comorbidity increases preventable hospitalizations and mortality among medicare beneficiaries with chronic heart failure. *J Am. Coll. Cardiol.* 203; **42**: 1226–33.

27 Fox K, Ford I, Steg PG, *et al.* Heart rate as a prognostic risk factor in patients with coronary artery disease and left ventricular systolic dysfunction (BEAUTIFUL): a subgroup analysis of a randomised controlled trial. *Lancet.* 2008; **372**: 817–21.

28 Flannery G, Gehrig-Mills R, Billah B, *et al.* Analysis of randomised controlled trials on the effect of magnitude of heart rate reduction on clinical outcomes in patients with systolic chronic heart failure receiving beta-blockers. *Am. J Cardiol.* 2008; **101**: 865–9.

29 Swedberg K, Komajda M, Bohm M, *et al.* Ivabradin and outcomes in chronic heart failure (SHIFT): a randomised placebo-controlled study. *Lancet.* 2010; **376**: 875–85.

30 www.thelancet.com/journals/lancet/.../PII50140-6736(10)61259-7

31 Smith D, Toff W, Joy M, *et al.* Fitness to fly for passengers with cardiovascular disease. *Heart.* 2010; **96**: ii1–ii16.

Useful reading

For health professionals

➤ British Society for Heart Failure: www.bsh.org.uk/

For patients

➤ www.netdoctor.co.uk

CHAPTER 19

Hypertension

Hypertension is common in older adults and is one of the major risk factors for cardiovascular disease. Systolic blood pressure tends to rise with age, whereas diastolic blood pressure rises until middle age and then falls. High systolic blood pressure is an independent risk factor for cardiovascular events than high diastolic blood pressure in individuals aged 50 or over and is often more difficult to control.[1]

Prevalence

Forty per cent of the adult population in the UK has hypertension, according to the British Hypertension Society, BHS IV and the NICE guidelines definition of hypertension.[2,3] The figure is as high as 70% for those aged 60 years or over.

Why included in QOF

The management of hypertension does and should take place in general practice. Only 10% of people have resistant or severe hypertension and only they should be referred to the secondary care.

➤ Hypertension is under-diagnosed and under-treated.[4] The QOF encourages GPs to correct this situation.
➤ Hypertension is one of the most important modifiable risk factors for premature morbidity and mortality.[5]
➤ Hypertension increases the risk of coronary heart disease, heart failure, stroke, peripheral vascular disease and dementia. A 2 mm rise in systolic blood pressure results in a 7% increase in risk of death from ischaemic heart disease and a 10% increase in the risk of death from stroke.[6] Inclusion in the QOF and its attached financial incentive can reduce the morbidity and mortality.
➤ GPs are ideally placed to offer lifestyle advice – exercise, advice and support to stop smoking and dietary and alcohol consumption advice.
➤ Control of blood pressure by rational use of anti-hypertensive drugs can reduce cardiovascular morbidity and mortality and the NHS financial strain – this can be easily done in the primary care sector.[7]

The facts

➤ More than one-quarter of the world's population has high blood pressure. This number is projected to rise to 1.56 billion (29%) by 2025.[8]
➤ Globally, high blood pressure is responsible for 7 million deaths every year.[4]
➤ Hypertension presents a major public health challenge in the UK. The incidence rises with advancing age in both sexes, so that by the age of 75 years and over, two-thirds of people have high blood pressure.[9]
➤ Hypertension in pregnancy should not be managed in the primary care sector but GPs should be vigilant about the problem. Pre-eclampsia is a leading cause of maternal and foetal morbidity and mortality and a significant number of affected women present to their primary care physician.[10]

QOF: hypertension indicators

Indicators and points: total points 81

BP 1

The practice can produce a register of patients with established hypertension.

Points 6

An accurate register is a prerequisite for disease management. Diagnosis has to be accurate for its inclusion in the QOF.

Hypertension should be diagnosed according to British Hypertension Society (BHS) guidelines.[2] Only those with a reading of ≥ 160/100 mm Hg should be coded. Accurate measurement of blood pressure is important prior to making a diagnosis. A one-off high reading should not be coded as hypertension. Blood pressure should be measured on at least three separate occasions. Automated sphygmomanometers are inaccurate in atrial fibrillation. Standing blood pressure should be checked in patients with postural hypotension. Patients with a reading of 140–159/90–99 mm Hg should only be included if they have end organ damage, diabetes or coronary heart disease or if their 10-year risk of cardiovascular disease is ≥ 20%.[11]

Ongoing management

BP4

The percentage of patients with hypertension in whom there is a record of the blood pressure in the previous nine months.

Points 18   Payment stages 40–90%

The BHS encourages self-monitoring of blood pressure. In general, blood pressure measured at home tends to be lower than in the surgery, and the correction factor often is 10/5 mm Hg.

The authors of this study compared the variability of blood pressure readings taken in the surgery, readings taken on a 24-hour machine and self-monitoring readings performed morning and evening for at least six weeks. The study concluded that self-monitoring over a one-week period provides more accurate readings than 24-hour ambulatory monitoring.[12]

Self-monitoring blood pressure devices are simple to use and relatively cheap. There are several websites that provide guidance about which validated device to buy (e.g. blood pressure: How to choose the right blood pressure monitor, www.bpassoc.org.uk; Blood Pressure Monitor, Best Blood Pressure Monitors for home use, www.blood-pressure-monitoring.org/blood-pressure-monitor.htm).

BP5

The percentage of patients with hypertension in whom the last blood pressure (measured in the previous nine months) is 150/90 or less.

Points 57   **Payment stages 40–70%**

The QOF target of 150/90 mm Hg is less vigorous than that recommended by NICE and the BHS.[2,5]

NICE recommends that drug treatment should be offered when blood pressure reaches 160/100 mm Hg, with the aim of reducing it to below 140/90 mm Hg, and that the drug treatment should start with an angiotensin converting enzyme for those under 55 years of age with no contraindications. An angiotensin II receptor antagonist should only be used in people who are not able to tolerate ACE inhibitors. For black patients of any age and those over the age of 55 years, a thiazide diuretic or calcium channel blocker should be used.[5,13] Contraindications of ACE include pregnancy and reno-vascular disease and caution is advised in renal impairment. Side-effects of ACE include dry cough and, rarely, angioedema, hyperkalaemia and renal impairment.

NICE, in conjunction with the BHS, launched updated clinical guidelines on the management of hypertension in adults. This partially updates the original guidelines, CG18, published in August 2004.[5,14] Beta blockers are now recommended as a step 4 therapy option in individuals with blood pressure above target despite treatment with ACE/ANG2, calcium channel blocker or thiazide diuretic each at full dose or in combination as these drugs are less effective, particularly in elderly.

Maximising quality points

GPs are well paid under the QOF and hypertension is so easy to control – so why some of us are not achieving the maximum? It could be the initiation of inappropriate drugs, low dose initiation with no dose titration, an unsuitable combination of drugs, poor patient compliance or not read coding properly.

➤ Use read code G20.
➤ Ensure all new patients with hypertension registering with the practice, including those in residential and nursing homes, are read coded.
➤ Run a repeat prescription search on patients taking anti-hypertensive medication and make sure they are on the register.
➤ Any hospital outpatient or discharge letter mentioning hypertension should be entered on the register.
➤ Do not read code a one-off high reading as hypertension.
➤ Do not read code pre-eclampsia as hypertension.

➤ Increase the number on your register by carrying out regular health checks on patients over 45 years. Do not forget annual health checks of those on your list aged over 75.

➤ Ensure an efficient call and recall system. It is very important that the patient goes home with an appointment for the next blood pressure check. Follow-up of the patient at regular intervals to monitor blood pressure and to reinforce the message about compliance to maintain blood pressure at the target level will maximise the points.

➤ Add a note to the repeat prescription with an appointment for a blood pressure check – this will save time and money on postage. Give a six-monthly appointment.

➤ Ensure the patients 'know their numbers' for both systolic and diastolic pressures and the importance of adhering to the pharmacological and non-pharmacological therapies.

➤ Remember, 10% of people with hypertension may have a secondary cause – this could that be the reason for poor control.

➤ Most patients will need at least two or sometimes more drugs to achieve good control. Simplifying drug dose regimens will improve concordance and achieve targets.

➤ Remember, with hypertension in pregnancy make a speedy referral to the hospital and do not read code hypertension.

➤ For white coat hypertension, enter read code (246M). Refer for 24-hour monitoring (8HR8) or ask the patient to undertake home reading. Enter in the register once the diagnosis confirmed.

➤ Exception reporting should be used with great care. The reasons for exception reporting must be clearly recorded in the notes, with a valid reason. Patients who are terminally ill or so frail that treating hypertension will make no significant difference to the quality or duration of life, where the patient exercises his or her right to 'informed dissent' and chooses not to have blood pressure treated and those who are on maximum tolerated medication can be exception reported.

➤ Ensuring influenza immunisation over the age of 65 years and one-off pneumococcal vaccination will score extra points.

Template GMS: Hypertension (V16)

Prompt	Code	Date	Coded subsets
Exception report: hypertension quality indicator	(9h3)		Except. hyperten. QI: Pt unsuit. (9h31) Except. hyperten. QI: inf. dis. (9h32)
Ethnic category – 2001 census	(9i)		*See ethnicity template, Chapter 17*
Monitoring	(662P)		
Hypertension resolved	(212K)		
Six month review	(662c)		
Annual review	(662d)		
O/E Weight	(22A)		
O/E Height	(229)		
Body Mass Index	(22K)		
WAIST CIRCUMFERENCE	(22N0)		
WCM DECLINE	(8IAf)		
IDEAL WEIGHT	(66CB)		
Smoking status			*See smoking status template, Chapter 25*
Alcohol consumption units/week	(136)		
Alcohol score (AUDIT C)	(9k17)		
Patient advised about alcohol	(8CAM)		
DIETARY ADVICE	(8CA4)		
HEALTH ED. – EXERCISE	(6798)		
LIFE STYLE COUNSELLING	(67H)		
Systolic BP	(2469)		(aim < 150/90)
Diastolic BP	(246A)		
BP refused (*I have never used this code*)	(8I3Y)		
Plasma random glucose	(44g0)		
Plasma fasting glucose	(44g1)		
FULL BLOOD COUNT	(424)		
TFT	(442J)		
REFERRAL FOR 24-HR BP	(8HR8)		
24-hr BP MONITOR	(662L)		
AVERAGE DAY SYSTOLIC	(246Y)		
AVERAGE DAY DIASTOLIC	(246X)		
AVERAGE NIGHT SYSTOLIC	(246b)		
AVERAGE NIGHT DIASTOLIC	(246a)		
STANDARD CHEST X-RAY	(535)		*Standard chest X-ray coded subsets same as in CHD template, Chapter 9*
Urine protein	(467)		Urine protein -ve (4672) Urine protein + (4674) Urine protein ++ (4675) Urine protein +++ (4676) Urine protein ++++ (4677)
Serum total cholesterol	(44P)		
Serum HDL cholesterol	(44P5)		

(continued)

Prompt	Code	Date	Coded subsets
Serum LDL cholesterol	(44P6)		
SERUM TRIGLYCERIDE	(44Q)		
SERUM CHOLESTEROL:HDL RATIO	(441F)		
LFT	(44D)		
CK	(44H4)		
Serum creatinine	(44J3)		
URINE ALBUMIN:CREATININE RATIO	(46TC)		
URINE MICROALBUMIN	(R1103)		
JBS SCORE	(662k)		JBS cardiovasc. risk < 10% in 10 yrs (662k) JBS cardiovasc. risk 10–20% in 10 yrs (662l) JBS cardiovasc. risk > 20–30% in 10 yrs (662m) JBS cardiovasc. risk > 30% in 10 yrs (662n) CVD risk assessment declined (90h9)
STATIN PROPHYLAXIS	(8B6A)		*Statin coded subsets same as in CHD template, Chapter 9*
12 LEAD ECG	(321B)		ECG requested (3211) ECG normal (3216) ECG abnormal (3217) ECG no LVH (3241) ECG LVH (3242)
Medication review	(8B3V)		
Hypertension monitoring	(662P)		
HYPERTENSION MONITORING 1st LETTER	(90I4)		
HYPERTENSION MONITORING 2nd LETTER	(90I5)		
HYPERTENSION MONITORING 3rd LETTER	(90I6)		
HYPERTENSION MONITORING TELEPHONE INVITE	(90I8)		
HYPERTENSION MONITORING VERBAL INVITE	(90I7)		
DNA HYPERENSION CLINIC	(9N4L)		
HYPERTENSION TREATMENT REFUSED	(8I3N)		
INFLUENZA VACCINATION	(65E)		*Influenza vaccination coded subsets same as in CHD template, Chapter 9*
PNEUMOCOCCAL VACCINATION	(6572)		*Pneumococcal vaccination coded subsets same as in CHD template, Chapter 9*

(Add the capitalised prompts to your template to maximise points and quality care)

Do something extra

➤ When treatment fails, check whether the patient is concurrently taking other medications or OTC items like NSAID. The use of recreational drugs such as cocaine, excess alcohol or even the 'liquorice allsorts' can cause treatment failure.

➤ Once the diagnosis is made, try to discontinue corticosteroids, combined oral contraceptive pills, NSAIDs and venlafaxine.

➤ Are you confident that the readings you are recording are really correct? Have you had your mercury sphygmomanometer calibrated – assuming your practice nurse still uses that. The same can be said of electronic machines.

➤ Buy some self-monitoring blood pressure devices and loan them to patients to carry out home measurements. They are relatively cheap and easy to use, and are useful for patients with white coat hypertension.

➤ Invest in an ECG machine. Carry out in-house ECGs.

➤ If yours is a teaching practice, get some audits done by the attached medical student – ACE initiation, U&E monitoring, statin prescribing. This will help your prescribing budget. (*An audit carried out in my practice showed that we were prescribing more ARBs than ACE for no clear reason.*)

References

1 Williams B. Systolic pressure is all that matters. *Lancet.* 2008; **371**: 2219–21.

2 Williams B, Poulter NR, Brown MJ, *et al*. British Hypertension Society Guidelines for management of hypertension: report of the fourth working party of the British Hypertension Society 2004 – BHS IV. *J Hum. Hypertens.* 2004; **18**: 139–85.

3 National Institute for Health and Clinical Excellence. *Hypertension: management of hypertension in adults in primary care: NICE clinical guideline 18.* London: NIHCE; 2004. www.nice.org.uk/guidance/CG018

4 World Health Organization. *The World Health Report 2001: reducing risks, promoting healthy life.* Geneva: World Health Organization; 2002.

5 National Institute for Health and Clinical Excellence. *Hypertension: management of hypertension in adults in primary care. NICE guideline CG34.* London: NIHCE; 2006. www.nice.org.uk/guidance/CG34

6 Lewington S, Clarke R, Qizilbash R, *et al*. Age-specific relevance of usual blood pressure to vascular mortality; a meta-analysis of individual data for one million adults in 61 prospective studies. *Lancet.* 2002; **360**: 1903–13.

7 Law MR, Morris JK, Wald NJ, *et al*. Use of blood pressure lowering drugs in the prevention of cardiovascular disease: meta-analysis of 147 randomised trials in the context of expectations from prospective epidemiological studies. *BMJ.* 2009; **338**: b1665.

8 Kearney PM, Whelton M, Reynolds K, *et al*. Global burden of hypertension: analysis of worldwide data. *Lancet.* 2005; **365**: 217–23.

9 Department of Health. *The Health Survey for England 2003. Summary of key findings.* London: Department of Health; 2003, p 8. Available at: www.dh.gov.uk/assetRoot/04/09/89/04098909.pdf (accessed 7 June 2006).

10 National Collaborating Centre for Women's and Children's Health. *Hypertension in pregnancy: the management of hypertensive disorders during pregnancy*. London: RCOG; 2010. Available at: www.nice.org.uk/CG107

11 Wood DA, Durrington PN, Poulter NR, *et al*. The joint British Societies recommendations on prevention of coronary heart disease in clinical practice. *Heart*. 1998; **80**(Suppl. 2): S1–29.

12 Warren RE, Marshall T, Padfield PL, *et al*. Variability of office, 24 hour ambulatory and self-monitored blood pressure measurements. *Br J Gen. Pract*. 2010; **60**: 675–80.

13 www.controllingbp.com

14 Sever P. New hypertension guidelines from the National Institute for Health and Clinical Excellence and the British Hypertension Society. *J Renin. Angiotensin Aldosterone Syst*. 2006; **7**: 61–3.

Useful reading

➤ www.bma.org.uk/ap.nsf/Content/QualityOutcomes
➤ British Hypertension Society guidelines for hypertension management 2004 (BHS-IV) summary. *BMJ*. 2004; **328**: 634–40.

Useful organisations

➤ British Hypertension Society: www.bhsoc.org.uk
➤ Blood Pressure Association: www.bpassoc.org.uk

Websites on blood pressure monitors and measurement techniques

➤ www.bhsoc.org/blood_pressure_list.stm
➤ www.bhsoc.org/how_to_measure_blood_pressure.stm

CHAPTER 20

Hypothyroidism

The onset of hypothyroidism is often insidious. The diagnosis of hypothyroidism relies on laboratory testing because the symptoms are non-specific and multi-systemic.

In addition to clinical examination, the diagnosis is confirmed with thyroid function tests. Generally, a rise in thyroid-stimulating hormone (TSH) with a low level of T4 (free thyroxine), low level of T3 (triiodothyronin) gives the earliest guide to the onset of hypothyroidism.

Prevalence

Prevalence of newly diagnosed overt hypothyroidism is 3–4 per 1000 and the probability of developing hypothyroidism increases with advancing age,[1] reaching 14 per 1000 in women aged between 75 and 80. Hypothyroidism has a tendency to occur in clusters in families, especially in female relatives.

Why included in QOF

➤ Hypothyroidism is a relatively common condition and can be easily managed in the primary care sector.
➤ The purpose of this indicator in the QOF is about quality improvement and improved patient care – making sure of the compliance with medication.
➤ The restoration and maintenance of TSH within the reference range can be undertaken in the primary care setting.
➤ The clinical improvement is fairly rapid with the right dose, similar to monitoring blood pressure and reaching a target value.
➤ Primary care is ideally placed to undertake case finding in women over 50 years of age or those with non-specific symptoms.
➤ Treatment is generally life-long and there are no serious drug side-effects.
➤ GPs know their patients well and can carry out regular monitoring of patients who are at high risk of hypothyroidism, for example, those who have had previous thyroid surgery and radioactive iodine treatment.

The facts

➤ Hypothyroidism is associated with hyperlipidaemia, particularly when the TSH level is greater than 10 mU/L.
➤ It is less commonly associated with anaemia, macrocytosis, hyperprolactinaemia and raised lactate dehydrogenase.
➤ In severe cases patients present with myxoedema coma, which is a life-threatening emergency.
➤ Few patients appear to be sensitive to different thyroxine preparations and may benefit getting the drug from the same manufacturer (*I have two such patients*).

QOF: hypothyroidism indicators

Indicators and points: total points 7

THYROID1

The practice can produce a register of patients with hypothyroidism.

Points 1

The register makes it possible for easy call and recall of patients and to ensure correct dose and compliance of the medication.

The register is a prerequisite for the organisation of good primary care service delivery to this group of patients.

A register will help you run an audit of the provision of care to these patients.

THYROID2

The percentage of patients with hypothyroidism with thyroid function tests recorded in the previous 15 months.

Points 6   **Payment stages 40–90%**

Serum TSH has a sensitivity of 89–95% and specificity of 90–96% for overt thyroid dysfunction.

Usually TSH alone is sufficient for monitoring replacement therapy. A full TFT profile may be necessary if non-compliance is suspected. In hypothyroidism secondary to deficiency of TSH, measurement of free T4 is necessary to guide replacement.

Dose changes of 25–50 μg should be made based on TSH levels measured two to three months after starting the treatment.

Maximising quality points

➤ Use the read codes:
— Acquired hypothyroidism (C04)
— Hypothyroidism (C04-3)
— Congenital hypothyroidism (C03).
➤ Patients taking thyroxine should have a diagnosis of hypothyroidism. A computer search of patients on thyroxine will identify the diagnosed patients in no time.

➤ The combination of a normal T4 and raised TSH is known as subclinical hypothyrodism. Do not enter the read code at this stage. Repeat the TFT in two to three months' time. If it persists, measure the (TPO) thyroid peroxidase antibodies. Enter the read code once the antibodies are positive.

➤ Check patients who have had radioiodine and thyroid surgery. Both can cause thyroid destruction leading to hypothyroidism.

➤ Amiodarone, lithium, alpha-interferon and anti-thyroid drugs can all cause hypothyrodism. Enter an alert message on these patients with a reminder note to check TFT every 12 months. Once confirmed biochemically, they must be added on the disease register.

➤ Carry out annual TFT screening of patients with Down's and Turner's syndromes due to increased association with hypothyroidism.

➤ Patients with type 1 diabetes should have a TFT annually. In type 2 diabetes, the recommendation is to check at the time of diagnosis, with no need to repeat regularly.

➤ Remember pregnant patients with hypothyroidism – check TFT every three months and adjust the dose. Raised TSH in the mother is associated with a slightly lower mean IQ and an increased risk of mental handicap in the child.

➤ Bear in mind iodine deficiency. This is common worldwide but absent in the UK. If your practice is registering people from third world countries, it is good clinical practice to check TFT at the time of the new patient health check.

➤ Patients with hypopituitarism and hypothalamic disease will be under the secondary care system. Make sure it is read coded if the specialist has confirmed hypothyroidism. Delegate the job of read coding hospital letters to one trained member of your staff.

➤ Ensuring influenza immunisation to those over 65 will earn extra points.

Template GMS: Hypothyroid (V16)

Prompt	Code	Date	Coded subsets
Exception report: hypothyroid quality indicator	(9h7)		Except. thyroid QI: Pt uns. (9h71) Except. thyroid QI: inf. dis. (9h72)
Ethnic category – 2001 census	(9i)		See ethnicity template, Chapter 17
O/E WEIGHT	(22A)		
O/E HEIGHT	(229)		
BODY MASS INDEX	(22K)		
WAIST IN CM	(22N0)		
SMOKING STATUS			See smoking status template, Chapter 25
ALCOHOL CONSUMPTION			See Alcohol, Chapter 27
PATIENT ADVISED REG. DIET	(8CA4)		
PATIENT ADVISED REG. EXERCISE	(8CA5)		
PATIENT ADVISED ABOUT ALCOHOL	(8CAM)		
WEIGHT PROGRAMME	(8HHH)		
Thyroid function test	(442J)		TFT normal (442H) TFT abnormal (442I)
Serum T3 level	(4424)		

(continued)

Prompt	Code	Date	Coded subsets
Serum T4 level	(4426)		
Serum TSH level normal	(442A0)		30 min. TSH level (442P) 60 min. TSH level (442Q) 90 min. TSH level (442R) 120 min. TSH level (442S) 150 min. TSH level (442T) Serum TSH level (442W)
T3 uptake test	(442D)		T3 uptake test normal (442D0) T3 uptake test abnormal (442D1)
Medication review done	(8B3V)		
FBC	(424)		
SERUM FERRITIN	(42R4)		
SERUM B12	(42T)		
CHOLESTEROL	(44PJ)		
HYPOTHYROID MONITORING 1st LETTER	(90j0)		
HYPOTHYROID MONITORING 2nd LETTER	(90j1)		
HYPOTHYROID MONITORING 3rd LETTER	(90j2)		
HYPOTHYROID VERBAL INVITE	(90j3)		
HYPOTHYROID TELEPHONE INVITE	(90j4)		
INFLUENZA VACCINATION	(65E)		Influenza vaccination coded subsets same as in CHD template, Chapter 9
PNEUMOCOCCAL VACCINATION	(6572)		Pneumococcal vaccination coded subsets same as in CHD template, Chapter 9

(Add the capitalised prompts to your template to maximise points and quality care)

Do something extra

➤ As part of health promotion, check height, weight, BMI and waist circumference. Ask history of smoking and alcohol intake and give advice accordingly.
➤ Patients on replacement therapy are exempt from prescription charges. Once diagnosed, fill the exemption form.

Reference

1 Tunbridge WMG, Evered DC, Hall R, et al. The spectrum of thyroid disease in the community: the Wickham Survey. *Clin. Endocrinol.* 1977; 7: 481–93.

Useful reading

➤ British Thyroid Association: www.british-thyroid-association.org
➤ Society for Endocrinology: www.endocrinology.org/
➤ UK guidelines for the use of thyroid function tests: www.british-thyroid-association.org/info-for-patients/Docs/TFT_guideline_final_version_July_2006.pdf

CHAPTER 21

Learning disability

Definition

Learning disability (LD), sometimes called a learning disorder or learning difficulty, is defined in *Valuing People*[1] and *The Same as You*[2] as a disability which started before adulthood (18 years) and with the presence of:
➤ a reduced ability to cope independently
➤ a significantly reduced ability to understand new or complex information and to learn new skills.

The definition does not include all those people who have a LD such as dyslexia.

The presence of an IQ below 70 should not be used in deciding whether someone has LD.

Prevalence

There are over 1.5 million people with LD in the UK, and the number is growing by around 3% every year. It is well known that people with LD find it harder to understand, communicate and learn.

The author of one study concluded that if LD was identified by research criteria there were no differences in gender, but if identified by general education teachers and/or special education teachers, there were twice as many boys identified than girls.[3]

Why included in QOF

➤ People with LD receive a poorer standard of healthcare than the rest of the population.[4] It is hoped that its inclusion in the QOF will provide a quality healthcare service to these patients
➤ LD patients have poorer health outcomes than the rest of the population, being at higher risk of epilepsy, diabetes and heart disease. Primary care physicians are best placed to screen, diagnose and provide necessary treatment.

➤ With the right support and intervention, and coordinating the execution of the intervention with parents, teachers and social workers, GPs can help people with LD to succeed in school and go on to be successful later in life.

➤ People with LD are 58 times more likely to die before their 50th birthday.[5] Providing structured healthcare in a primary care setting can prolong their life.

➤ People with LD are discriminated against in the NHS. A small financial incentive could stop that. After a full assessment, the GP can determine what is needed – for example, special equipment (talking calculators, books on tape, text-to-speech and speech-to-text programmes).

➤ Over the past three decades, almost all the long-stay NHS beds for people with LD have closed and all these people are now living in the community and cared for by their GP.

➤ LD people are treated with neglect or lack of dignity, which can result in various psychological and emotional problems. QOF inclusion can help identifying these people. GPs are best placed to decide whether an assessment by a clinical psychologists or neuropsychologists could be useful.

The facts

➤ There is a lack of training and specific guidelines among healthcare professionals to meet the needs of those with LD.

➤ Seventy-five per cent of GPs have received no training to help them treat people with a LD.

➤ Mencap has recently launched a 'Getting it right' campaign, calling on health authorities to sign up to a charter which has nine goals to ensure that LD people have access to good-quality healthcare.

➤ Annual health checks can pick up problems before they worsen.

➤ Children with LD are often socially excluded, and eight out of 10 LD children are bullied.

➤ One in two families with a LD child live in poverty.

➤ One in three people with LD take part in some form of education or training.

➤ Fifty-eight thousand people with LD are supported by day-care services.

QOF: learning disability indicators

Indicators and points: total points 4

LD1

The practice can produce a register of patients aged 18 years and over with learning disabilities.

Points 4

The creation of a register is important to make sure that all LD people have access to good-quality healthcare. Diagnosis has to be correct before putting them on the register.

A person should display following criteria before being diagnosed as LD:

➤ intellectual impairment
➤ social dysfunction
➤ both.

IQ score is one way to diagnose and categorise LD into mild, moderate, severe or profound.

You may have children on your list with challenging behaviour – could they have LD? Have you, on your list, any patient with social dysfunction – dependant on their parents, needing help with washing, dressing and feeding. Add them to your register. A child with writing disability or dysgraphia brought in by his or her mum or reported by the health visitor or school nurse should be on the register.

Maximise quality points

➤ Do a computer search of patients with Down's syndrome and Fragile X syndrome.
➤ Learning disabilities often run in the family – check if the family members are registered with you.
➤ Problems during birth, for example, low birth weight, premature or prolonged labour, foetal exposure to alcohol or drugs may result in LD. Check the notes of mothers with alcohol or drug abuse problems.
➤ Cerebral palsy is not a LD but many people with cerebral palsy also have a LD. Add them to the register.
➤ Thirty per cent of people with a LD have epilepsy – make sure they are on both the registers.
➤ Fifty per cent of people with autism may have a LD. Check and put them on the register.
➤ William's syndrome – enter them on the register.
➤ Asperger's syndrome – a form of autism – if any patient is read coded with Asperger's syndrome, check whether they have LD.
➤ Ring the social worker attached to the practice – they may have patients on their list cared for in the community.
➤ Run a computer search of patients asking for pads for urinary or faecal incontinence. Have they got LD?

Template GMS: Learning disabilities (V16)

Prompt	Code	Date	Coded subsets
On LD register	918e		
LD annual check	9HB5		
LD action plan review	9HB2		
Ethnic category – 2001 census	(9i)		*See ethnicity template, Chapter 17*
O/E WEIGHT	(22A)		
O/E HEIGHT	(229)		
BODY MASS INDEX	(22K)		
WAIST IN CM	(22N0)		

(continued)

Prompt	Code	Date	Coded subsets
WCM DECLINE	(8IAf)		
SYSTOLIC BP	(2469)		
DIASTOLIC BP	(246A)		
O/E PULSE RATE	(242)		
SMOKING STATUS			*See smoking template, Chapter 25*
ALCOHOL CONSUMPTION			*See Alcohol, Chapter 27*
H/O RECREATIONAL DRUGS	(146E)		
DRUG DEPENDENCE	(E24)		
SUSPECTED DRUG ABUSE	(1J1)		
REFER TO DRUG ABUSE COUNSELLOR	(8H7x)		
PATIENT ADVISED REG. DIET	(8CA4)		
PATIENT ADVISED REG. EXERCISE	(8CA5)		
PATIENT ADVISED ABOUT ALCOHOL	(8CAM)		
FBC	(424)		
TFT	(442J)		
PLASMA RANDOM GLUCOSE	(44g0)		
URINE PROTEIN TEST – TRACE	(4673)		*Urine protein test coded subsets same as in diabetes template, Chapter 15*
Incontinence of urine	(1A23)		
Incontinent of faeces	(19E3)		
Normal vision	(668A)		
Wears glasses	(22EG)		
Hearing normal	(1C11)		
Feet examination	(66AE)		
Health education Breasts	(6795)		
Health education Testes	(679B)		
Chronic disease	(661)		
General contraception	(611)		
Disability	(13VC)		
Action plan completed	(9HB4)		
Referrals	(8HHP)		
EXCLUDED LD	(9hL0)		
INFORMED DISSENT			
EXCLUDED LD	(9hL1)		
PATIENT UNSUITABLE			
LD ANNUAL HEALTH CHECK INVITATION 1st LETTER	(9mA20)		
LD ANNUAL HEALTH CHECK INVITATION 2nd LETTER	(9mA21)		
LD ANNUAL HEALTH CHECK INVITATION 3rd LETTER	(9mA22)		

(Add the capitalised prompts to your template to maximise points and quality care)

Do something extra

➤ Make sure you have good access to your premises and make reasonable adjustments if necessary.

➤ Allow more consultation time. Give a double appointment – 20-minute consultation time.

➤ Observe the attitudes of your reception staff towards learning disability patients and address if necessary.

➤ Involve the family members and carers in decisions about treatment.

➤ School psychologists can coordinate the execution of the intervention with teachers and parents. Involve them if necessary.

➤ Identify the gaps in your own learning needs, understand mental capacity laws and attend a training course. (*Make sure your practice nurse and healthcare assistant are trained too.*)

References

1 Department of Health. *Valuing People: a new strategy for learning disability in the 21st century*. Cm. 5086. London: Department of Health; 2001. www.publications.doh.gov.uk/learningdisabilities/access/

2 Scottish Executive. *The Same as You? A review of services for people with learning disabilities*. Edinburgh: Scottish Executive; 2000. www.scld.org.uk/information/employment/publication/policy

3 Bandian NA. Reading disability defined as a discrepancy between listening and reading comprehension. A longitudinal study of stability, gender differences and prevalence. *Journal of Learning Disabilities*. 1999; **32**(2): 138–48.

4 ICM Research surveyed a sample of 1084 doctors and nurses online between 25 May and 7 June 2010.

5 Hollins S, Attard MT, von Fraunhofer N, *et al.* Mortality in people with learning disability: risks, causes and death certification findings in London. *Developmental Medicine and Child Neurology*. 1998; **40**: 50–6.

CHAPTER 22

Mental health

Mental health quality indicators cover schizophrenia, bipolar disorders and other psychoses. Schizophrenia is strongly affected by many different genes that interact with each other and the environment. In psychosis there is a loss of contact with reality as a result of delusional beliefs and/or hallucinations. Mood variability is the main feature of bipolar disorder, with clear-cut manic and depressive episodes.

Prevalence

The lifetime risk of schizophrenia and bipolar disorder is 0.8%. The mean age of onset of schizophrenia is 23 years in males and 26 years in females, early twenties in bipolar and late twenties in psychotic disorders. Schizophrenia affects both sexes equally, but psychosis is more common in women than men by 2:1.

Why included in QOF

➤ Approximately 25% of patients with psychotic illness receive most or all of their care with their GPs. Patients with schizophrenia are big users of primary care consultations. With this level of contact, GPs are well placed to provide care and support.

➤ The WHO has estimated that bipolar disorder is the fourth most important cause of disability in 15–45-year-olds.

➤ Diabetes, CVD and respiratory illness are all significantly more common in schizophrenia. Overall morbidity for people with schizophrenia is much higher than average, with life expectancy shortened by about 10%. Its inclusion in the QOF encourages GPs to provide a systematic health assessment.

➤ Schizophrenia has an insidious onset. Early detection of the first episode is important because the longer the duration of undiagnosed psychosis, the greater the likelihood of a slower recovery. GPs are well placed to make early detection of the first episode.

➤ Schizophrenia often seems to follow a relapsing and remitting course. Eighty per cent of patients suffer a relapse. GPs are well placed to detect a relapse. Early intervention can return the patient to a good level of functioning.

➤ Lifetime risk of suicide is around 5% in schizophrenia, the risk being highest in the first five years after the onset of illness. Early intervention by the GP can improve the prognosis.

➤ Patients should remain on an anti-psychotic medication for at least two years following an acute psychosis. Providing support and compliance can be best delivered by a working partnership between the GP, patient and carer.

The facts

➤ Bipolar disorder is strongly heritable.

➤ An average GP list will contain about 20–40 patients with bipolar disorder.

➤ Maternal drug use, alcohol use, winter birth, urban birth (three times higher risk in a large town compared with a rural village), life events, lower social class, smoking cannabis and particular migrant groups (African-Caribbean in the UK) are the risk factors for schizophrenia.

➤ Cannabis is a modest risk factor for schizophrenia in vulnerable individuals.

➤ Bipolar disorder runs a remitting and relapsing course in 90% of patients. The average annual risk of relapse after one episode is about 20%.

➤ The awareness of bipolar disorder has increased following media interest in the celebrity sufferer Stephen Fry.

➤ Over time, it is the depressive episodes that cause most disability for most patients.

➤ Lithium is the first line drug treatment of choice in type 1 bipolar dosorder,[1] and remains superior to valproate for relapse prevention.[2]

➤ Atypical anti-psychotics appear to be well tolerated in schizophrenia.[3] They appear to have fewer extra-pyramidal side-effects but possibly more metabolic side-effects such as weight gain and diabetes.

QOF: mental health indicators

Indicators and points: total points: 39

Records

MN8

The practice can produce a register of people with schizophrenia, bipolar disorders and other psychoses.

Points 4

The quality indicators cannot be delivered unless a register is kept. Identifying patients in need of mental healthcare, assessing their needs and proactively planning their care can only be possible if a proper register is maintained.

Bipolar disorder is often misdiagnosed. Think of bipolar disorder in a patient with recurrent episodes of depressive disorder. Use reliable diagnostic criteria such as DSM-IV to make a proper diagnosis. Sub-typing bipolar on the basis of history can be difficult. For type 1, the patient must have experienced an episode that met criteria for mania lasting at least seven days or led to hospital admission. For type 2, the patient must have experienced an episode that met the criteria for hypomania which lasted at least four days.

Characteristic features of schizophrenia are:
➤ disorganised speech
➤ flattened affect, apathy
➤ hallucinations (mostly auditory – running commentary or voices talking)
➤ delusions (bizarre)
➤ catatonic behaviour.

Characteristic features of mania are:
➤ elevated mood
➤ increased energy
➤ reduced attention
➤ loss of social inhibition – increased spending, inappropriate sexual encounters.

Characteristic features of psychotic depression are:
➤ weight loss
➤ poor sleep
➤ loss of energy
➤ reduced concentration
➤ reduced libido
➤ depressed mood
➤ anhedonia
➤ increased guilt
➤ suicidal thoughts
➤ hallucinations – auditory, olfactory, visual
➤ delusions (illness, guilt).

Ongoing management

MH9

The percentage of patients with schizophrenia, bipolar disorder and other psychosis with a review recorded in the preceding 15 months. In the review there should be evidence that the patient has been offered routine health promotion and prevention advice appropriate to their age, gender and health status.

Points 23   **Payment stages 40–90%**

➤ Forty-six per cent of people with bipolar disorder and 61% of people with schizophrenia smoke, compared with 33% of the general population. Smoking cessation advice or a referral to a specialist smoking cessation clinic, if available, should be offered. Respiratory illnesses, CHD and premature deaths are more common in people with mental illness.

➤ Obesity is common in patients with schizophrenia, particularly women. Nutritional assessment and weight loss interventions should be provided at the time of review. Referral to a health trainer, if available in your area, for dietary advice on avoiding high calorie food is recommended.

➤ Exercise programmes can be effective in patients with mental illness. They may need a higher level of persuasion to engage in any exercise programme. Encouraging, offering free exercise on prescription, a free swimming pass and realistic goal setting can work.

➤ Alcohol and drug misuse are common. Enquire and give advice regarding illicit drug use. Cannabis is a risk factor for schizophrenia. Give advice.

➤ Patients with bipolar disorder should be advised not to drive when acutely unwell and to inform the DVLA.

MH4

The percentage of patients on lithium therapy with a record of serum creatinine and TSH in the preceding 15 months.

Points 1   **Payment stages 40–90%**

Achieving this one point is easy. A simple blood test is all that is needed.

MH5

The percentage of patients on lithium therapy with a record of lithium levels in the therapeutic range within the previous six months.

Points 2   **Payment stages 40–90%**

This indicator has been introduced because monitoring of lithium is important due to narrow therapeutic range of lithium. Whatever the source of lithium initiation, it remains your responsibility to make sure that the blood level is in the therapeutic range. It does not necessarily mean that the blood test has to be done by the GP.

NICE guidance is as follows:

➤ check serum lithium level every three months

➤ monitor weight, especially with rapid weight gain

➤ monitor older patients carefully for symptoms of lithium toxicity.

MH6

The percentage of patients on the register who have a comprehensive care plan documented in the records agreed between individuals, their family and/or carers as appropriate.

Points 6   **Payment stages 25–50%**

The involvement of the patient's family and good communication between family members decreases the relapse rates and the admission rates.

The choice of medication is jointly made with the patient, involving the carer, side-effect profile, gender and age.

Monitoring of early warning signs, providing education about the illness and promoting regular patterns of eating and sleeping form part of the care plan involving the patient's family and/or carer.

MH7

The percentage of patients with schizophrenia, bipolar affective disorder and other psychoses who do not attend the practice for their annual review who are identified and followed up by the practice team within 14 days of non-attendance.

Points 3   **Payment stages 40–90%**

Just get them in – you have no choice.

Maximising quality points

This is one of the easiest indicators to achieve, with 39 points attached to it, with a positive approach to the illness, early detection and intervention, checking the patient's compliance to the prescribed medication, team work with patient, carer and other healthcare workers and attention to the patient's unmet needs.

➤ There are two different ways by which patients are included in the mental health QOF box. Issuing a lithium prescription in the six months before 1 April each year and any patient with a read code of psychosis added at any time in the past.

The codes which will trigger a mental health review are:
— E10–E10z.
— E110–E110z
— E111–E111z
— E114–E114z
— E11y–E11yz
— E11z–E11zz
— E13–E13z
— E2122
— Eu30–Eu30z.

➤ The read code 9H7, which has been removed from the mental illness register, no longer works.

➤ The following codes are not mental health codes:
— bereavement (13Hc)
— grief reaction (E2900)
— depressed mood (1BT).

➤ You may have patients who have recovered and no longer need a mental health review. There is no code that may be entered which would remove these patients from the register. You have an option of just doing the mental health review even if it is not needed – see the patients opportunistically or invite them. You can add the code mental health: patient unsuitable 9h91 and this has to be repeated next year. You can change the old codes to H/O psychosis (146H), H/O manic depression (146D), H/O schizophrenia (1464). If you are changing the codes, add a note as to why, and you may have to explain at the time of the QOF visit.

➤ Height, weight, BMI, blood pressure, smoking, alcohol, dietary and exercise advice must be given at every review. This will help achieve obesity, smoking and alcohol DES points.

➤ While checking the lithium level, do other bloods like TFT, cholesterol, U&E and blood sugar. You may pick up some undiagnosed diabetics, CKD3 or hypothyroid patients.

➤ Read code DNA and invite within 14 days of DNA. This should be documented. Invitation can be given by phone or in writing.

➤ The details of the carer, care worker, mental health worker and their phone numbers must be recorded. This is a piece of evidence for the MH6 indicator.

➤ If, unfortunately, you have no patient taking lithium, the prevalence within that indicator is zero and you lose all the points under that indicator. Beg, borrow or steal a patient who is on lithium!

Template GMS: Mental health (V16)

Prompt	Code	Date	Coded subsets
Exception report: mental health quality indicator	(9h9)		Except. M.H. QI: Pt unsuit. (9h91) Except. M.H. QI: inf. dis. (9h92)
Ethnic category – 2001 census	(9i)		See ethnicity template Chapter 17
Mental health review	(6A6)		
DNA mental health review	(9N4t)		
O/E weight	(22A)		
O/E height	(229)		
BMI	(22K)		
SMOKING STATUS			See smoking template, Chapter 25
ALCOHOL UNITS/WEEK	(136)		
ALCOHOL SCORE AUDIT C	(9k17)		See Alcohol, Chapter 27
PATIENT ADVISED ABOUT ALCOHOL	(8CAM)		
PATIENT ADVISED REG. DIET	(8CA4)		
PATIENT ADVISED REG. EXERCISE	(8CA5)		
LIFE STYLE COUNSELLING	(67H)		
Mental health medication review	(8BM0)		
Lithium stopped	(665B)		
Psych., schiz. + bip. aff. dis. res.	(212T)		
Standard CPA level	(8CG4)		Enhanced CPA level (8CG3) Standard CPA level (8CG4)
Mental health personal health plan	(8CR7)		
Psych. care plan	(8CM2)		
Systolic blood pressure	(2469)		
Diastolic blood pressure	(246A)		
Mini mental exam.	(388m)		
Mini mental score	(388v)		
Serum TSH level normal	(442A0)		See TSH coded subsets in hypothyroidism template, Chapter 20

(continued)

Prompt	Code	Date	Coded subsets
Serum creatinine	(44J3)		
Lithium level therapeutic	(44W80)		Serum lithium level (44W8) Lithium level ther. (44W80) Lithium level high – toxic (44W81) Lithium level low (44W82) Lithium stopped (665B)
On injectable phenothiazine	(6656)		
TOTAL CHOLESTEROL	(44PJ)		
SERUM LDL	(44P6)		
SERUM HDL	(44P5)		
SERUM CHOLESTEROL:HDL RATIO	(44PG)		
JBS CARDIOVASCULAR RISK < 10%	(662k)		*JBS coded subsets same as in hypertension template, Chapter 19*
PLASMA RANDOM GLUCOSE	(44g0)		
PLASMA FASTING GLUCOSE	(44g1)		
Suicide risk	(1BD4)		High suicide risk (1BD5) Moderate suicide risk (1BD6) Low suicide risk (1BD7)
Suicide attempt	(TK)		
[X]Intentional self-harm	(V2)		
Patient's condition worsened	(2127)		Patient's condition improved (2126) Patient's condition worsened (2127) Patient's condition the same (2128)
Psychiatric referral	(8H49)		
Refer mental health worker	(8H7A)		
Other referral	(8H7)		Voluntary social agency (8GC) Day centre care (8GE6) Refer to social worker (8H75) Refer to psychologist (8H7T) Refer to other health worker (8H7Z)
Carer's details	(9180)		Care from relatives (8GEA) Care from friends (8GEB) Other social care NOS (8GEZ) [V]No able carer in household (ZV604)
F/H SCHIZOPHRENIA	(EU20)		
F/H BIPOLAR AFF. DIS.	(1287-1)		
Housing dependency scale	(13F)		Independent housing, not alone (13F1) Lives alone – help available (13F2) Lives alone – no help available (13F3) Warden attended (13F4) Part III accommodation (13F5) Nursing/other home (13F6) Residential institution (13F7) Hospital patient (13F8) Living in hostel (13F9) Living in B&B (13FA) Living in lodgings (13FB)

(continued)

Prompt	Code	Date	Coded subsets
			Living in bedsitter (13FC)
			Rehoused (13FE)
			Housing problems – eviction (13FF)
			Squatter (13FG)
			Lives with relatives (13FH)
			Planning to move (13F1)
			Living rough (13FL)
			Housed (13FN)
			Long stay hospital inpatient (13FS)
			Lives in old peoples' home (13FT)
			Housing NOS (13FZ)
Work status	(13J)		Unemployed (13J5)
			Retired (13J5)
			Unfit for work (13JJ)
			Full time employment (13JA)
MENTAL HEALTH MONITORING 1st LETTER	(90I0)		
MENTAL HEALTH MONITORING 2nd LETTER	(90I1)		
MENTAL HEALTH MONITORING 3rd LETTER	(90I2)		
MENTAL HEALTH MONITORING VERBAL INVITE	(90I3)		
MENTAL HEALTH MONITORING TELEPHONE INVITE	(90I4)		
MH review due	(6A6)		
INFLUENZA VACCINATION	(65E)		Influenza vaccination coded subsets same as in CHD template, Chapter 9
PNEUMOCOCCAL VACCINATION	(6572)		Pneumococcal vaccination coded subsets same as in CHD template, Chapter 9

(Add the capitalised prompts to your template to maximise points and quality care)

Do something extra

➤ Refer the patient with bipolar disorder to structured psychotherapy – group psycho education, cognitive behavioural therapy (CBT), family focussed therapy. NICE recommends that structured psychotherapy should be offered to patients who have depressive symptoms after an acute episode.

➤ Advise patients to take precautions against unplanned pregnancy and to avoid valproate if possible.

➤ Do not prescribe anti-depressants for patients with a recently unstable mood or a past history of anti-depressant-induced mood stabilisation

➤ Anti-depressants should be discontinued early after remission except in unipolar disorder, where anti-depressants should be continued for six months.

➤ Help patients claim all the benefits they are entitled for while never abandoning their hope of eventual return to work.

References

1 National Collaborating Centre for Mental Health. *Bipolar Disorder. The management of bipolar disorder in adults, children and young people in primary and secondary care.* 2005. www.nice.org/uk/page.aspx?0=278260

2 Geddes JR, Goodwin GM, Rendell J, *et al*. Lithium plus valproate combination therapy versus monotherapy for relapse prevention in bipolar 1 disorder (BALANCE); a randomised open-label trial. *Lancet.* 2010; **375**(9712): 385–95.

3 Liberman JA, Stroup TS, McEvoy JP, *et al*. Effectiveness of antipsychotic drugs in patients with chronic schizophrenia. *N. Engl J Med.* 2005; **353**: 1209–23.

Useful reading

➤ National Institute for Health and Clinical Excellence. *Schizophrenia: core interventions in the treatment and management of schizophrenia in primary and secondary care: NICE guideline CG1.* London: NHICE; 2002. www.nice.org.uk/guidance/GC1

➤ National Institute for Health and Clinical Excellence. *The Management of Bipolar Disorder in Adults, Children and Adolescents, in Primary and Secondary Care: NICE guideline CG38.* London: NHICE; 2006. www.nice.org.uk/guidance/GC38

➤ NHS choices: www.nhs.uk/Conditions/Bipolar-disorder/.../Introduction.aspx

➤ The British Association for Psychopharmacology guideline: www.bap.org.uk/pdfs/18062009_BAP_bipolar_disorder_guidelines_PR.pdf

CHAPTER 23

Obesity

Obesity continues to be a growing problem. It is a risk factor for many serious diseases. Some patients see their GP specifically for advice on their weight, some may be receiving treatment for a medical condition caused by obesity, for example, coronary heart disease, osteoarthritis of weight-bearing joints, diabetes, while others attend with depression or psychological problems caused by obesity.

Prevalence

The prevalence of obese and overweight adults in England has trebled in the past 25 years. In 2004, almost 24 million – two-thirds of adults – were either obese or overweight.[1] In 2008 in England, 57% of women and 66% of men had a BMI > 25 kg/m², and within this 25% of women and 24% of men had a BMI > 30 kg/m².[2]

Why included in QOF

➤ The life expectancy of obese patients is shortened by an average of around seven years – more if the obesity starts early in life or the condition is severe.[3]

➤ Obesity is more harmful to health than drinking, smoking or poverty.[4]

➤ The WHO predicts that by 2015, 700 million people globally will have a BMI of 30 kg/m² or greater.

➤ A typical GP practice with a list size of 6000 patients will have around 1500 adult patients who are obese. As the number of people who are obese increases alongside the ageing population, primary care will encounter more cases of elderly patients who are obese.[5]

➤ Some medications can induce weight gain: insulin, anti-psychotics, anti-depressants, corticosteroids, alpha-blockers, oral hypoglycaemics, anti-convulsants and anti-histamines. GPs are well aware of patients taking these medications. The inclusion of obesity in the QOF means paying special attention to these patients and providing early dietetic management.

➤ Obesity in pregnancy is as harmful as smoking. GPs involved with providing pre-, ante- and post-natal care along with the midwife are best placed to advise women to achieve a healthy weight before becoming pregnant and maintaining a healthy weight during and after pregnancy.

➤ With an ever-increasing problem, there is an increasing physical and psychological cost to the patient, not forgetting the financial cost to the NHS. Primary care is best placed to make a real impact on prevention, early diagnosis and appropriate management helping the patient and the NHS.

➤ Obese patients are at increased risk of hypertension, diabetes, dyslipidaemia, obstructive sleep apnoea, depression and other mental health problems. GPs are well placed to screen for obesity-related co-morbidities.

➤ Even a brief intervention regarding obesity during any consultation goes a long way. Such opportunistic management is only possible in primary care.

➤ GPs are ideally placed to assess whether a patient has any motivation to lose weight and any past history of weight loss attempts, successful or otherwise, including diets or drugs. The inclusion of obesity in the QOF means that GPs are able to decide whether the patient's expectations are realistic and whether they are really motivated. Such patients can then be directed to appropriate professionals – health trainers, dieticians or counsellors.

➤ Primary care is able to obtain a detailed history of the physical activity of the patient, both routine daily activity and any committed sport time, and reasons for sedentary behaviour. These patients can then be referred to appropriate primary care professionals.

➤ Modest weight loss of only 5–10% can result in significant benefits to health.[6] GPs and their teams are in a position to make a real impact on the treatment of obesity and overweight people.

➤ Spending an extra five minutes with these obese patients and calculating the caloric requirement (not difficult to do), can be easily done in the primary care. Teach your practice nurse how to do this.*

➤ NICE endorses the use of orlistat in patients aged between 18 and 75 years with a BMI of > 30 kg/m^2 or > 28 kg/m^2 with co-morbidities. It is the first evidence-based medicine approved for 'OTC' use. Providing orlistat through GPs and regular monitoring of weight by the practice nurse can result in weight loss and improvement in health risk.

➤ If your practice includes a population of South Asian origin, educational material or even the use of interpreters may be useful. QOF inclusion may help GPs to organise their resources towards these patients.

---

* How to calculate calorific requirement: modified Harris Benedict equation

(Takes five minutes of nurse's time **but** benefits outweigh the time input.)

BMR ♂ = 66 + (13.7 x weight in kg) + (5 x height in cm) − (6.8 x age)

BMR ♀ = 655 + (9.6 x weight in kg) + (1.8 x height in cm) − (4.7 x age)

Then multiply by a physical activity factor:
- Sedentary = BMR x 1.2
- Light activity (1–3 days/week) = BMR x 1.375
- Moderate activity (3–5 days/week) = BMR x 1.55
- Vigorous activity (6–7 days a week) = BMR x 1.725
- Extreme activity = BMR x 1.9

Subtract 500–600 calories from the calorific requirement to create a personal regime that will induce weight loss at around 1–2 lb per week.

Or use the online calculator at www.shapeup.org/interactive/rmr1.php

---

The facts

➤ Cardiovascular disease. There is a 40% increased risk of death from cardiovascular disease for every 5 kg/m^2 increase in BMI above 25 kg/m^2.[2]

➤ Obesity increases the risk of type 2 diabetes, stroke, osteoarthritis, post-menopausal breast cancer, gall bladder disease and obstructive sleep apnoea.

➤ Increased risk of pre-eclampsia, gestational diabetes and miscarriage.

➤ Severely obese men and women are more likely to suffer from cancer.[7]

➤ Depression is more common in obese and overweight people because of poor body image, a sense of failure and social stigma.

➤ Obesity affects sexual behaviour. Obese women are 30% less likely to have had a sexual partner within the previous year and men who are obese are less likely to have had more than one sexual partner in the past year.[8]

QOF: obesity indicator

Indicator and points: total points 8

Records

OB1

The practice can produce a register of patients aged 16 and over with a BMI greater than or equal to 30 in the previous 15 months.

Points 8

At present, the QOF requirement is the establishment of disease register. This is not difficult at all.

There is no point in recording the data and then conveniently forgetting about the problem. It is important that the advice should be tailored according to the risk profile and patient's preference.

Advice should be given to all women with a BMI of 30 or over to lose weight before becoming pregnant.

It is equally important to offer a structured weight loss programme to those who remain obese at the time of post-natal examination.

Regardless of the reason for consultation, obesity should be positively addressed and managed as per the NICE guidelines.

Maximising quality points

➤ The most accurate method of identifying obesity is visual. It is obvious as soon as a patient enters the consulting room.
➤ Check the weight in kg and height in cm and enter the readings in the new patient health check at the time of registration, adult health examination, over-75 year assessment template, or the disease specific template (the patient may have obesity-related co-morbidities like diabetes, asthma, heart disease or depression). The BMI is calculated automatically by the computer.

Build up your template by adding the following codes (good for audit).

Overweight	BMI 25–29	22K4
Obesity	BMI 30+	22K5
Severely obese	BMI 40+	22K7

➤ Measure waist circumference. Waist circumference is measured at the height of the uppermost border of the iliac crest, making sure the patient is relaxed with arms crossed on their chest and feet shoulder-width apart. Ensure that the tape is snug without indenting the patient's skin and is not twisted. The measurement should be taken at the end of a normal expiration to the nearest 0.1 cm. It is a good practice to enter the waist circumference read code in all disease templates (practice nurses and healthcare assistants are less likely to forget to take the measurement).

Waist circumference	22N0
Waist circumference declined	81Af
Waist hip ratio	22N7

➤ People with a larger waistline and high triglyceride levels may be at a greater risk of heart disease. One study found that patients with a phenotype of waistline of at least 90 cm and a triglyceride level of 2 mmol/L or more were at a greater risk of CHD.[9] It is good clinical practice to measure waist circumference since more than 50% of obese patients have metabolic syndrome. The global prevalence of metabolic syndrome seems set to increase in coming years as a consequence of rising rates of obesity.[10] In a community-based longitudinal study in the US, the risk of developing diabetes over 11 years among obese patients was increased tenfold in those with the syndrome, and the risk of developing CVD was increased twofold.[11]

Table 23.1 Modified International Diabetes Federation (IDF) criteria for metabolic syndrome12

Essential	Central obesity
	Waist circumference ≥
	94 cm European males
	≥ 90 cm in South Asian, Chinese, and Japanese males
	≥ 80 cm in females
Plus two of:	Raised triglycerides
	≥ 1.7 mmol/L
	or receiving specific treatment
	Raised blood pressure
	systolic ≥ 130 mm Hg
	diastolic ≥ 85 mm Hg
	Raised fasting blood sugars
	≥ 5.6 mmol/L
	or previously diagnosed diabetes
	Reduced HDL-cholesterol
	< 1.03 mmol/L in males
	< 1.29 mmol/L in females
	or receiving specific treatment

➤ Waist:hip ratio (WHR). No QOF points for recording this. If you are a trainer or a GP with special interest (GPwSI) in obesity, you should be focussing more on this than the more traditional BMI. WHR is a better marker for predicting underlying coronary and aortic atheroma.[13] Waist circumference and WHR are strongly associated with risk of death.

➤ BMI check at the time of prescribing or advising contraception, during a pre-pregnancy health check and at the time of post-natal examination.[14]

➤ Offer lifestyle advice. Add the appropriate codes under the BMI recording in all the templates. The only two valid codes are:
— 67H (lifestyle counselling)
— 67H8 (lifestyle advice regarding hypertension).

➤ It is easy to fail to score on the lifestyle advice code if it is not added to the template of hypertension. As a GP, it is also equally important to discuss increasing activity, focussing on those activities which fit easily into patients' lives, and quality of diet and improvement in eating behaviour. Moderate fixed energy-deficit diets of 500–600 Kcals per day have been shown to be effective for inducing sustained and consistent weight loss of about 0.5 kg per week. Patients can be advised to use online calculators (available at: www.shapeup. org/interactive/rmr1.php).

To prevent relapse following weight loss, 60–90 minutes of moderate exercise a day may be needed. For this, a referral to an exercise class or a free gym membership pass, if available in your area, can be given to the patient.

➤ Patients with a BMI of 40, or 35 with a co-morbidity, must be referred for bariatric surgery as per NICE and SIGN guidelines. If your practice is in an area where the primary care trust does not follow NICE/SIGN advice on whom to offer bariatric surgery, or has rationed the procedure by raising the BMI threshold to 50 or 60, you cannot do anything. Fifty-five per cent of primary care trusts (PCTs) do not follow NICE/SIGN advice. The reasons these restrictions are in place is lack of resources. It is hoped that GP consortia could improve access to obesity surgery by adhering to NICE advice.

➤ Providing influenza vaccination to obese patients aged over 65 and those with or without chronic disease will boost your immunisation targets.

Template GMS: Obesity (V16)

Prompt	Code	Date	Coded subsets
Ethnic category – 2001 census	(9i)		See ethnicity template, Chapter 17
Obesity monitoring	(66C)		Obesity monitoring (66C) Initial obesity assessment (66C1) Follow-up obesity assessment (66C2)
Obesity monitoring admin (90K)			Attends obesity monitoring (90K1) Refuses obesity monitoring (90K2)
Obesity resolved	(212Q)		
SMOKING STATUS			See smoking template, Chapter 25
ALCOHOL CONSUMPTION			See Alcohol, Chapter 27
Systolic blood pressure	(2469)		
Diastolic blood pressure	(246A)		
Blood pressure refused	(8I3Y)		
O/E height	(229)		
O/E weight	(22A)		
Ideal weight	(66CB)		
Target weight	(66CF)		
Target weight reached	(66CK)		
Waist circumference	(22N0)		
WAIST CIRCUMFUMFERENCE DECLINED	81Af		
WAIST HIP RATIO	(22N7)		
Body Mass Index	(22K)		
BM1 25–29	(22k4)		
BMI 30+	(22k5)		
BMI 40+	(22k7)		
THYROID FUNCTION	(442J)		
SERUM TOTAL CHOLESTEROL	(44PJ)		
SERUM LDL	(44P6)		
SERUM HDL	(44P5)		
SERUM TRIGLY.	(44Q)		
SERUM CHOLESTEROL:HDL RATIO	(441F)		
PLASMA RANDOM GLUCOSE	(44g0)		
PLASMA FASTING GLUCOSE	(44g1)		
SERUM ALT.	(44GB)		
Patient advised reg. diet	(8CA4)		

(continued)

Prompt	Code	Date	Coded subsets
Patient advised reg. exercise	(8CA5)		
Patient advised about alcohol	(8CAM)		
LIFE STYLE COUNSEL.	(67H)		
Follow-up obesity assessment	(66C2)		
OBESITY MONITORING 1st LETTER	(90K4)		
OBESITY MONITORING 2nd LETTER	(90K5)		
OBESITY MONITORING 3rd LETTER	(90K6)		
OBESITY MONITORING VERBAL INVITE	(90K7)		
OBESITY MONITORING TELEPHONE INVITE	(90K8)		

(Add the capitalised prompts to your template to maximise points and quality care)

Do something extra

➤ Approach your friendly drug reps for free pedometers.
➤ Use exercise on prescription schemes if they exist in your area.
➤ Ask your practice manager to check if there are any organised walks, rambling or cycling groups in the area.
➤ Display lots of educational material in the waiting area.
➤ Get interpreters if you have patients of Asian origin.

References

1 NHS Health and Social Care Information Centre. *Health Survey for England 2004. Uupdating of trend tables to include 2004 data.* London: NHS Health and Social Care Information Centre; 2005.

2 Logue J, Sattar N. Tackling obesity in adults in primary care. *The Practitioner.* 2010; **254**(1730): 31–4.

3 Peeters A, Barendregt JJ, Willekens F, *et al.* Obesity in adulthood and its consequences for life expectancy; a life table analysis. *Ann. Intern. Med.* 2003; **138**: 24–32.

4 Sturm R, Wells KB. Does obesity contribute as much to morbidity as poverty or smoking? *Public Health.* 2001; **115**: 229–35.

5 Corbett J, Given L, Gray L, *et al. The Scottish Health Survey.* 2008. Edinburgh: Scottish Government; 2009, **1**: 191–228. 2009 symposium abstracts available at: www.rcpe. ac.uk/journal/abstracts/.../care-for-the-elderly_abstracts_2010.pdf

6 Scottish Intercollegiate Guidelines Network. *Obesity in Scotland: integrating prevention with weight management. A national clinical guideline recommended for use in Scotland.* Edinburgh: SIGN; 1996.

7 Calle EE, Rodriguez C, Walker-Turmond K, *et al.* Overweight, obesity and mortality from cancer in prospectively studied cohort of US adults. *N. Engl. J Med.* 2003; **348**: 1625–38.

8 Bajos N, Wellings K, Laborde C, *et al.* Sexuality and obesity, a gender perspective: results from French national random probability survey of sexual behaviour. *BMJ.* 2010; **340**: c2573.

 9 Quebec QC, Benoit A. Triglyceride and waist measurements predict heart-disease risk. *Canadian Medical Association Journal.* Epub. 19 July 2010. www.theheart.org/article/1100179.do
10 Wild S, Byrne CD. *The Global Burden of the Metabolic Syndrome and its Consequences for Diabetes and Cardiovascular Disease. The Metabolic Syndrome.* Chichester: John Wiley & Sons; 2005.
11 Meigs JB, Wilson PW, Fox CS, *et al.* Body mass index, metabolic syndrome and risk of type 2 diabetes or cardiovascular disease. *J Clin. Endocrin. Metab.* 2006; **91**: 2906–12.
12 Alberti KG, Zimmet O, Shaw J. The metabolic syndrome – a new worldwide definition, *Lancet.* 2005; **366**: 1059–62.
13 See R, Abdullah SM, McGuire DK, *et al.* The association of differing measures of overweight and obesity with prevalent atherosclerosis: the Dallas Heart Study. *J Am. Coll. Cardiol.* 2007; **50**: 752–9.
14 National Institute for Health and Clinical Excellence. *Weight Management Before, During and After Pregnancy: NICE guideline PH27.* London: NHICE; 2010. www.nice.org.uk/guidance/PH27

Useful reading

➤ National Institute for Health and clinical Excellence. *Obesity: guidance on the prevention, identification, assessment and management of overweight and obesity in adults and children.* London: NICE; 2006.
➤ www.nice.org.uk/Guidance/CG43
➤ Obesity: Department of Health. *Public Health.* www.dh.gov.uk/Home/Publichealth
➤ www.foresight.gov.uk/Obesity/Obesity.html
➤ www.scotland.gov.uk/Publications/2008/11/26155748/6
➤ http://nationalobesityforum.org.uk/
➤ www.wlsinfo.org.uk/
➤ British Obesity Surgery Patient Association: www.bospa.org/information.aspx

CHAPTER 24

Palliative care

Matthias Hohmann

Palliative care means that we are moving beyond cure into an area of increasing uncertainty, which as physicians we can find uncomfortable or difficult to deal with. With so many advances in treatment, we continue to see that many patients live longer with their conditions. It is advisable to discuss end-of-life wishes, living with uncertainty and the concerns surrounding possible sudden death with all patients who are diagnosed with a terminal illness.

A new quality of death index has shown substantial variations in end-of-life care in different countries across the world. Analysis of the quality of death index for 40 different countries found that the UK scored highly on the quality of end-of-life care, access to pain control, good availability of training and doctor–patient transparency. Many rich nations lag a long way behind, including Denmark (22nd), Italy (24th) and Finland (28th) because of poor quality, availability of care and total lack of policy coordination.[1]

Why included in QOF

➤ Three-quarters of patients wish to die at home[2] but less than a quarter currently do so.[3]
➤ Primary care has the potential to deliver high-quality domiciliary palliative care.
➤ The primary care physician is the person the patient often turns to for advice and information. A GP can fulfil the patient's wishes with the help of an integrated nursing team which is skilled in palliative care.
➤ GPs can deliver high-quality, patient-centred care throughout the critical phase cost-effectively.
➤ The primary care team is able to provide advice over the phone quickly to patients who are cared for at home. An admission to a hospice or hospital can be arranged if distressing symptoms cannot be managed at home or in the case of an acute emergency such as peritonitis.

➤ Common problems like pain, constipation, nausea, vomiting and nutritional support can be easily addressed in the primary care sector.

➤ Oxygen at home or the use of syringe driver for pain control, for which patients were admitted to hospital or hospice previously, if done in their home setting, ensures that the patient is able to enjoy the time they have left.

➤ Advance care planning will allow the GP to identify and respect the patient's wishes, enhance family satisfaction and reduce the risk of depression in surviving relatives.

➤ GPs are ideally positioned to provide the best possible quality of life through psychological, social and spiritual support, relief of pain and other distressing symptoms, helping patients to live as actively as possible until death – the principles of modern palliative care.[4]

➤ In spite of the time constraints of modern general practice, GPs are ideally placed to deliver truly holistic patient care – the principle of modern palliative care.[4]

QOF: palliative care indicators

Indicators and points: total points 6

Records

PC3

The practice has a complete register available of all patients in need of palliative care/support irrespective of age.

Points 3

The register should include not only cancer but also non-cancer conditions such as motor neurone disease, end-stage COPD and heart failure. One of the central elements of the Gold Standards Framework (GSF) is that all patients who are expected to die within the next 12 months should be included in the register whether suffering from cancer or a non-malignant, life-limiting disease.

You can use a colour coding system in the register:

➤ green representing a prognosis of several months
➤ amber representing a prognosis of weeks
➤ red representing the last few days of life.

All red patients should be on the Liverpool Integrated Care Pathway.

Avoid giving exact prognoses – you will almost always be wrong. Talking in 'days', 'weeks' or 'months' can give families some indications, but remind them of the unreliability of these predictions.

Ongoing management

PC2

The practice has regular (at least three-monthly) multi-disciplinary case review meetings where all patients on the palliative care register are discussed.

Points 3

Although the QOF recommends three-monthly meetings to review patients on the register, *in my practice we hold monthly meetings*. At any given time there are two or three patients on the register and it is not difficult to have a monthly practice meeting involving the district nurse, Macmillan nurse (who has a specialist training in palliative care and is skilled in counselling, support and symptom control), practice nurse, social worker and a head receptionist or practice manager. Do not forget to invite the named pharmacist, if involved in the delivery of medication to the patient's home. Address the ethical dilemmas in the team meeting by balancing the moral principles: beneficence, respect for autonomy, justice and non-maleficence.

Follow the GSF and Liverpool Integrated Care Pathway.

Goals of Gold Standards Framework (GSF)

This is a practice-based system to improve the quality and organisation of the care of patients in their last year of life in the community. The 7Cs of GSF (www. goldstandardsframework.nhs.uk) are:

➤ Communication
➤ Coordination
➤ Control of symptoms
➤ Continuity out of hours
➤ Continued learning
➤ Carer support
➤ Care in the dying phase.

Liverpool Integrated Care Pathway[5]

➤ A multidisciplinary pathway for the last few days and hours of life.
➤ Aims to discontinue all obsolete treatments and interventions and allow a dignified and peaceful death, free from distressing symptoms.

The central elements of the multi-disciplinary meetings are as follows.

Symptom control

➤ High standards of symptom management – pain, nausea, vomiting, constipation, insomnia, depression, confusion, restlessness, nutrition.
➤ Anticipation of symptoms and anticipatory prescribing.
➤ Liverpool Integrated Care Pathway.

Continuity of care

➤ A handover to out-of-hours services for all amber and red patients on the register.
➤ Do not attempt resuscitation (DNAR) form in patient's notes and ambulance.
➤ Provision of an appropriate medication/palliative care bag.
➤ Important phone numbers in case of emergency.

Advance care planning and preferred place of care

➤ This is a GMC good practice.

➤ The multidisciplinary team must know the patient's preferred place of care and preferred place of death.
➤ Make sure that patients who are approaching the end of life have been encouraged by the members of the team to participate in advance care planning. This should include beliefs and values and must be taken into account in the event of incapacity.
➤ For patients who lack capacity, check the records to see if an advance decision has been documented and enquire whether they have appointed an attorney. If there is no attorney and you are responsible for decision making, you must consult those close to the patient regarding their views and wishes and document these in the notes.

Carer support
➤ Carer's needs and specific support.
➤ Is the system in place if they need help in their bereavement counselling or time off work?

NICE focus on end-of-life care

(See www.nice.org.uk/aboutnice/whatwedo/...endoflifecare.jsp?) Good progress has been made in improving end-of-life care, but more needs to be done. The UK's Care Service Minister has highlighted the importance of ensuring everyone gets the highest quality of care, in the setting of their choice. Key areas of progress highlighted in the report include the following.
➤ The allocation of a £40 million capital grant for hospices to improve the environment in which they provide the care and the launch of e-learning on end-of-life care for health and social care staff.
➤ The establishment of end-of-life-care locality register pilots to improve coordination of care.
➤ The launch of the National End of Life Care Intelligence Network.
➤ National survey of bereaved relatives (VOICES).

Tips to achieve maximum points

It is not difficult to achieve six QOF points if you have a system in place. Palliative care means the proactive and holistic management of patient.
➤ It is easy to make a mistake in coding. The palliative register is not only for cancer but also end-stage COPD, heart failure and motor neurone disease.
➤ Follow the three main end-of-life care tools in three-monthly multi-disciplinary case review meetings:
   — Gold standard framework (GSF)
   — Advance Care Planning (ACP) and Preferred Priorities of Care (PPC)
   — Liverpool Integrated Care Pathway.

Template GMS: Palliative care (V16)

Prompt	Code	Date	Coded subsets
Exception report: palliative care quality indicator	(9hB)		Except. pall. care QI: Pt unsuit. (9hB0) Except. pall. care QI: inf. dis. (9hB1)
Ethnic category – 2001 census	(9i)		*See ethnicity template, Chapter 17*
Form Ds 1500 completed	(9EB5)		
On Gold Standard palliative care framework	(8CM1)		
Liverpool Care Pathway dying	(8CM4)		
Palliative care plan review	(8CM3)		
Specialist palliative care	(8BAP)		Terminal care (8BA2) Sp. pall. care treat. – day care (8BAS) Sp. pall. care treat. – outpt. (8BAT) Anticipatory pall. care (8Bae)
Palliative treatment	(8BJ1)		
Preferred place of death	(94Z0)		Preferred place of death: home (94Z1) Preferred place of death: hospice (94Z2) Preferred place of death: community hospital (94Z3) Preferred place of death: nursing home (94Z5) Preferred place of death: hospital (94Z4)
Refer to palliative care services	(8H7g)		Ref. to terminal care consultant (8H6A) Ref. for terminal care (8H7L) Ref. com. spec. pall. care team (8HH7)

Do something extra

➤ Respect the patient's wishes as an individual and make sure they spend meaningful time with close family and friends.[6]

➤ A good and honest communication with the patient and their carer is very important. Being the patient's GP, you will have a pretty good idea of the patient's understanding of the illness, their socio-economic conditions and the ability of their carer. Discuss the place of death and document it. A meta-analysis of death patterns has evaluated several factors likely to determine where the death occurs.[7] A long illness and a low functional status were associated with death at home[7] but a haematological malignancy was associated with death in hospital. Towards the terminal stage, with worsening of the symptoms, the patient or the carer may change their mind. Allow them to do so.

➤ Remember, palliative care is not exclusive to patients with cancer. A quantitative study of 40 patients with heart failure showed that the palliative care values of a good death from cancer may not be the same for an elderly patient with heart failure. If patients are not keen to continue with medication, respect their wishes. Over-medication of elderly people, not asking whether they would prefer quality or quantity of life, is not acceptable.

➤ Make sure carers are well supported. They are key allies in community end-of-life care. They must be treated as team members.

➤ The carer must be given an influenza vaccination.

➤ As the patient's GP you may not know everything. Do not hesitate to ask for help. In some areas, specialist palliative care advice is available 24 hours a day. Chapters on palliative prescribing in the BNF and the symptom control algorithm in the Liverpool Integrated Care Pathway are useful and informative.

➤ The palliative drug bag must be in the patient's home. Good pain relief is important.

➤ Discuss with the carer how to access care at different times. Specifically, calling 999 is very seldom appropriate.

➤ Rehearse the final days of life with them.

➤ The GMC has published important guidance on the treatment and care of patients who are likely to die within the next 12 months.[8] The guidance takes account of the Mental Capacity Act 2005, the government's end-of-life care strategy[6] and GMC guidance on consent.[9] Keep yourself up to date.

➤ Regular review and discussion of the disease process is important to make sure that the care provided is as good as possible. Remember, acute breathlessness is often due to panic or fear.

References

1 Mayor S. UK is ranked top out of 40 countries on quality of death. *BMJ*. 2010; **341**: c3836. Available at: www.bmj.com/content/341/bmj.c3836

2 Karlsen S, Addington Hall J. How do cancer patients who die at home differ from cancer patients who die elsewhere? *Palliat. Med*. 1998; **12**: 279–86.

3 Bosanquet N. New challenges for palliative care. *BMJ*. 1997; **314**: 915–18.

4 World Health Organization. *Definition of Palliative Care*. 2010. www.who.int/cancer

5 See www.mcpcil.org.uk/liverpool-care-pathway/ for further information.

6 Hunt R, McCaul K. A population-based study of the coverage of cancer patients by hospice services. *Palliat. Med*. 1996; **10**: 5–12.

8 Gomes B, Higginson IJ. Factors influencing death at home in terminally ill patients with cancer: systematic review. *BMJ*. 2006; **332**: 515–18.

7 Slaon J. *A Bitter Pill; How the Medical System is Failing the Elderly*. Margate: Greystone Books; 2009.

9 Gott M, Small N, Barnes S, *et al*. Older peoples' views of a good death in heart failure. Implications for palliative care provision. *Soc. Sci. Med*. 2008; **67**: 1113–21.

Useful information

➤ Marie Curie Cancer Care: www.mariecurie.org.uk

➤ Macmillan Cancer Support: www.macmillan.org.uk

Useful reading for health professionals

➤ Royal College of General Practitioners. *End of Life Care Strategy*. Available at: www.nelm.nhs.uk/.../RCGP-/launches-ante-mortal-End-of-Life-Care_Strategy/

➤ GMC ethical guideline. *Treatment and Care Towards the End of Life: good practice in decision making*. Available at: www.gmc-uk.org/guidance/ethical_guidance/6858.asp

CHAPTER 25

Smoking

Smoking is a substantial cause of deaths and hospital admissions in the UK. It is the main factor behind the social inequalities in life expectancy,[1] killing over 86 500 people in England each year and 106 000 people across the UK. The number of hospital admissions with a primary diagnosis of a smoking-related disease has increased steadily since 1996/97 – from 1.1 million admissions in 1996/97 to 1.4 million in 2007/08. The cost of treating smoking-related diseases is estimated to be £5.2 billion a year, which is about 5.5% of total healthcare costs.[2]

Prevalence

The prevalence of smoking in the UK has declined relatively slowly over the last decade and more than 20% of the adult population are still smokers.[3] Of those who smoke, the highest prevalence is those aged 20–24 years. The lowest prevalence is in those aged 60 or older.[2]

Why included in QOF

The provision of a high-quality NHS stop smoking service remains a government priority and forms a key element of the UK's national tobacco control policy. NICE estimates that each GP will see about one new patient requesting smoking cessation support every two weeks. Only about 4–7% of people are able to quit smoking on any given attempt without medicines or other help. Between 25% and 33% of smokers who use medicines can stay smoke-free for over six months.[4]

The 2004 Department of Health Public Service Agreement (PSA) target for smoking is to reduce adult smoking rates to 21% or less by 2010,[5] with the reduction in prevalence in routine and manual worker groups to 26% or less.

This led to the inclusion of smoking in the QOF.[6] Additional reasons are as follows.

➤ Smoking cessation at any age provides life extension.[7] Stopping smoking does not just add years to life, it adds life to years. Ex-smokers can expect not only a longer life than those who continue to smoke, but also a healthier life. Half of all lifelong cigarette smokers die from smoking, typically losing 10 years of life.[8]

➤ Smoking cessation in older adults reduces the risks of cardiac events during the first year of quitting and the risks continue to decline more gradually over many years.[9]

➤ Male older smokers who stop smoking also have reduced risks of dying of COPD after 10–15 years of abstinence.[9]

➤ Smoking is associated with increased risk of coronary heart disease.[10]

➤ Patients who have suffered a stroke remain at an increased risk of a further stroke – between 30 and 40% – within five years. High priority should be given to these patients for lifestyle modifications, including stopping smoking.[11]

➤ The single most cost-effective intervention to stop the progression of COPD is stopping smoking.[12]

➤ Smoking increases the risk of depression. The association between smoking and depression is in part due to a causal relationship. One should routinely target smoking cessation when treating depressed smokers.[13] Between one in three and one in four depressed smokers are willing to attempt cessation.[14] This can be easily achieved in a primary care setting.

➤ GPs are ideally placed to give advice and treatment. Even brief advice from a primary care physician to stop smoking leads to 1–3% of patients stopping smoking for at least six months.[15]

➤ Most smokers claim that they do want to quit (67%),[2] but those that are reluctant to do so could be advised by the primary care sector at least to consider the possibility of quitting or be referred to a smoking cessation clinic.

➤ It is never a waste of time advising smokers to quit. The primary care team is best placed to give simple opportunistic advice at the time of any and every consultation.

The facts

➤ In the UK, routine and manual workers have a higher smoking prevalence of 26%[16] compared with the UK national average of 21%[17] and make up 44% of the smoking population.[18]

➤ The lower socio-economic groups generally have poorer health outcomes and it is important to help them stop smoking.[19]

➤ The cost of stop-smoking services has risen by 30% between 2007/08 and 2009/10, but quit rates have remained almost unchanged. The new analysis estimates that if smoking cessation clinics provided nicotine replacement therapy (NRT) or varenicline (Champix) for more than three months, they could increase the quit rates by 13–19%.[20]

➤ A recent Finnish study showed that smoking in mid-life increased the risk of dementia in patients with apolipoprotein E carriers (APOEe4).[21]

QOF: smoking indicators

Indicators and points: total points 60

SMOKING 3

The percentage of patients with any or any combination of the following conditions: coronary heart disease, stroke or TIA, hypertension, diabetes ,COPD ,CKD, asthma, schizophrenia, bipolar affective disorder or other psychosis whose notes record smoking status in the previous 15 months.

Points 30   **Payment stages 40–90%**

The practical and effective approach is to enter the smoking status coding in all the disease templates, including the new patient registration template. Recording smoking status should be a priority for all health professionals if we are significantly to reduce the enormous burden on the NHS and the suffering that smoking causes.

SMOKING 4

The percentage of patients with any or any combination of the following conditions: coronary heart disease, stroke/TIA, hypertension, diabetes, COPD, CKD, asthma, schizophrenia, bipolar affective disorder or other psychosis whose notes contain a record that smoking cessation advice or referral to a specialist service, where available, has been offered within the previous 15 months.

Points 30   **Payment stages 40–90%**

In any one year, one-third of smokers make a quit attempt. Without support, less than 3% of attempts are successful. With treatment, one-year quit rates of 15–20% can be achieved. Assisting even a small proportion of these smokers to quit would bring health benefits. It is a good idea to ask about smoking history at every consultation – this can never be counterproductive.

➤ Use the AAA approach. **Ask, Assess and Assist**.
➤ Either provide yourself or direct the patient to a flexible, readily accessible and quality service.
➤ The patient must be ready and motivated.
➤ Use a SMART – Specific, Measurable, Achievable, Realistic and Time-scaled – action plan.
➤ Set carbon monoxide targets for each consultation.
➤ Agree target date for reduction in the number of cigarettes smoked each day with in a certain timescale.
➤ Everyone motivated to stop smoking should be offered a choice of interventions – NRT, varenicline (Champix).
➤ Provide a good follow-up service.
➤ Chase the DNA.
➤ Provide specific management for any issues arising as a result of quitting. For example, increasing exercise to help manage stress.

Maximising quality points

➤ At every opportunity, ask the patient about smoking and advise them not to. This should be read coded.

➤ Smoking status should be a part of the history of any and every clinical condition. No history and/or examination is complete without smoking history.

➤ Make sure that the practice nurse, healthcare assistant, district nurse, community matron and/or locum doctor ask the smoking status and read code it. There is no excuse for ignoring this.

➤ The code never smoked tobacco (1371) needs to be entered only once.

➤ The code current non-smoker (137L) no longer exists – make sure this code is removed from your templates.

➤ Use:
— current smoker (137R)
— ex-smoker (137S)
— never smoked tobacco (1371).

➤ Use the exception code if a patient declines to give their smoking status history. (*I have never used this code. The information can be obtained by saying, 'Help is available if you wish to stop'.*)

➤ A patient documented as ex-smoker for three consecutive years does not need coding. This patient is permanently exempted from any further recording of the smoking status. For example, with a patient coded as:
— ex-smoker on 5 November 2008
— ex-smoker on 4 November 2007
— ex-smoker on 4 November 2006,
do not ask again about the smoking status.

➤ A patient aged 26 years and documented and coded as never smoked after reaching 25 needs smoking status recording only once. It is assumed that a person who confirms non-smoker after the age of 26 years is unlikely to start smoking again.

➤ Patients aged 15–25 years who are coded as never smoked tobacco must have smoking status recorded every 15 months (not every 27 months) to score Records 23 (Smoking 3).

➤ There is no need to record smoking status for anyone under 15 years old.

➤ Run a regular audit of smoking status.

➤ Smoking appears in the QOF box which stares at you when you open up the patient medical record screen.

➤ Read code those not interested in stopping smoking (137d), but ask and offer advice at every opportunity.

➤ Thinking about stopping smoking is **another** useful code (137c).

➤ Excepted codes are patient unsuitable (9hG0) and informed dissent (9hG1). (*I do not think these have any place and they should not be used.*)

Template GMS: Smoking status (V16)

Prompt	Code	Date	Coded subsets
Ethnic category – 2001 census	(9i)		See ethnicity template, Chapter 17
O/E Weight	(22A)		
O/E Height	(229)		
Body Mass Index	(22K)		
Waist circumference	(22N0)		
Ideal weight	(66CB)		
Never smoked tobacco	(1371)		Never smoked tobacco (1371) Pipe smoker (137H) Cigar smoker (137J) Rolls own cigarettes (137M) Cigarette smoker (137P) Current smoker (137R) Ex-smoker (137S) Ex cigarette smoker (137j) Ex roll-up cigarette smoker (137l)
Stopped smoking	(137K)		
Trying to give up smoking	(137G)		
Ready to stop smoking	(137b)		Ready to stop smoking (137b) Thinking about stopping smoking (137c) Not interested in stopping smoking (137d)
Nicotine replacement therapy	(8B2B)		
Smoking cessation therapy	(745H)		Smoking cessation therapy (745H) Nic. rep. ther. nic. patches (745H0) Nic. rep. ther. nic. gum (745H1) Nic. rep. ther. nic. inhalator (745H2) Nic. rep. ther. nic. lozenges (745H3) Smoking cessation drug ther. (745H4) Smoking cessation ther. NOS (745Hz)
OTC nicotine replacement therapy	(8B3Y)		
Health education	(679)		Health education smoking (6791) Preg. smoking advice (67A3) Smoking cessation advice (8CAL)
Brief intervention smoking cessation	(67H6)		
Referral: smoking cessation advisor	(8H7i)		Ref. smoking cessation advisor (8H7i) Ref. to stop-smoking clinic (8HTK) Ref. to NHS stop-smoking service (8HkQ)
EXCEPTION REPORT: SMOKING QUALITY INDICATOR	(9hG)		Except. smoking QI: Pt uns. (9hG0) Except. smoking QI: inf. dis. (9hG1)
Alcohol screen – AUDIT C	(9k17)		

(continued)

Prompt	Code	Date	Coded subsets
Alcohol consumption screen	(68S)		Teetotaller (1361) Stopped drinking alcohol (1367) Suspect alcohol abuse – denied (1369) Social drinker (136J) Hazardous alcohol use (136S) Harmful alcohol use (136T) Alcohol assessment declined (9k19)
DEPRESSION SCREEN USING QUESTIONNAIRE	(6896)		
HAD ANXIETY	(388N)		
HAD DEPRESSION	(388P)		
PHQ-9 SCORE	(388f)		
PATIENT ADVISED REG. DIET	(8CA4)		
PATIENT ADVISED REG. EXERCISE	(8CA5)		
PATIENT ADVISED ABOUT ALCOHOL	(8CAM)		
INFLUENZA VACCINATION	(65E)		Influenza vaccination coded subsets same as in CHD template, Chapter 9
PNEUMOCOCCAL VACCINATION	(6572)		Pneumococcal vaccination coded subsets same as in CHD template, Chapter 9

(Add the capitalised prompts to your template to maximise points and quality care)

Do something extra

➤ Smoking cessation interventions are more cost-effective than most medical life-saving interventions.
➤ Do spirometry screening on all smokers. They will respond and will be more interested in quitting if spirometry shows poor lung function.
➤ Do blood pressure check and fasting lipid profile on all smokers. Calculate JBS 2 score and initiate statin therapy if indicated.
➤ Ask your PCT for an in-house smoking cessation counsellor (*if you have not already got one*).
➤ Make sure you give the information and support in the client's language.
➤ Neither advanced age nor length of time a smoker should exclude a patient from being encouraged to stop smoking. Keep encouraging and keep advising as giving up at any age is beneficial.

References

1 Jha P, Peto R, Zatonski W, *et al*. Social inequalities in male mortality, and in male mortality from smoking. *Lancet*. 2006; **368**: 367–70.
2 National Statistics. The Information Centre for Health and Social Care. *Statistics on Smoking*. 2009. www.nhs.uk/.../smoking09/Statisticson_smoking_England_2009.pdf (accessed 24 February 2010).
3 Goddard E. *General Household Survey, 2006: smoking and drinking among adults, 2006*. Newport: Office of National Statistics; 2008.
4 www.cancer.org/.../guidetoquitsmoking/guide-to-quittingsmoking-success-rate/

5 Department of Health. *Spending Review 2004 Public Service Agreement.* www.guidance. nice.org.uk/nicemedia/live/11925/40611/40611.doc

6 HM Treasury. *2004 Spending Review.* London: HM Treasury; 2004.

7 Taylor D, Hasselblad V, Henley J, *et al.* Benefits of smoking cessation for longevity. *Am. J Public Health.* 2002; **92**: 990–6.

8 Doll R, Peto R, Boreham J, *et al.* Mortality in relation to smoking. *BMJ.* 2004; **328**: 1519.

9 LaCroiz A, Omenn G. Older adults and smoking. *Clin. Geriatr. Med.* 1992; **8**: 69–87.

10 European Society of Cardiology. *CVD Prevention in clinical practice (European Guide-lines on).* www.escardio.org/knowledge/guidelines/CVD_Prevention_in_Clinical_Practice.htm

11 Stroke risk factors – Smoking. www.wehct.nhs.uk/...strokeservices/...stroke/...strokeriskfactors-smoking.htm

12 www.goldcopd.com/

13 Berk M. Should we be targeting smoking as an intervention? *Acta Neuropsychiatrica.* 2007; **19**: 131–22.

14 Hitsman B, Borrelli B, McChargue DE, *et al.* History of depression and smoking cessation outcome; a meta-analysis. *J Consult. Clin. Psychol.* 2003; **71**: 657–63.

15 McEwen A, Vangeli E. Smoking cessation: advice and treatment in general practice. *Prescriber.* 2008; **19**: 48–56. Available at: www.prescriber.co.uk

16 Department of Health. *Tackling Health Inequalities: targeting routine and manual smokers of the public service agreement smoking prevalence and health inequality targets.* London; Department of Health; 2009.

17 Office for National Statistics. *General Lifestyle Survey 2008: smoking and drinking among adults, 2008.* London: Office for National Statistics, 2010.

18 Department of Health. *NHS Stop Smoking Services: service and monitoring guidance 2010/11.* London: Department of Health; 2009.

19 Department of Health. *Health Inequalities. Progress and next steps.* London: Department of Health; 2008.

20 Coleman T, Agboola S, Leonardi-Bee J, *et al.* Relapse prevention in UK Stop Smoking Services: current practice, systematic reviews of effectiveness and cost-effectiveness analysis. 2010. www.hts.ac.uk/fullmono/mon1449.pdf

21 Rovio S, Ngandu T. Midlife smoking, apolipoprotein E and risk of dementia. *Dement. Geriatr. Cogn. Disord.* 2010; **30**: 277–84.

Useful information

For health professionals

➤ Smoking Cessation Service Research Network (SCSRN): www.scsrn.org

➤ NHS Stop Smoking Services Service and monitoring guidance 2009/10.6. April 2010: www.dh.gov.uk/en/Publicationsandstatistics/Publications/PublicationsPolicyAndGuidance/DH_096886

For patients

➤ NHS Smoking Helpline: 0800 022 4 332 (free).

➤ NHS stop smoking website: www.gosmokefree.nhs.uk

➤ QUIT: www.quit.org.uk

➤ No Smoking Day: www.nosmokingday.org.uk

CHAPTER 26

Stroke and TIA

Stroke is the leading cause of disability in the UK[1] and the third leading cause of death in most Western countries.

A transient ischaemic attack (TIA) is defined as a rapid onset of focal neurological deficit lasting less than 24 hours with no apparent cause other than disruption of blood supply to the brain. The majority of TIAs resolve within one hour and episodes of transient monocular blindness (amaurosis fugax) commonly last less than five minutes. A TIA lasting several hours could be due to a complete cerebral infarction or a small cerebral haemorrhage.

Prevalence

Stroke is a common condition affecting around 150 000 people every year in the UK. At any given time, there are about 2500 stroke patients in an average health district. An average GP will see only three to four new cases of stroke each year. It is one of the most common causes of disability and psychological burden upon relatives.

Approximately 20 000 TIAs occur in England every year,[2] with the risk of stroke in the first month following a TIA as high as 32% in some patient groups.[3]

While the incidence increases with age, 25% of all strokes occur in people under the age of 65 years. Approximately 15% of strokes are haemorrhagic and the rest are ischaemic.

Why included in QOF

➤ The management of any chronic disease is appropriately coordinated by the primary care physician and stroke/TIA is no exception. Effective secondary prevention used to be slow and patchy, resulting in unnecessary strokes, as shown by previous audits. Its inclusion in the QOF with emphasis on secondary prevention will contribute towards a better quality of care.

➤ The risk factors for stroke – hypertension, diabetes mellitus, obesity, smoking, recreational drugs and high cholesterol – can be effectively addressed and managed in the primary care sector.

➤ Inclusion in the QOF means GPs take a leading role in the identification of TIAs, their early management and the organisation and provision of long-term rehabilitation.

➤ Stroke is associated with large economic costs.[4]

➤ The financial cost of stroke is increasing. It costs the NHS and the wider economy £7 billion per year.[5] Its inclusion in the QOF hopefully will reduce the financial burden.

➤ Stroke is the third most common cause of death in the UK.[6] Thirty per cent of people die after their first myocardial infarction (MI), while after a stroke approximately 23% die within 30 days. Of the initial stroke survivors, only 30–40% are alive after three years. Inclusion in the QOF means that GPs remain closely involved in the delivery of care once the patient is discharged from hospital.

➤ A blood pressure fluctuation is a warning sign of stroke. Two retrospective analyses, a meta-analysis and a review article, examined the data from a UK TIA aspirin trial[7,8] and an Anglo-Scandinavian Cardiac Outcomes Trial-Blood Pressure Lowering Arm (ASCOT-BPLA) trial[9] and found that in patients with prior stroke, variability in systolic blood pressure measured in the clinic was a strong predictor of stroke and coronary heart disease, independent of mean systolic blood pressure. Targeting variable blood pressure is easily achievable in the primary care setting and will prevent some strokes. Maximum systolic blood pressure was more predictive than mean systolic blood pressure and patients with stable hypertension had a better prognosis than those whose hypertension was episodic.

The facts

➤ Patients who have had a TIA have a two-day stroke risk of approximately 4%, a seven-day stroke risk of approximately 5.5%, a 30-day stroke risk of approximately 7.5% and a 90-day stroke risk of approximately 9%. The risk may be stratified using the ABCD2 scoring system (see Table 26.1 below).[10]

➤ For every minute a stroke goes untreated, 1.9 million brain neurons die.

➤ Reduction in mortality and dependency is seen in patients treated in a dedicated stroke unit compared with conventional care.

➤ Very few stroke survivors make a complete recovery. About 12–18% are left with speech problems, 25% are unable to walk and 24–53% remain dependent on carers for day-to-day activities.

QOF: stroke and TIA indicators

Indicators and points: total points 24

STROKE 1
The practice can produce a register of patients with stroke or TIA.

Points 2

Accurate disease registers underpin high-quality primary care. To recall people and ensure they are managed according to best practice, it is important to maintain a good quality disease register.

The QOF expects accurate coding. This means that miscoded people will miss out on any recalls. Misdiagnosis can occur when people are labelled as having a stroke but there is no objective evidence. This may result in medical harm and wastage of NHS resources.

STROKE 13

The percentage of new patients with a stroke or TIA who have been referred for further investigations.

Points 2   **Payment stages 40–80%**

In order to risk stratify patients presenting with a possible TIA, use the scoring system shown in Table 26.1. Make posters and hang one in the reception and another one in the examination room.

Table 26.1 ABCD2 scoring system10

Clinical feature	Score*
Age 60 or older	1
BP > 140/90 mm Hg	1
Clinical features	
Unilateral weakness	2
No weakness	1
Duration of symptoms	
> 60 minutes	2
10–59 minutes	1
Diabetes	1

Score	Two-day stroke risk
0–3	1%
1–5	4%
1–7	8%

* Scores range from 0–7, with 7 being at highest risk.

Those patients with an ABCD2 score ≥ 4 are classified as 'high risk' and should have a specialist assessment and investigations within 24 hours. The patients with a score of < 4 are classified as 'low risk' and should have specialist assessment and investigation within one week.

The new NICE guidelines emphasise the importance of diagnosing these patients early and starting management in a timely manner.[11] If a patient is outside the surgery or ringing for an appointment with symptoms suggestive of TIA, a validated FAST test tool should be used. Primary care staff, including the receptionist, must be aware of the UK Stroke Association Act FAST Campaign.[12]

All suspected stroke patients must have full blood count (FBC), urea and electrolytes (U&E), liver function tests (LFT), thyroid function tests (TFT), cholesterol and blood sugar levels measured to assess any haematological or biochemical derangement, in addition to brain scanning – CT or MRI. The most commonly used is CT scanning due to its ease of use and availability. MRI is more expensive and can be claustrophobic.

STROKE 5

The percentage of patients with stroke or TIA who have a record of blood pressure in the notes in the preceding 15 months.

Points 2   **Payment stages 40–90%**

This should not be difficult. A record of blood pressure and entering the reading gives you two easily achievable points.

STROKE 6

The percentage of patients with a history of stroke or TIA in whom the last blood pressure reading (measured in the previous 15 months) is ≤ 150/90 mm Hg.

Points 5   **Payment stages 40–70%**

It is well known that the key to success is to eliminate any risk factors that might worsen the symptoms or predispose to further thrombotic or bleeding episodes. Maintaining blood pressure with anti-hypertensive drugs is essential.

All patients should have their blood pressure checked and high blood pressure persisting for over two weeks should be treated. The British Hypertension Society guidelines are as follows.

➤ In non-diabetic patients with hypertension, the optimal blood pressure treatment goals are:
— systolic blood pressure < 140 mm Hg and
— diastolic blood pressure < 85 mm Hg.
➤ For patients with diabetes mellitus the optimal goals of control are 130/80 mm Hg.
➤ For QOF the target is 150/90 mm Hg or less.

STROKE 7

The percentage of patients with stroke or TIA who have a record of total cholesterol in the last 15 months.

Points 2   **Payment stages 40–90%**

Use the district nurse, community matron or phlebotomist attached to the practice to carry out blood cholesterol testing of housebound patients. Blood pressure can be updated at the same time.

STROKE 8

The percentage of patients with stroke or TIA whose last measured total cholesterol (measured in the previous 15 months) is ≤ 5 mmol/L.

Points 5   **Payment stages 40–60%**

Prescribe appropriate lipid-lowering cost-effective statin – Simvastatin 40 mg is an effective statin for secondary prevention.

STROKE 10

The percentage of patients with stroke or TIA who have had influenza immunisation in the preceding 1 September to 31 March.

Points 2   **Payment stages 40–85%**

Involve the district nurse or community matron for housebound patients. Housebound patients will be known to them.

STROKE 12

The percentage of patients with a stroke shown to be non-haemorrhagic, or a history of TIA, who have a record that an anti-platelet agent (aspirin, clopidogrel, dipyridamole or a combination), or an anticoagulant is being taken (unless a contraindication or side-effects are recorded).

Points 4   **Payment stages 40–90%**

For patients with thrombotic or embolic strokes, reducing blood viscosity is a mainstay of treatment. Anti-platelet drugs are highly effective in secondary prevention. Anti-coagulation should be started in every patient with persistent or paroxysmal atrial fibrillation (AF) unless contraindicated.

Specific treatment for TIA involves giving aspirin 300 mg immediately and a combination of aspirin 75 mg daily in combination with dipyridamole 200 mg modified release twice daily subsequently. Clopidogrel monotherapy is an alternative in aspirin-intolerant patients.

Giving aspirin in doses above 75 mg daily to patients who have had an ischaemic stroke reduces the risk of a further stroke by about 13% and the stroke risk per year from 7% to 6%. This equates to one stroke being prevented for every 100 patients prescribed aspirin.

Once 14 days have passed from onset of symptoms, guidelines suggest anti-coagulation rather than anti-platelet therapy to prevent ischaemic stroke of cardioembolic origin.

There is a reluctance to start warfarin, but warfarin reduces the risk of stroke in patients with a previous cerebrovascular event in comparison with aspirin.[13]

Do not start anti-coagulation therapy until brain imaging has excluded haemorrhage.

More specifically, intra-arterial thrombolysis could be an option for treatment of selected patients who have had a major stroke of less than six hours' duration due to occlusion of the middle cerebral artery.

The common side-effects, contraindications and cautions for aspirin, clopidogrel and dipyridamole are shown in Table 26.2.

Table 26.2 Common side-effects, contraindications and cautions for aspirin, clopidogrel and dipyridamole

	Aspirin	Clopidogrel	Dipyridamole
Side-effects	Nausea Heartburn Abdominal pain GI haemorrhage Heamorrhagic stroke	GI haemorrhage GI upset Intracranial haemorrhage	Vomiting Diarrhoea Dizziness Low BP Flushing Tachycardia
Contraindications	Aspirin allergy Active peptic ulcer Haemophiliacs	Clopidogrel allergy Breast feeding Severe liver impairment Active pathological bleeding	Dipyridamole allergy
Cautions	Asthma Renal impairment Peptic ulcer disease	Patients at increased risk of bleeding	Severe CAD Unstable angina/recent MI Coagulation disorders

In patients with aspirin-induced dyspepsia, add a proton pump inhibitor or change to clopidogrel. Adding a proton pump inhibitor is the more cost-effective option.

Maximising quality points

➤ There are a number of diagnoses that may mimic stroke or TIA, such as hypoglycaemia, syncope, migraine, space occupying lesion. Do not read code these as stroke/TIA. If in doubt, refer the patient for further investigations.

➤ Migraine, sometimes associated with visual aura, unilateral sensory disturbance, dysphasia and motor weakness, can be easily misdiagnosed and miscoded as TIA/stroke. Refer this patient for imaging first.

➤ Isolated vertigo is rarely a presenting symptom of TIA. Do not read code as TIA.

➤ TGA-transient global amnesia, an abrupt disorder of memory where the patient suffers from anterograde amnesia and asks the same questions repetitively. This is a common reason of confusion in the middle-aged and elderly, and is often assumed to be a TIA. Do not read code this as TIA/stroke.

➤ Blackout does not mean TIA. TIAs rarely present with loss of consciousness.

➤ Do not enter a read code until the CT/MRI scan results are reported by the hospital.

➤ Do a stroke update on the template at the time of registering a new patient with a past history of stroke.

➤ Blood pressure fluctuation is a warning sign of stroke. Do not ignore variations in blood pressure. Prescribe an effective drug to lower blood pressure.

➤ Make a list of housebound patients with stroke. The stroke template can be updated at the time of the home influenza immunisation visit.

➤ Enquire about the patient's history of smoking and offer smoking cessation advice and support. This will help you achieve smoking 3 and 4 indicators.

➤ Patients under the age of 45 years must be referred for ECG to exclude AF/MI. If AF is diagnosed, put these patients on the AF register as well.

➤ Some patients may not tolerate rigorous blood pressure lowering due to dizziness and pre-syncope. In these cases it is sensible to add a code of maximum tolerated anti-hypertensive therapy – you may be asked to explain at the time of the QOF visit.

➤ Give an appointment of patient's/carer's choice. Most stroke patients will be dependent on someone. This will reduce your DNA/CNA.

➤ Although no QOF points are awarded, you will achieve maximum clinical satisfaction points by making sure that the patient receives coordinated support from a speech therapist, physiotherapist and dietician. Sometimes patients are discharged into the community without a support package.

Template GMS: Stroke and TIA (V16)

Prompt	Code	Date	Coded subsets
Exception report: stroke quality indicators	(9h2)		Except. stroke QI: Pt unsuit. (9h21) Except. stroke QI: inf. dis. (9h22)
Ethnic category – 2001 census	(9i)		See ethnicity template, Chapter 17
Stroke monitoring	(662M)		
Systolic BP	(2469)		(Aim ≤ 140/85 mm Hg)
Diastolic BP	(246A)		
Blood pressure procedure refused	(8I3Y)		
O/E height	(229)		
O/E weight	(22A)		
Body Mass Index	(22K)		(Aim < 25 kg/m²)
WAIST CIRCUMFERENCE	(22N0)		
WAIST CIRCUMFERENCE DECLINED	(81Af)		
WAIST HIP RATIO	(22N7)		
O/E PULSE RATE	(242)		
Smoking status			See smoking status template, Chapter 25
ALCOHOL CONSUMPTION			See Alcohol, Chapter 27
PATIENT ADVISED REG. DIET	(8CA4)		
PATIENT ADVISED REG. EXERCISE	(8CA5)		
PATIENT ADVISED ABOUT ALCOHOL	(8CAM)		
H/O RECREATIONAL DRUGS	(146E)		
CURRENT DRUG USER	(13c7)		
Serum cholesterol	(44P)		
FULL BLOOD COUNT	(424)		
PLASMA RANDOM GLUCOSE	(44g0)		
PLASMA FASTING GLUCOSE	(44g1)		
HBA1c < 7%	(42W1)		
URINE PROTEIN TEST+	(4674)		Proteinuria (R110) Albuminuria (R1100)
URINE BLOOD TEST	(469)		
STANDARED CHEST X-RAY	(535)		
12 LEAD ECG	(321B)		
ULTRASOUND HEART SCAN	(5853)		

(continued)

Prompt	Code	Date	Coded subsets
STANDARD CHEST X-RAY	(535)		*Standard chest X-ray coded subsets same as in CHD template, Chapter 9*
CAROTID DOPPLER	(585Q)		
Computerised axial tomography	(567)		CAT scan requested (5671) CAT scan normal (5672) CAT scan abnormal (5673) Refer for CAT scan (8HQ4)
Nuclear magnetic resonance	(569)		NMR requested (5691) NMR normal (5692) NMR abnormal (5693) Refer for NMR scanning (8HQ3)
MRI brain – abnormal	(5694)		MRI brain abnormal (5694) MRI brain normal (569F) Refer for MRI (8HQ3-1)
Patient on maximum tolerated dose	(8BL)		Pt on max. tolerat. antihypert. therapy (8BL0) Pt on max. tolerat. lipid lowering therapy (8BL1)
Anti-coagulation contraindicated	(8I2R)		Anticoag. prescribed by 3rd party (8B2K) Anticoag. contraind. (8I2R) Anticoag. declined (8I3d) Anticoag. not indic. (8I6N) Anticoag. not tolerat. (8I7A)
Aspirin			*Aspirin coded subsets same as in CHD template, Chapter 9*
Warfarin contraindicated	(8I25)		*Warfarin coded subsets same as in CHD template, Chapter 9*
Clopidogrel contraindicated	(8I2K)		*Clopidogrel coded subsets same as in CHD template, Chapter 9*
H/O Dipyridamol allergy	(14LX)		*Dipyridamol coded subsets same as in CHD template, Chapter 9*
Statin prophylaxis	(8B6A)		*Statin coded subsets same as in CHD template, Chapter 9*
Influenza vaccination	(65E)		H/O influenza vaccine allergy (14LJ) Influenza vaccination (65E) No consent – influenza imm. (68NE) Influenza vaccination contraind. (8I2F) Influenza vaccination not indicat. (8I6D) Influenza vaccination declined (9OX5) Influenza vaccination other health provider (65E2) First pandemic flu vaccination (65E0) Second pandemic flu vaccination (65E1)
Pneumococcal vaccination	(6572)		Pneumococcal vaccination (6572) Pneumococcal vaccination given (65720) Pneumococcal vaccination contraind. (8I2E) Pneumococcal vaccination declined (8I3Q)
Stroke/TIA referral	(8HBJ)		

(continued)

Prompt	Code	Date	Coded subsets
Referral to stroke clinic	(8HTQ)		
Medication review done	(8B3V)		
Stroke monitoring	(662M)		
STROKE/TIA MONITORING 1st LETTER	(90m0)		
STROKE/TIA MONITORING 2nd LETTER	(90m1)		
STROKE/TIA MONITORING 3rd LETTER	(90m2)		
STROKE/TIA MONITORING VERBAL INVITE	(90m3)		
ADVISE REG. DRIVING	(8CAJ)		

(Add the capitalised prompts to your template to maximise points and quality care)

Do something extra

➤ Exercise reduces the risk of recurrent stroke and myocardial infarction. Between 30 and 60 minutes of aerobic exercise three to five times a week is beneficial. Refer these patients to the local supervised exercise class.

➤ Advising on reducing salt intake to less than 6 g/day will help reduce blood pressure to its target level.

➤ Give advice regarding alcohol intake. Excess alcohol of > 21 units in men and 14 units in women increases the risk of both haemorrhagic and ischaemic stroke.[14]

➤ Check FBC, blood glucose and routine urine for protein. Other investigations include ECG, ECHO and carotid Doppler.

➤ Address the needs of the carers, even though this is not included in the QOF.

➤ Provide information to patient and their family about the statutory and voluntary organisations services specific to their needs.

➤ The patient must be advised not to drive for one month.

➤ Provide influenza vaccination to the carer as well.

➤ Patients diagnosed with significant carotid stenosis (50–90%) must have carotid endarterectomy within two weeks of the symptoms. (Make sure the patient has an appointment.)

➤ Run a regular audit of secondary prevention, aiming to improve patient outcomes. For example, cholesterol and blood pressure targets.

➤ Any patient with reduced activity at six months or later after stroke should be assessed for further targeted rehabilitation.

➤ Calcium supplements without co-administration of vitamin D may increase the risk of stroke. Run a computer search of patients who are either at risk of or with established osteoporosis and are on calcium supplements. Many of these could be elderly and may also be at a high risk of cardiovascular disease.[15]

➤ Warn the patients against taking vitamin E supplements because of an increased risk of haemorrhagic stroke.[16]

References

1 MacKay J, Mensah G. *The Atlas of Heart Disease and Stroke*. Geneva: World Health Organization; 2004.

2 National Audit Office. *Reducing Brain Damage: faster access to better stroke care*. HC 452. 2005–06.

3 National Institute for Health and Clinical Excellence. *Final Stroke Scope*. Available at: www.nice.org.uk/nicemedia/pdf/StrokeFinalScope050608.pdf (accessed 10 May 2010).

4 Vila EM, Irimia P. The cost of stroke. *Cerebrovasc. Dis*. 2004; **17**(Suppl. 1): 124–9.

5 Public Accounts Committee. *Reducing Brain Damage: faster access to better stroke care*. Available at: www.publications.parliament.uk/pa/cm/2005506/cmselect/.../911.pdf

6 Wolfe C, Rudd T, Beech R. *Stroke Services and Research*. London: Stroke Association; 1996.

7 Farrell B, Godwin J, Richards S, *et al*. The United Kingdom transient ischaemic attack (UK-TIA) aspirin trial. *J Neurol. Neurosurg. Psychiatry*. 1991; **54**(12): 1044–54.

8 Vermeer SE, Sandee W, Algra A, *et al*. The Dutch TIA trial: protective effects of low-dose aspirin and atenolol in patients with transient ischaemic attacks or nondisabling stroke. The Dutch TIA Study Group. *Stroke*. 1988; **19**; 512–17. Available at: www.stroke.ahajournals.org/cgi/content/short/19/4/512

9 Dahlof B, Sever PS, Poulter NR, *et al*. Prevention of cardiovascular events with an antihypertensive regimen of amlodipine adding perindopril as required versus atenolol adding bendroflumethiazide as required, in the Anglo-Scandinavian Cardiac Outcomes Trial-Blood Pressure Lowering Arm (ASCOT-BPLA): a multicentre randomised controlled trial. *Lancet*. 2005; **366**: 895–906.

10 Johnston SC, Rothwell PM, Nguyen-Huynh MN, *et al*. Validation and refinement of scores to predict very early stroke risk after transient ischaemic attack. *Lancet*. 2007; **369**(9558): 283–92.

11 National Institute for Health and Clinical Excellence. *Diagnosis and Initial Management of Acute Stroke and Transient Ischaemic Attack (TIA): NICE guideline GC68*. London: NHICE; 2008. www.nice.org.uk/guidance/GC68

12 The Stroke Association. *Suspect a Stroke? Act FAST*. www.stroke.org.uk/document.rm?id=1586

13 European Atrial Fibrillation Trial (EAFT) Study Group. Secondary prevention in non-rheumatic atrial fibrillation after transient ischaemic attack or minor stroke. *Lancet*. 1993; **342**: 1255–62.

14 National Institute for Health and Clinical Excellence. *Hypertension: management of hypertension in adults in primary care. NICE guidance: CG34*. London: NHICE; 2004. www.nice.org.uk/guidance/CG34

15 Bolland MJ, Avenell A, Baron JA, *et al*. Effect of calcium supplements on risk of myocardial infarction and cardiovascular events: meta analysis. *BMJ*. 2010; **341**: c3691.

16 Schurks M, Goldstein LB. Vitamin E may pose slight bleeding stroke risk. 5 November 2010. *BMJ* online. www.doctorslounge.com.index.php/nesw/hd/15403

Useful reading

➤ *Primary Care Concise Guidelines for Stroke 2004. National Institute for Health and Clinical Excellence Concise Guideline on Acute Stroke* . Available at: www.slcsn.nhs.uk/files/stroke/events/240510/stroke.pdf

➤ Department of Health. *National Service Framework for Older People.* London: Department of Health; 2001.

CHAPTER 27

Alcohol: directed enhanced service

Four clinical Directed Enhanced Services (DES) – Alcohol, Learning disability, Oste-oporosis and Ethnicity were first introduced for 2008/09.

Alcohol DES is a means of case-finding followed by simple alcohol advice. The aim is to make the person recognise that they are drinking harmful amounts of alcohol and that help is available if they are motivated.

The UK has a drink problem. Teenagers are drinking twice as much as they did in 1990.[1] As a nation, our alcohol consumption has been rising for decades, and with it the harms associated with this consumption. Department of Health figures suggest that more than 10 million people drink over the recommended limits (this group consumes 75% of all alcohol consumed and 2.6 million drink over the safe limits). A total of 3.5 million of us are dependent on alcohol.[2] Continued hazard-ous and harmful drinking can result in dependence and tolerance. It can also cause damage to any organ or system of the body.[3]

Why included in DES

➤ Alcohol-related admissions to hospital have increased in England by 69%, representing rises of around 70 000 per year between 2002/03 and 2007/08.[4] This accounts for more than 6% of all hospital admissions.
➤ The cost to the NHS of treating acute and chronic drinking is estimated at up to £2.7 billion a year.[5] In 2007, there were 134 429 items prescribed in primary care settings and NHS hospitals in the UK for drugs relating to the treatment of alcohol dependence.[6]
➤ The rate of increase in alcohol-related deaths has risen most steeply among middle and older age groups: those in their 30s, 40s and 50s are at a much higher risk of an early death due to heavy drinking.[7]

The DES pays practices to undertake alcohol screening in patients aged 16 or over using the Fast Alcohol Screen Test (FAST) or, for newly registered patients only, the Alcohol Use Disorders Identification Test Consumption (AUDIT-C) questionnaire tool. It pays £2.33 for each newly registered patient screened by their GP.

DES ALC 1: New patients alcohol screening

The number of newly registered patients aged 16 and over with in the financial year who have had the short, standard case-finding test (FAST or AUDIT-C).

DES ALC 2: Full alcohol assessment

The number of newly registered patients aged 16 and over who have screened positive using the above tool to determine hazardous, harmful or likely dependent drinking.

DES ALC3: Brief alcohol intervention

The number of hazardous or harmful drinkers who have received a brief intervention to help them.

Unfortunately there are no points attached for alcohol screening under the QOF, not even in relation to hypertension, CHD, stroke, epilepsy, depression or diabetes, and some GPs argue that this is too small a DES payment.

While death rates from diabetes, stroke and cancer have been declining, mortality from liver disease has increased fivefold in people under 65.[7]

As primary care physicians, we cannot ignore this worrying and ever-increasing problem just because there are no QOF points attached to alcohol. A French study showed that, compared with regular drinkers, men who drank more than 50 g of alcohol at least once a week were at twice the risk of MI or coronary deaths.[8] As GPs, we must reinforce the effects on the heart of high alcohol consumption to patients who binge drink.

In June 2010, NICE published its 100th clinical guideline, focussing on the diagnosis and management of alcohol-related complications in adults and children aged over 10 years.[3] The guideline covers acute alcohol withdrawal, liver disease, pancreatitis and Wernicke's encephalopathy. The NICE recommendations are not specific to a clinical setting.

There is a growing body of evidence documenting the effectiveness of alcohol reduction and blood pressure control. Alcohol misuse and mood disorders go hand-in-hand. Advice from a GP, practice nurse and other members of the primary healthcare team is likely to be taken seriously. GPs know their patients well. Asking and addressing alcohol consumption, like smoking history, at every consultation is essential to allow patients to reach an informed decision.

Recognition of alcohol withdrawal, assessment of its severity and determining which patients need admission for treatment, although a challenge, can be achieved by a vigilant GP. Early detection of end organ damage such as pancreas or liver and recognition, assessment and treatment of those with hazardous drinking problems can be delivered if adequate community alcohol services are in place. Ideally the healthcare professionals, whether primary or secondary care, caring for the patients with alcohol problems should work together to nationally agreed standards.

Hopefully, the NICE recommendations will help to raise awareness of alcohol-related physical conditions. In order to raise standards of care and reduce the cost to the NHS of treating acute and chronic drinking, alcohol must be added to the QOF like smoking cessation and obesity.

The read codes shown in Table 27.1 can be easily added in all chronic disease templates. A total of 5+ on AUDIT-C indicates hazardous drinking. These patients should be referred to an alcohol counsellor.

AUDIT-C (Alcohol Use Disorders Identification Test Consumption) can be downloaded from www.cquaimh.org/pdf/tool_audit c

Table 27.1 Alcohol read codes to add to all chronic disease templates

Prompt	Code
Alcohol screen – AUDIT-C	(9k17)
Alcohol consumption screen	(68S)
Teetotaller	(1361)
Stopped drinking alcohol	(1367)
Suspect alcohol abuse – denied	(1369)
Social drinker	(136J)
Hazardous alcohol use	(136S)
Harmful alcohol use	(136T)
Alcohol assessment declined	(9k19)
Patient advised about alcohol	(8CAM)

References

1 Information Centre for Health and Social Carers. *Smoking, Drinking and Drug Use among Young People in England in 2006: headline figures.* National Centre for Social Research, National Foundation for Educational Research; 2007. www.natcent. ac.uk/...centre/...new-findings-from-the-survey-of-smoking-drinking-and-drug-use-amongst-11–15-years

2 Singleton N, Bumpstead R, O'Brien M, *et al. Psychiatric Morbidity among Adults Living in Private Households.* London: National Statistics; 2000. Available at: www.statistics. gov.uk/downloads/theme_health/psychmorb.pdf

3 National Clinical Guideline Centre for Acute and Chronic Conditions. *Alcohol Use Disorders: diagnosis and clinical management of alcohol related physical complications.* London: RCP; 2010.

4 Hospital Episode Statistics. Available at: www.hesonline.nhs.uk

5 Department of Health. *The Cost of Alcohol Harm to the NHS in England: an update to the Cabinet Office (2003) study.* London: Department of Health; 2008. Available at: www.dh.gov.uk/en/Consultations/Liveconsultations/DH_086412?IdcService=GET_FILE&dID=169373&Rendition=Web

6 The NHS Information Centre. *Statistics on Alcohol, England 2009.* London: The Health and Social Care Information centre; 2009. Available at: www.ic.nhs.uk/statistics-and-data-collections/health-and-lifestyles/alcohol/statistics-on-alcohol-england-2009-%5Bns%5D

7 British Liver Trust. *Analysis of Office for National Statistics Mortality Statistics covering All Deaths related to Liver Dysfunction.* 7 May 2009. www.britishlivertrust.org.uk/home.../facts-about-liver-disease.aspx

8 Ruidavets J-B, Ducimetière, P, Evans A, *et al.* Patterns of alcohol consumption and ischaemic heart disease in culturally divergent countries: the Prospective Epidemiological Study of Myocardial Infarction (PRIME) [Research]. *BMJ.* 2010; **341**: c6077.

Useful reading

➤ National Institute for Health and Clinical Excellence. *Alcohol Use Disorders: preventing the development of hazardous and harmful drinking: NICE guideline PH24*. London: NHICE; 2010. www.nice.org.uk/guidance/PH24

➤ National Institute for Health and Clinical Excellence. *School-based Interventions on Alcohol: NICE guideline PH7*. London: NHICE; 2007. www.nice.org.uk/guidance/PH7

CHAPTER 28

QOF: the assessment process

John Stephen Kelly

There have been many changes to the payment structure of general practice since I first became a principal 28 years ago. One of the most radical, far-reaching and, at times, controversial has been the Quality and Outcomes Framework (QOF) introduced as part of the new GMS contract in 2004.

I was at the outset, and still remain, an enthusiastic supporter of the principles of the QOF in spite of its imperfections, and the encouragement of improvements to the quality of care provided to patients in ways which can demonstrate specific benefits is clearly a good thing. The financial support for this process has also been welcomed and for most practices this now represents a significant proportion of practice income.

The QOF therefore provides benefits for patients in terms of health outcomes, for GPs in terms of financial rewards for the work they undertake and for primary care trusts (PCTs) in terms of measurable improvement in the quality of care provided to their population. I therefore felt sufficiently enthusiastic about the process to become the QOF lead for our nine-doctor suburban practice and later agreed to become a clinical assessor for our PCT.

The phrase 'poacher turned gamekeeper' came to mind when I first took up the role, but given that the inspection process is an essential part of ensuring financial probity in relation to the QOF, I felt that an experienced local GP who understood the process, the pressures of day-to-day general practice and the local health economy would be best placed to fill that role.

I attended several training events when I first took on the role, which were designed to ensure that the assessors had a good working knowledge of the QOF domains and individual indicators as well as an understanding of the assessment process and what the PCT is trying to achieve at the inspection visit. Meetings are also held at the beginning of each visiting year to agree priorities for that round of visits and to try to agree a timetable for the visits so that practices can be given adequate notice. These meetings involve the GP assessors, the clinical governance team and the lay assessors to ensure a uniform approach whichever team happens to be involved in visiting a particular practice. Meetings also take place after the round of visits to reflect on what went well, what could be improved upon and any problem areas which were identified.

The reason the assessment process is so important relates to the large sums of money involved. A sum of £1.1 billion is invested in primary care through the QOF process and it is therefore not surprising that the government wants reassurance that the funds are being invested wisely and appropriately.

The process itself is based on a number of important principles; it is required to be robust but not unnecessarily intrusive or officious. The original guidelines laid down the basic principles of the process.

> *The practice quality review will be founded on the development of a relationship between the practice and the PCO based on the principles of high trust, evidence base, appropriate progression and development within the practice context, minimising bureaucracy and ensuring compliance with the statutory responsibilities of the PCO.*

There is clearly a balance to be struck between the need for accountability for the investment of such large sums of public money and the avoidance of unnecessary administrative work and disruption to the running of the practice. My experience with our own PCT has been very positive and I have been impressed by its genuine concern to be supportive to practices striking, what seems to me, to be a fair balance between the needs of clinical governance and clinical care. Indeed, had I not been comfortable with the approach taken I would certainly not have been happy to be part of the inspection process over the last six years. Moreover, an amicable atmosphere during the inspection visit is more likely to allow people to feel relaxed and therefore engage more fully with the process – the inspection visit is more successful for both parties.

Preparation is an essential ingredient for a successful outcome and the PCT team will have done their 'homework' in advance, and relevant documents such as practice profile, staff changes, prevalence data and previous achievement figures will have been circulated to members of the visiting team. The practice will normally have several weeks' notice of the date and time of the visit, and a morning or afternoon should be put aside for the visit itself. It is vitally important that key members of the practice are available during the visit and should not have appointments booked, but otherwise the practice should continue to run normally. A room of adequate size should be available, as should any documentary evidence such as policies and procedures or minutes of significant event meetings, which may have been requested by the clinical governance lead. Interruptions should be kept to the minimum and, as always, regular offers of refreshment in the form of tea, coffee and biscuits are most welcome.

There is a certain amount of flexibility built into the inspection process and PCTs vary a great deal in the method, style and frequency of the assessments undertaken. In the early years it was usual to visit all practices every year and a wide range of indicators was examined. In my area, the inspection team consists of a member of the clinical governance team, a quality improvement facilitator (usually with a background in practice nursing), a lay assessor, a GP assessor and a clerk to provide secretarial support. The practice team must include the practice manager, the lead GP and the practice nurse involved in chronic disease management. This number of people descending on a small practice could seem rather intimidating at times and could be very disruptive to the running of the practice on the day of the visit. The clinical team will discuss the processes involved in maintaining registers, call and recall systems, chronic disease management and explore the practice approach to the QOF as a whole. The lay assessors will look round the premises from a patient's perspective and discuss aspects of the patient survey, etc. At the end of the visit everyone comes together for a feedback session and the findings of the visit are summarised for the practice. Any action points or training needs are agreed, with an appropriate timescale, and following the visit a full written report is sent to the practice.

As the process evolved, this changed to a rolling programme of visits for each practice every three years, with a more focussed approach on specific indicators reflecting the PCT's priorities for that year.

More recently, the visits were targeted on those practices with the lowest QOF scores based on the previous year's performance, with particular emphasis on areas of unusually high or low prevalence.

Some PCTs now do very few visits, relying mainly on the information available through the QMAS (the Quality Management and Analysis System) and other computer-based tools together with prescribing data and the evidence required to support indicators relating to the organisational domain.

In addition to the assessment visits, QOF clinical assessors are also involved in the two other parts of the inspection process.

Pre-payment verification takes place after the practice claims have been submitted via QMAS. The PCT is required to confirm the accuracy of all the achievement information before the payment can be made. Data is examined and information on such things as prevalence rates compared with local and national averages, rates of exception reporting and unusual patterns of activity via the Apollo system, which can remotely look at values in anonymised versions of patient records. These assessments are usually performed at the PCT and specific queries may be sent to practices for a response or, occasionally, a further visit may be required.

The third form of assessment is the post-payment verification process in which 5% of practices are chosen in a random procedure witnessed by senior members of the PCT and local medical committee for a more detailed analysis of the information which has given rise to the QOF payment. It is important to emphasise the random nature of this process and that being chosen for one of these visits in no way indicates any suspicion of wrongdoing.

The visiting team on this occasion includes the PCT quality and outcomes primary care lead, an external auditor, usually from a nearby PCT, and a GP clinical assessor. The purpose of this visit is:

> To ensure that the PCT has robust assurances to support QOF payments made to the practice and that there is specific assurance that no fraudulent transactions have been carried out.

The policies and procedures related to the QOF are discussed with relevant members of the practice team and clinical processes are reviewed by the GP assessor via random spot-checking of the transactions underpinning the claims, with cross-reference to appointment records where appropriate. The areas sampled are, understandably, often related to the high value indicators and records are examined to ensure that all the relevant information is in the medical record to substantiate the entry in the notes of, for example, 'dementia review'.

The work of a QOF clinical assessor is therefore interesting, varied and helpful in developing a greater knowledge and understanding of the QOF process. It is a useful opportunity to become more familiar with the workings of the PCT and gives useful insights into the varied ways in which colleagues approach the challenges of the QOF. There are also opportunities to try to spread 'best practice' throughout the area and use some of the experience gained to develop one's own practice.

Relationships between GPs and their respective PCTs vary a good deal and although areas of conflict are inevitable given their differing priorities, agendas, directives, etc., a good working relationship brings benefits to patients and GPs alike. This relationship can be encouraged, fostered and strengthened by a constructive and supportive approach to QOF assessments by the PCT, but, conversely, the wrong approach can cause untold damage to these relationships.

Unfortunately, the current financial climate will increase the pressure on PCTs (or their successors) to limit expenditure in all areas across the health economy and the QOF will be no exception. This means that QOF payments will come under greater scrutiny and the assessment process may well be adversely affected. I hope that these changes do not affect things too severely and that I am able to continue in the role of clinical assessor – if I am not happy with the approach in the future then the gamekeeper may just have to return to being a full-time poacher!

Index